Business Process Redesign
A View from the Inside

Business Process Redesign
A View from the Inside

edited by Ashley Braganza, Cranfield School of Management
and Andrew Myers, Independent Consultant

INTERNATIONAL THOMSON BUSINESS PRESS
I(T)P® An International Thomson Publishing Company

London • Bonn • Boston • Johannesburg • Madrid • Melbourne • Mexico City • New York • Paris
Singapore • Tokyo • Toronto • Albany, NY • Belmont, CA • Cincinnati, OH • Detroit, MI

Business Process Redesign A View from the Inside

A division of International Thomson Publishing Inc.
The ITP logo is a trademark under licence

British Library Cataloguing-in-Publication Data
A catalogue record for this book is available from the British Library

---

First published by International Thomson Business Press 1997

Typeset by J&L Composition Ltd, Filey, North Yorkshire
Printed in the UK by Clays Ltd., St Ives Plc.

ISBN 1-86152-187-1

International Thomson Business Press
Berkshire House
168–173 High Holborn
London WC1V 7AA
UK

International Thomson Business Press
20 Park Plaza
13th Floor
Boston MA 02116
USA

http://www.itbp.com

Contents

List of figures

List of tables

Acknowledgements

Our thanks go to the 'insiders' who put in a great deal of time and effort to craft their contributions. The weekends and evenings you spent are much appreciated. Our thanks also extend to their organizations for allowing them to provide the insider's view. And behind the scenes there were others: Martin Shotbolt, Janet Price, Oscar Weiss, Daniel Kusio, Jim Harvard, Jane Clarke, Ingmar Folkmans, Sophie Durlacher (our tireless production editor) and Lisa Williams. Many thanks!

Ashley Braganza
Andy Myers

Introduction

The proactive management of business processes is just beginning in organizations. There are a plethora of books on the market which purport to explain what Business Process Redesign (BPR) is, why organizations should undertake fundamental, radical changes, the methods that can be employed and the benefits to be gained. Many, if not most, of the books are written by scholars and consultants, based upon their research or consultancy assignments, or occasionally a combination of the two.

But what about the people who experience BPR? What do they think? What do they feel? How has it affected them? Many of the books referred to above report the views and experiences of managers; however, these are still second-hand accounts of what actually happened. Hence, one of the central drivers for publishing this book is to release the first-hand views of the people who have had to live BPR: to hear it from the redesigner's mouth.

We are told that managers who enter into a redesign or re-engineering initiative are embarking upon a journey. They need to plan the journey, but once they start they must demonstrate qualities such as leadership, tenacity, patience and courage. But the path is strewn with frustration, pain and risks. We hope that the reader will recognize many of the vast range of emotions experienced by the contributors.

For the purposes of this book the terms 'business process redesign' and 're-engineering' are used interchangeably. The key criteria for selection of the cases was that the organizations focused upon the process, that is, implemented changes that have crossed functional boundaries, albeit to varying degrees of radical transformation.

Structure of the book

The book comprises seven chapters. Chapter 1 sets out current issues in BPR. It highlights the debates which appear to cause confusion in the minds of managers, and sets the scene for the cases. Chapter 2 examines the transformational changes that have taken place in Texas Instruments. Specifically the critical issues surrounding the re-engineering of the Semiconductor Group are revealed. Chapter 3 takes a detailed look at how Rank Xerox combine radical and incremental change. This chapter explores the work done in Rank Xerox (UK) to change the culture of the organization. Chapter 4 provides an insight into First Direct, the UK's first 24-hour, 365-day-a-year telephone bank. This chapter exposes the difficulties in making radical changes in an organization that is highly successful. Chapter 5 demonstrates the power of BPR when applied to the supply chain. Robert Bosch Limited used the 'process' as the basis for getting closer to the customer by re-engineering their supply chain. Chapter 6 is an examination of information technology to support redesign in an automotive company in order to make it more competitive. This is a unique example of an organization and a consultancy, acting as the change agent, operating in partnership. Here, the viewpoint of Perot Systems, who have gained a great deal of 'insider knowledge', describes the change process. The last chapter pulls together the key messages to emerge from the cases, and points to a potential future for process-managed organizations.

Style

The book is intended for practitioners and researchers; the aim is to let the reader enter the experiences of the authors in their organization. Hence we have let the authors set the style and tone of their chapter. We have tried to ensure that as little jargon as possible is used, and, wherever possible, organization-specific terms are defined. Each chapter begins with background and the story of the organization. Key issues affecting the organization are then explored. The chapters then end with the key lessons learned, which should be helpful for any organization wishing to undergo a similar initiative.

1

Ashley Braganza and Andrew Myers

Business process redesign – an outsider's view

Introduction

It is estimated that 75 per cent of re-engineering initiatives are unsuccessful, which is a worrying failure rate. In spite of this, increasing numbers of organizations are turning to BPR in order to deal with current and future challenges; moreover, a BPR initiative is often a high-risk endeavour for any organization.

It is this apparently high failure rate that has sparked the authors' attempt to investigate why this should be true. The following sections highlight how those within the organization, the 'insiders', could become confused by the whole issue of re-engineering.

A substantial amount of the BPR literature focuses upon two key topics, namely classifying and planning a BPR initiative. A number of authors provide anecdotes and illustrations of organizations to add weight to their particular argument. Practitioners may be misled by the conclusions of various authors' debates, as they often focus on what actions organizations should or should not take. We feel that a number of commentators have identified 'what' an organization should do, but do not go into any detail as to 'how' an organization should go about doing it. Little evidence, empirical or qualitative, exists which highlights the ways in which organizations have implemented different BPR initiatives, or identifies the issues that are critical to implementation, or the degree of difficulty faced by managers when implementing the issues.

The 'how to' debate is addressed in later chapters by way of actual examples and the key learning points associated with each case should provide a useful source of information for other practitioners who find themselves potentially in the position of having to undertake such an initiative within their organization.

Why undertake a BPR initiative in the first place?

BPR has been identified as a key change initiative for achieving business improvements for organizations in the 1990s. Issues such as providing value for money, increasing customer focus and improving cost-efficiency are seen as important areas for organizations to concentrate on.

A survey of North American and European organizations undertaken by CSC in 1994 identified two key forces that drive an organization to implement BPR. These are changing customer demands and increasing competition. Re-engineering draws organizations to do it with promises of radical benefits being achieved. Several organizations from a variety of sectors, including services, manufacturing and government agencies, have presented the benefits they have achieved at BPR symposia held at Cranfield since 1992. Examples include organizations that have achieved 200 per cent improvements in product development times, and reductions in order processing times from several weeks to minutes.

Another key reason as to why an organization may begin to re-engineer is that it is a useful way for an organization to realize its strategy and, hence, ultimately gain a competitive advantage.

Porter (1980) suggested that organizations needed to do three things to achieve competitive advantage:

- examine the business structure of the industry;
- agree on a strategy;
- implement the business strategy.

A BPR initiative is one way in which organizations can implement their business strategy.

Following a line of argument that structure follows strategy, organizations experimented with different types of structure in the 1980s – product-centred, geographic and matrix, to mention a few. However, the underlying functional structure remained intact in all options. What has become apparent is that organizations are increasingly unable to respond to competitive pressures when they are structured vertically, that is by function. Although these organizations are able to achieve high-levels of functional excellence and efficiency, they are slow to change, ill-equipped to learn and unable to adapt to new challenges. The major problem with vertical organizations is that of coordination between departments and functions. A new organization design – namely the 'horizontal' organization, which is built around business processes that cut across-functional boundaries – is called for. Rockart and Short (1989) describe process orientation as disintegrating the value chain boundaries of the organization. The notion of moving from a functional to a process organization is at the heart of redesign.

There is a tendency for consultants and scholars to take the view that in the redesigned process organization the functional silos are removed or disbanded completely, and that the entire organization works in cross-functional teams. This view is at best naive and at worst impractical. At the end of the day the decision to implement radical BPR has to be agreed to by the board, who are functional directors, and it is perhaps naive to expect these managers to vote themselves out of their hard-earned position, and the status and power it represents. As organizations have resource constraints, it may also be necessary to keep certain activities in functional silos. For example, it would be extremely inefficient and expensive to have a recruitment activity or an accounts-payable activity in *all* the processes in the organization. We would argue that there is a quite valid argument for 'functionalizing' certain activities. Hence it is apparent that managers need to find a balance between function and process to support the strategy.

Consensus or divergence

The many definitions used for BPR, the types of classification derived, the planning of an initiative and the management and implementation of the project are areas where confusion seems to exist when inspecting management texts on the subject. These we will discuss further to highlight that there is a greater degree of divergence than convergence.

Definitions

What is generally understood by the term 'business process re-engineering'? There are a number of definitions of BPR. Yet, when reading through later chapters, the reader will see that a number of 'insiders' make reference to Hammer and Champy (1993) and their work. According to them:

> Re-engineering is the fundamental rethinking and radical design of business processes to achieve dramatic improvements in critical, contemporary measures of performance, such as cost, quality, service, and speed.
>
> (Hammer and Champy 1993: 32)

A key problem that practitioners have identified in the past is that there is no one common definition that is agreed upon. Two other definitions can be cited to highlight the point:

> Re-engineering has been simply defined as the analysis and redesign of business and manufacturing processes to eliminate that which adds no value.
>
> (Parker 1993)

> Re-engineering is a radical new process or organizational change that many companies are using to renew their commitment to customer service.
>
> (Janson 1992–3: 45)

The implications of these different definitions can be represented in terms of:

- *Level* – the whole organization or process;
- *Focus* – 'waste elimination', 'customer focus' or 'performance';
- a combination of all of the above.

Other commentators have defined re-engineering in terms of a continuum. For example, Chait and Lynch (1995) argue that BPR can take place on a continuum from continuous improvement to transformational change. Is it any wonder that the phrase itself causes confusion in the minds of practitioners?

The characteristics and classification of BPR initiatives

Delving beyond the phrase, we note that three issues tend to characterize BPR initiatives. The first issue associated with re-engineering is radical change. Change is often presented as a continuum that ranges from incremental to radical; BPR initiatives are associated generally with large-scale change, as opposed to incremental change, upon the organization. Hammer (1990) states that businesses have made minor improvements by tinkering with work practices that existed in vertical silos. CEOs, he stresses, should not 'pave cowpaths'. He calls upon managers to question all organizational assumptions and sacred cows. He states that:

> at the heart of re-engineering, is the notion of discontinuous thinking – of recognizing and breaking away from the outdated rules and fundamental assumptions that underlie operation. Unless we change these rules, we are merely rearranging the deck chairs on the Titanic.
>
> (Hammer 1990: 107)

The second issue that characterizes a BPR initiative is that it encompasses an holistic perspective of the organization with a view to transforming departmental teams into coordinated cross-functional or process teams. The third issue is that a BPR initiative will require managers to reconsider the way in which they view their organization; this requires changes in the organization's culture, structure, systems and people.

Although this is not commonly recognized, it could be argued that there is another type of change, namely breakthrough change which goes beyond the radical. This gives managers the opportunity to develop processes outside the existing way of doing things. An example of this is First Direct, which redesigned the delivery mechanism of personal banking services in the United Kingdom. This is a step more than radical design, as significant parts, but not all, of the organization were designed from scratch.

It is generally agreed that when classifying BPR initiatives, two dimensions are required. These can be summarized as follows:

- *Scope:* which refers to the number of vertical silos that are co-ordinated to create the process;
- *Scale:* which refers to the extent to which the organization's BPR project will be radical.

The two dimensions are well established in the literature (Davenport and Nohria 1994; Morris and Brandon 1993; Rockart and Short 1989). However, it is not surprising that, as we found when in discussion with practitioners, they are confused by the degree of subjectivity that can be applied to the interpretation of the two dimensions. This becomes apparent in the interpretation of Heygate's model, for example.

Heygate's model (1993) classifies BPR initiatives on the basis of how radical each is. He likens 'radical' to the number of re-engineering initiatives an organization implements. Heygate attempts to relate different methods to different grades of

Levels of process redesign

Increasing radicalism →

	Single-process redesign	*Multiple-process redesign*	*Single major business model change*	*Multiple, integrated business model changes*
Level of ambition for change	Quick hits	Continuous incremental improvement	Major investment to be world class in one element of business system	Total commitment to becoming a world leader
Type of programme needed	Project-oriented improvement	Bottom-up initiatives (e.g. total quality management)	Major process-specific investment	Total commitment to permanent change

Figure 1.1 Heygate's framework for BPR.
Source: Heygate (1993: 80).

radical design. His model has two dimensions: scope and performance yield (see Figure 1.1). Scope is defined in terms of the number of re-engineering initiatives – a single project involving one process or multiple projects which are organization-wide. Performance yield starts at 'quick hits' and leads to an organization becoming world class.

Two criticisms become apparent when using the number of re-engineering initiatives as a gauge of how radical an organization is. First, using simply the number of initiatives means that one cannot take into consideration the nature of the changes. A large number of minor change projects may add up to a radical change. Second, Heygate confuses the concepts of radical and of risk. It is likely that the greater the number of radical re-engineering initiatives, the greater the potential risk of failure. His model is also open to a great degree of subjectivity. Several organizations claim to be committed to attaining world-class status; however, senior managers are often unwilling to create the conditions to achieve such status.

Planning BPR initiatives

This section brings together the current dilemmas facing organizations in planning a BPR initiative. The literature on BPR planning methods is reviewed, highlighting the need for BPR plans and underlying the major issues that are disputed in this area. Organizations face a choice: should they adopt a planned method or a 'just-do-it' (JDI) approach when implementing BPR? There is much confusion, even within the planned approach, on the specific steps that an organization should take to move re-engineering towards implementation.

According to Legge, a planned organizational change is one where the management team have a desired future state for the business and 'conscious efforts are made on the part of those responsible for its initiation and implementation' (Legge 1984: 18). Others, too, have argued that different types of change initiatives require a plan. For example, Savage and Lycoming (1991) suggest that total quality initiatives have been broadly successful as such changes have had a planned implementation. Information systems- and information technology-related (IS/IT) changes should be supported by a plan (Ward et al. 1990). Managers responsible for implementing re-engineering in their organization need to understand 'how to implement' BPR. They also need to be in a position to manage the critical issues that will adversely affect implementation. The BPR literature sets out different planning steps and identifies the issues that are critical to the success of BPR.

The literature also highlights two issues. One is a view that businesses need not, in fact should not, plan a re-engineering initiative – the suggestion is that a JDI approach to re-engineering is the most appropriate method. The second view holds that the steps of the various plans that organizations could use for implementation have very little in common. It is upon these two issues that we shall now focus.

The BPR planning debate – to plan or not to plan

Davenport and Short (1990) put forward a five-step plan which should lead an organization through the implementation of a BPR project. Hammer, on the other hand, argues that: 're-engineering cannot be planned meticulously and accomplished in small and cautious steps' (Hammer 1990: 105). This perspective has wide-ranging consequences: formal plans which take an organization through a structured approach to re-engineering an organization are apparently redundant. Thus the debate on 'how to do' re-engineering is crystallized: the planned approach and the JDI approach. The former posits that organizations should implement re-engineering based upon a set of planned steps. Proponents of the latter approach suggest a number of issues managers should use to benchmark the progress the organization makes towards successful implementation.

This debate has continued over the last few years and remains unresolved. Kaplan and Murdock (1991) and Harrington (1991) hold differing perspectives on re-engineering. Kaplan and Murdock take the view that re-engineering involves radical transformation across the entire business. They state that 'the scope of the effort, therefore, requires that companies take a broadly-based, structured, and phased approach (to undertake re-engineering)' (Kaplan and Murdock 1991: 35). Harrington states that organizations should make incremental as opposed to radical changes. None the less, he makes clear that organizations should use sophisticated and detailed plans. Morris and Brandon (1993) put forward a planned approach for 'how' re-engineering initiatives should be implemented. They suggest that organizations should adopt a structured and uniform implementation plan for re-engineering. Belmonte and Murray (1993), however, take the alternative view. They argue that re-engineering needs a certain degree of creativity and formal plans give managers a false sense of security. Belmonte and Murray argue that businesses should utilize several different descriptive frameworks to facilitate discussion and creative thinking amongst managers.

The JDI approach is tempered by some authors, for example Hagle (1993) and Heygate (1993). These commentators suggest a series of self-diagnostic questions which managers should use to gauge whether plans developed by the business will result in a successful re-engineering initiative. Other authors present a combination of a planned and a JDI approach. For example, Dichter et al. (1993) put forward a 'road map' which consists of a number of structured phases which organizations should use to implement re-engineering. However, one of the phases calls upon organizations to create their *own* plans. Tapscott and Caston (1993) also set out a plan and a range of guidelines to implement re-engineering. Hammer and Stanton (1995) continue to hold the view that re-engineering cannot be planned. They identify several mistakes organizations make in re-engineering, and state that one mistake is that 'they (companies) formulate careful and detailed plans; they develop precise milestones for every stage of the upcoming journey'. They claim that organizations taking this approach are 'doomed to failure', and argue that organizations should recognize that:

> Re-engineering cannot be carefully planned like a traditional project. Re-engineering begins with a vision, a mandate, a concept, not with detailed specifications. The shape of the outcome does not emerge until one is well into it . . . Attempting to achieve a high degree of precision and completeness before the beginning is at best a waste of time and at worst disastrous.
>
> (Hammer and Stanton 1995: 31)

Implications of the two views

While this debate may continue in the literature, there is a key issue which is of practical importance to organizations: that the basis upon which managers choose a planned or a JDI approach is not apparent. One research survey (IMPACT 1993) found that organizations adopt different approaches when implementing re-engineering, and that each approach resulted in major improvements in business performance measures such as time, cost and quality. The survey concludes that a critical question is yet to be resolved: 'are certain approaches to BPR more desirable in given situations?' (IMPACT 1993: 17). However, the authors do not go on to describe what the 'given situations' are.

According to Morris and Brandon (1993), the re-engineering plan would depend upon the initiative's nature and scope. Heygate (1993) argues that organizations should select a method based upon the degree of change, that is, the level of 'radicalism' and the scope of integration; in other words, single-function or whole-organization. A further practical consideration for organizations is that the structured plans, as presented in the literature, differ widely. A cursory glance at Figure 1.2 reveals the differences. The step identified by six out of the seven authors advises organizations to identify their processes. However, two authors suggest this should be the first step an organization should take, three make it the second step, one makes it a third step and one does not even include it in the planned approach. Developing a vision and mapping current processes are also popular themes. However, it is not apparent whether organizations should create a vision in each re-engineering initiative or only for certain initiatives.

Little consensus exists in relation to the ways in which each step could be carried out. For example, businesses are advised to 'measure current processes'. According to Davenport and Short (1990), this should be undertaken using the 80/20 rule and based upon the re-engineering initiative's objectives. On the other hand, Harrington (1991) makes it clear that detailed process flowcharts should be produced for actual and elapsed cycle times, and that cost measures would need to be calculated.

Stages	Author (see key below)						
	D&S	BC	K&M	H	M&B	D	T&C
Develop a vision	✓ ①	✓ ①	✓ ④			✓ ①	✓ ①
Develop objectives	✓ ①	✓ ①				✓ ①	
Set stretch targets	✓ ①					✓ ①	✓ ②
Identify processes	✓ ②	✓ ②	✓ ①	✓ ①	✓ ②	✓ ③	
Map current processes	✓ ③		✓ ③	✓ ②	✓ ④		✓ ②
Measure current processes	✓ ③		✓ ②	✓ ②	✓ ④		
Identify IT enablers	✓ ④			✓ ③	✓ ⑤		✓ ②
Brainstorm	✓ ④				✓ ⑤		
Design prototype	✓ ⑤				✓ ⑤	✓ ③	
Implement	✓ ⑤		✓ ⑤		✓ ⑧		✓ ③
Redesign the processes		✓ ②		✓ ③	✓ ⑤		✓ ②
Establish new management structure		✓ ③		✓ ③		✓ ④	✓ ②
Gain staff commitment		✓ ④					
Develop new IS		✓ ⑤				✓ ④	
Measure/benchmark new process			✓ ②	✓ ④ ✓ ⑤		✓ ②	
Map information flows			✓ ③		✓ ⑤		
Create BPR team				✓ ①		✓ ②	
Appoint BPR champion				✓ ①			
Define process scope, mission and boundaries				✓ ②	✓ ③		
Identify BPR initiative					✓ ①		
Do a high-level cost analysis and process map					✓ ②		✓ ①
Select redesign initiative					✓ ③		
Evaluate cost of each initiative					✓ ⑥		
Select the best alternative					✓ ⑦		
Update models and document					✓ ⑨		
Identify opportunities/benefits							✓ ②
Develop a migration strategy							✓ ②
Continuous improvement							✓ ④

Key:

BC • Butler Cox (1991)
D • Dichter et al. (1993)
D&S • Davenport and Short (1990)
H • Harrington (1991)
K&M • Kaplan and Murdoch (1991)
M&B • Morris and Brandon (1993)
T&C • Tapscott and Caston (1993)

Figure 1.2 Stages of a BPR plan.
Note: The numbers refer to the order in which each stage should be carried out.

Managing a BPR initiative

When an organization decides to undertake a BPR initiative what has to be taken into consideration are the influences this can have on various aspects of the organization. We shall now discuss the influences such an initiative could have on individuals, structure and systems.

Influences on the individuals

Re-engineering initiatives will affect people's roles and responsibilities, their skills, the ways in which they are assessed and the criteria used, reward structures, and many require some people to leave the organization and others to join it again. In a vertically organized business an individual's role, responsibilities and skills are of a specialist nature and defined narrowly. The work may involve several 'hand-offs', as it passes from one expertise to another. In a process-oriented business individuals are likely to need a wider set of skills. Most, if not all, vertical businesses reward individuals with an element of cash, usually related to their performance, perks and a percentage based upon the organization's profit. In a process business other options may be possible: for instance, using the process's performance as one element, team-based reward or some combination of these.

Influences on the structure

This refers to the extent to which the re-engineering initiative will affect issues such as reporting lines, the business's hierarchy, process ownership, process teams and power bases. For example, in a process business power may need to shift from departmental heads to process owners. There may be areas where management is able to create a flatter structure, thus influencing the hierarchy. One financial services organization reduced by half the number of management layers when it implemented its process changes.

Influences on systems

Re-engineering initiatives also affect the organization's information systems, service level agreements, information flows and budgeting procedures. Sadler (1991) states that when businesses reduce the role played by functions this usually means either introducing new systems and procedures or abandoning those already in place.

Implementing a re-engineering initiative

It is likely that managers will need to concentrate on key success factors when implementing a re-engineering initiative. We have tabulated the key issues identified in some of the BPR literature. These key issues have been examined by the authors and Figure 1.3 summarizes these.

An analysis of the issues shows that there is virtually no consensus on which are the key issues that are likely to lead to successful implementation of a re-engineering

	Author (see key below)									
Key issue to be managed	D&S	BC	K&M	IMPS	Ha	EY ICL	He	Hag	Hall	B&M
Gain executive commitment	✓	✓	✓	✓	✓	✓	✓	✓	✓	✓
Use cross-functional team	✓	✓	✓	✓						
Use a process structure	✓									
Use a matrix structure	✓	✓								
Facilitated by IT	✓			✓						✓
Question assumptions					✓					
Change culture		✓								
Recognize need for change		✓								✓
Flexible implementation						✓				
One-step implementation					✓					
Phased implementation		✓	✓							
Brainstorm/creative			✓	✓			✓			
Understand/map current processes			✓							
Avoid exhaustive current process maps								✓		
Get quick wins			✓							
Set clear/stretch goals				✓		✓	✓	✓	✓	✓
Align BPR with strategic vision				✓	✓	✓				
Achieve critical mass for change							✓			
Set correct scope for BPR initiative							✓	✓		
Strong BPR team leader								✓		
Use correct method								✓		
Allocate budget/resources for change				✓						
Communicate BPR plans										✓
Gain staff commitment						✓				
Owned by business not IT				✓						
Invest in training/education				✓						
Conduct a pilot									✓	
Learn from other organizations										✓

Key:

B&M • Belmonte and Murray (1993)
BC • Butler Cox (1991)
D&S • Davenport and Short (1990)
EY/ICL • Ernst and Young/ICL Survey (1992)
Ha • Hammer (1990)
Hag • Hagle (1993)
Hall • Hall et al. (1993)
He • Heygate (1993)
IMPS • IMPACT Survey (1993)
K&M • Kaplan and Murdoch (1991)

Figure 1.3 Key issues to be managed.

initiative if managed well. Only one issue – gaining executive support, as one would expect – attracts unanimous support. It is also unclear whether the issues in Figure 1.3 are vital for every re-engineering initiative or for particular types of initiatives.

Empirical evidence

Managers facing a re-engineering initiative would find little empirical evidence to help guide their choice of approach. IMPACT (1991) and Ernst & Young/ICL (1992) carried out surveys of businesses that commenced re-engineering initiatives. The results show that businesses tend to develop plans of their own. The IMPACT report uses the literature on BPR and interviews with senior managers of businesses implementing re-engineering. The report concludes that several methodologies and plans are used by organizations to implement re-engineering.

An independent survey, based upon a sample of 100 businesses from the Times Top 1000 firms, was carried out on behalf of Ernst & Young and ICL (1992). Directors and senior business managers from thirty-seven organizations were taken through a comprehensive telephone interview. IT directors formed one-third of the respondents, while the rest were drawn from other functions. Twenty-seven businesses claimed to have started a re-engineering initiative, but had used quite different implementation methods.

The surveys and figures mentioned above are useful as they highlight issues to which businesses can attach some level of importance. However, what is not apparent is the level of difficulty that exists in resolving each issue; nor is the relative importance of each issue clear.

At Cranfield we carried out an exploratory study to gauge managers' perceptions on the level of difficulty and importance they attach to a range of issues. We felt this would be useful as this area is rarely explored in the literature. The organizations included in the study were implementing one or more re-engineering initiatives.

The study

The study addresses among other things, awareness of re-engineering at different levels in the organization, the rationale for making the change and the relationship between re-engineering and other change initiatives such as total-quality and strategic reviews. The study was carried out during a two-day symposium held at Cranfield on the subject of re-engineering.

We issued to the delegates attending the Cranfield symposium a short questionnaire to glean qualitative and quantitative data. The delegates were from public and private sector businesses. The questionnaire was issued to all delegates, sixty-five in total. As not all businesses represented at the symposium had started a re-engineering initiative, and since others were unlikely ever to start an initiative in the future, we used only relevant respondent data – for example, information relating to the awareness of re-engineering within the business. We wished to concentrate on those organizations that had commenced a re-engineering initiative. Obviously the effect of this decision was to reduce the sample size from sixty-five to twenty-three. These twenty-three organizations represented several different industry sectors, including finance/banking; utilities; aerospace; publishing; telecommunications; pharmaceuticals; food/drink/tobacco; and the public sector.

The twenty-three organizations undertaking re-engineering are best described as large in terms of sales (a combined total of approximately £29 billion) and the number of employees (representing a total of 380,250 employees). The sales of the twenty-three organizations range from a low of £23 million to a high of £15 billion – with an average of £1.5 billion. The average number of employees per organization was around 22,500 – with a low of 150 and a high of 160,000.

We are cognisant of the fact that we have a modest sample size; hence, we would not feel comfortable in drawing specific conclusions. Yet the data could reveal a few meaningful insights which could be useful for practitioners. Organizations may find it useful to address some issues as part of their re-engineering strategy.

Results and discussion

The data from the questionnaires was analysed and key findings are examined below under four headings: level of awareness throughout the organization; key reasons for implementation; the relationship with other change initiatives; and the use of external advice.

Level of awareness in the organization

The organization's chief executive appeared to have the highest level of re-engineering awareness. This supports the CSC Index (1994) survey, which shows that re-engineering is a top-down initiative. Senior managers such as information technology managers and functional managers also appeared to have a high degree of re-engineering awareness compared with those in the rest of the organization (see Table 1.1). IT managers seem to have a greater degree of awareness compared to functional managers and others in the organization.

This last point would reinforce the notion that re-engineering may still be perceived by managers to be an IT rather than a business issue. Perhaps managers still fall into the trap of considering re-engineering as a short-term cost-cutting exercise which automates manual activities rather than as a means, among other things, of enhancing customer satisfaction.

Table 1.1 Degree of awareness

	Mean
Chief Executive	4.7
Functional directors	4.4
Line managers	3.4
IT manager	4.5
The organization	2.8

Note: 1 = not aware, 5 = highly aware.

It would appear that the people in the rest of the organization are barely aware of re-engineering when compared with senior management.

Key reasons for doing BPR

The questionnaire enquired about the organization's rationale for implementing BPR. The most frequently cited reason was cost reduction in relation to the overall process. Only one person specifically mentioned headcount reduction as the main rationale for doing BPR; perhaps the others were being politically correct.

The second most frequently mentioned reason was a reduction in cycle times. This would support what many organizations see as a key competitive issue in the 1990s – that is, shortening timescales for new product development, order processing and delivery and customer response times. The major pharmaceutical companies are busy shortening their new product development cycle times through the use of processes rather than the traditional silo structure.

Improving customer service came out as the third most common reason. This is a worthy aim and invariably would be on most managers' wish list. However, it is not apparent how this will be achieved if BPR is seen as an IT issue or if only senior managers are aware of BPR while those in the rest of the organization 'continue as normal'. It is also not at all clear how organizations will achieve this aim when 'ability to focus on customer' was a requirement only four respondents would seek in a cross-functional BPR team.

Relationship between re-engineering and other change initiatives

Duck (1993) states that organizations usually have different change initiatives being implemented concurrently. She says that 'an organization may simultaneously be working on TQM [Total Quality Management], process re-engineering, employee empowerment, and several other programs' (Duck 1993: 110). Morris and Brandon (1993) argue that a business should position its re-engineering initiative(s) alongside other change initiatives. The results of the survey seem to support these views. They reveal that the relationship between re-engineering and other types of change – specifically quality management, strategy review, culture change and IS/IT change – are fairly strong (see Table 1.2).

Table 1.2 BPR in relation to other change initiatives

	Mean
Total quality	5.1
Strategy review	5.4
Culture change	4.5
IS/IT change	4.7

Note: 1 = very weak, 7 = very strong.

Use of external advice

About half, thirteen out of the twenty-three respondents, indicated that their organization had employed external consultants to assist with re-engineering. The majority of these respondents (ten) said that the consultants were used primarily for skills transfer. Consultants were rarely used for the implementation of re-engineering. It would appear that organizations wish to take ownership of the implementation of re-engineering. This result is encouraging as it reveals that managers can control the implementation of the re-engineering initiative by developing change management capabilities within the organization. A potential implication is that businesses may implement the initiative in quite different ways. This would make the development of a generic plan to implement BPR an improbable dream.

Summary

This chapter has provided an insight into current issues concerning BPR initiatives. It has focused on three key debates in the field, namely classifying, planning, and implementing. As examples are rare, the following chapters provide further empirical evidence as to the issues and reasons for organizations and practitioners wishing to undertake a BPR initiative, and 'how' the initiatives were implemented.

The Semiconductor Group, Texas Instruments
Janis Jesse

2

Achieving the vision and surviving a major manufacturing re-engineering project

Introduction

Since the early 1990s Texas Instruments (TI) has done a significant amount of work internally and externally in the business process engineering (BPE) and re-engineering arena. TI used this and other projects as a basis for the development of a methodology, training classes and advisory services. These are used extensively on internal projects and they are offered to companies in an attempt to make them self-sufficient in the area of business process improvement. The belief at TI is that understanding and managing business processes is central to the improvement that companies throughout the world must undergo to keep pace with the phenomenal rate of change.

One of the fundamental assumptions at TI regarding the business process engineering activities is that it is important to continue to share and seek information on the topic. Since this is the first core process re-engineering activity to follow the methodology from start into transition/implementation, the purpose of this chapter is to share the insights and lessons we have learned from the practitioner's perspective. At this time, this project is still underway and TI is still learning. Since it is such a large project, it was felt that a long list of topics had been compiled and the intention was to capture them as early as possible.

Re-engineering a core business process is one of the most difficult but rewarding things a company can do, if it is done well. It is difficult and consumes a lot of time and resources. But if the decision has been made that re-engineering is the answer, hopefully some of the insights discussed in this chapter will help during the countless times you question the wisdom of the decision to re-engineer.

This chapter is split into a number of different sections. There is an overview of the re-engineering environment at TI and of the Order Fulfilment Project in the Semiconductor Group (SC) – the Order Fulfilment Project is the main source of the lessons learned in the rest of the sections and of the next steps in SC's journey.

The Texas Instruments story

Entering the 1990s, TI was no different from the majority of other American-based global companies. Things were changing faster than we could get our minds around them. We had been successful in the semiconductor business, but that success was being eroded. Our defence business was undergoing a major upheaval. We had world-class information technology capability but, when examined closely, we were not getting the business value from that capability.

In our information technology group we were asked to explain why some information technology projects were much more successful than others at providing business value. A study revealed that major successes occurred when the business first defined the change in work that must occur. The big gains were seen when information technology was applied as an enabler to do the newly defined work.

In the Semiconductor Group (SC) in 1990–91, the business defined a major work change that had to occur. SC had to make a transition from being a high-volume commodity supplier to being a custom-product supplier. More than 50 per cent of the revenue in the mid-1990s had to come from custom-products or SC was not going to be a viable player in the semiconductor market. SC's past strength was commodity business, not custom-products. We had built and excelled at a business structure to build these commodity products. We were struggling to fit the custom-products into the existing business processes and infrastructure. We were struggling so much that our customers were pointing out our failures very loudly. So change was required for survival.

A team of four people working on an information strategy plan to address this SC transition by developing new information systems reached the conclusion in late 1990 that the way work was done would have to change. New or enhanced information systems would not provide the answer. This supported the findings of the information technology study. Information technology alone was not enough.

We now had the ideal opportunity to try the new premise that the business should define the work, and information technology would then be used to enable that work. Great premise, but how were we to start? As fate would have it, we had recently attended a seminar on re-engineering by Dr Michael Hammer and made the connection between his philosophy of dramatic change to business processes and SC's need to change the business dramatically. With corporate support and funding, the SC Order Fulfilment Project began in early 1991.

The project team consisted of five key SC business representatives, three business process engineering practitioners, and two SC Vice-Presidents, one a strong process advocate and the other a long-range thinker. Their support was invaluable in the start-up phase of the project. This team had been motivated by Dr Hammer's seminar, but basically were starting from scratch on 'how' to re-engineer.

The team knew the first thing that was necessary was to set the scope of the project. The direction so far had been to 'fix the custom-products business'. We stumbled on to the idea that we should define the high-level business processes of SC. From this, we could set the scope of the project. Three months later, the SC High-Level Business Process Map (cited in Hammer and Champy 1993: 119) emerged. This would prove to be the most valuable deliverable of the entire project.

In the High Level Business Process Map, seven high-level business processes were defined. Executive owners were assigned to each of the seven processes. From this map, in August 1991 the SC executives made the decision to re-engineer the Order Fulfilment Process. The Order Fulfilment Process starts with the identification of a customer's production need and ends when the product is delivered to the customer. The decision to re-engineer this process was made because it received the most complaints from customers. We knew there were other problems in the other processes, but the decision was made to start with the one generating the most customer concerns and complaints. We now had our scope and our process owner.

At this time the scale of the project was set to Application Specific Integrated Circuits (ASICs), a product family in the Application Specific Products business unit. The bulk of the current custom-product base of SC could be found in this product family. Six months later the scale was increased to the entire business unit. Roughly six months after that, it was decided that the entire SC Order Fulfilment Process should be changed. This increasing scale caused some delays in the project, but the larger scale allowed for the largest impact to TI.

The need to rethink the SC Order Fulfilment Process was clear. The move from a commodity-product base to a custom-product base had to be made. The primary impact of that move was that SC had to shift from a 'cost' decision base to a 'time' decision base. In a commodity business, you have the luxury of using inventory to cover product movement around the world in search of lower variable costs. In a custom business that luxury does not exist. Time becomes the critical element. Our customers are depending on our product to get their product market. The entire end-customer need may be satisfied with one production lot of product, so any scrap, loss or other variability may be catastrophic. All these differences required a new way of looking at the business.

When we first measured our process, to be 95 per cent confident it took us 186 days from the time we recognized a customer's need until we delivered it to the dock. We had information that one of our competitors could accomplish this in four weeks. This was the case for action we would use repeatedly. We knew our competitor would continue to improve its process, so we set the new process design goal to reaching a two-week cycle time on the Order Fulfilment Process in 1995.

We spent from April 1991 through to October 1991 understanding the Order Fulfilment Process, learning as much as we could about new technological advancements, talking to experts and experiencing some of the first signs of resistance. In late 1991 we unveiled the new process design to our sponsors and process owner. It would reach the goal of two weeks from start to finish for custom-products. It threw away some of the basic premises of the existing SC operations.

The most dramatic change defined in the vision was the statement that complete

Table 2.1 Project summary

- Case for Action – transition from commodity to customer products
- Competitor could do Order Fulfilment in four weeks to our twenty weeks
- Scope – total semiconductor Order Fulfilment
- Scale – Product line, moving to business unit, moving to total semiconductor
- Start – April 1991
- Implementation Plan – through to 1998
- Impact – worldwide, 15,000 people, forty-four sites, 160,000 products, eighteen databases, 500+ handoffs

factories had to be built under one roof. The existing factories were in 44 countries and many products had to travel across several oceans before fabrication, assembly and test were completed. A semiconductor factory costs in excess of $US500 million to build. We had a huge existing asset base that could not be changed. This was a critical point for the project. The executives allowed the vision to stand, but created a bounded vision that defined the transition plan from the current factory situation to a more 'vision-like' plan, one that made worldwide manufacturing sites link as if they were one site. They made the decision to use the 'factory under one roof' criteria for future factory decisions.

The bounded vision was accepted in early 1992. Since that time the project has been in the implementation phase. The project directly impacts approximately 15,000 people in the United States, Asia Pacific Region, Europe and Japan. Much of the time has been spent setting short-term goals toward the two-week vision, giving the 15,000 people the necessary knowledge and skills to achieve the goals, coordinating the multitude of activities required for transition to the vision, and communicating the vision at every opportunity.

Is the SC Order Fulfilment Project a success? Well, the SC group has reduced its 95th percentile cycle time by more than 50 per cent since mid-1992. The variability of the process has been reduced by 75 per cent. Both finished goods and work-in-process inventory have been dramatically reduced (multimillions of dollars), a common language concerning the Order Fulfilment Process and its vision have been established and factories around the world are sharing lessons learned (both good and bad) for the first time as they reach for common goals. In the words of the Order Fulfilment Process Owner, now President and CEO of Texas Instruments, Tom Engibous, 'This is the most significant change in the history of SC'.

In spite of this, there are still huge pockets of resistance three years into the project. The roadmap to reach the vision extends into 1998 and consists of seventeen (at the last count) projects currently underway that will direct SC to the vision. But there is a vision guiding all these projects and the gains are indisputable. We do not know what the definition of success is for this re-engineering project. We do know we have learned a lot in the first three years (see Table 2.1 for a project summary).

Educating and communicating with the executive sponsors and owners

At TI, we formalized a business process engineering (BPE) methodology based on our prior experience, the SC project and other internal re-engineering projects. This was done to ensure repeatability of our successful re-engineering efforts and to avoid the mistakes made in our not so successful ones. The methodology is composed of four basic phases:

1. Project Initiation;
2. Process Understanding;
3. New Process Design;
4. Business Transition.

Also included are suggested tools and techniques to be used at appropriate points in each of the phases. What are not included, however, are the just-in-time creative tips and techniques that we have learned the hard way. These have proven invaluable as we share them across our internal projects. The objective here is to capture them and share them externally. This section is devoted to those that helped us build a high-level commitment and understanding.

Included are the lessons learned and descriptions of some of the actual situations where these lessons were encountered. Each lesson learned is highlighted with relevant information and examples.

Get the information in front of your sponsors and stakeholders creatively

One of the key challenges we faced was how to make our executives familiar with what we were doing. By executives we mean the President of SC, the three Strategic Business Unit (SBU) managers, the vice-presidents of all the enabling activities, and the head of research and development. We were asking for such a high level of support that it was important for them to be able to justify the time and energy we were asking of them. We wanted a specific time commitment from them but were never fortunate enough to get it. So we had to create opportunities to supply them with information. This was a risky business because we had to ensure the information we were giving them was valuable to them as well as to us.

Related to educating the top-level executives was the task of getting the stakeholders reporting to them to believe the executives were really committed. To address both of these issues, we used as many different creative techniques as we could imagine to get information and signs of commitment in front of the executives and the stakeholders. Some of the techniques we used are outlined below.

We persuaded our executive process owner to speak at a Hammer Re-engineering Forum. He was to give a thirty-minute presentation and then answer questions. We volunteered to create the presentation, to spend as much time with him as was required to make sure he was familiar with the presentation and to prepare a set of potential questions and answers. We had three one-hour sessions with him to review the proposed presentations. This was one of our most beneficial early victories because:

- during these sessions we could feed him our thoughts as we reviewed the proposed slides;
- his feedback on the slides gave us an excellent indicator of his level of understanding and his ideas on what was important;

- the prepared questions and answers allowed us to present many of our ideas to him to review and question;
- we transcribed the actual presentation and have used it as motivational material, for standardization of internal presentations, as a basis for external presentations and as a change management tool to convince some of our resident sceptics of executive commitment to the process.

Through one-on-one meetings, articles and messages from other executives, we were able to convince the executives that the process perspective was so important we should hold quarterly business process reviews to review the status of the Order Fulfilment Project as well as the work going on in the other processes. These meetings were held quarterly for eighteen months and were great forums for reviewing the business process activity and resolving any between-process issues; they also served as a change management barometer. The Order Fulfilment team scribed these sessions and published action items to ensure all issues and actions were documented. Based on the informal executive and stakeholder change management assessments made during the meeting, actions were defined by the Order Fulfilment team to work with these critical players.

We have several internal newsletters. We asked our executive owner if he would be willing to do a question and answer series to be included in these newsletters. The questions to be included were those we heard most often from people affected by the project and questions we wanted him to think about and discuss with us. We volunteered to screen the questions and write the proposed answers for his critique. This gave us the opportunity to write down the questions we were hearing the most frequently and also suggest answers that would give us leverage. It gave us an opportunity to highlight some key points we thought were critical at this time in the project.

We have monthly global satellite broadcasts scheduled to all our US, and sometimes European, sales offices. We used several of these to have our executive owner give status updates and answer call-in questions.

We had video tapes made of the semiconductor executives stating their thoughts on the re-engineering effort and the cycle time goals. These were then distributed to everyone for use in their department or staff meetings.

We prepared quarterly updates for Board of Director presentations giving status and key accomplishments. We also wrote impact statements to be included in annual stockholder reports.

The executive staff in SC have been very cooperative in giving the initial 'kick-off' speeches when a new activity was started or when an activity needed a jump-start. Depending on how comfortable the executive was with the re-engineering activity, we volunteered to prepare certain portions of the material. We found that if we prepared a slide with a good quote for the executive to endorse, we could use it in the presentation and in future presentations with other stakeholders. We used several of these executive quotes in preparing the orientation for our Change Agent (Jonah) Network, which will be discussed later. These quotes were a significant factor in showing management commitment.

The communication/commitment message that had the most impact was one used by our executive owner. It was a surprise to us. He was giving a lunch presentation to our Jonah (Change Agent/Cycle Time Expert) Network. The audience was international. His message was simple and he had one slide. His message was 'I am committed'. On his slide were three things: his office, home and car phone numbers.

'If you hit a barrier or obstacle you cannot overcome, call me anywhere, anytime.' It was a great message.

Our team leader volunteered to track near-term cycle time data for the process owner. This was not a primary concern of the re-engineering team, but it provided an opportunity for the team leader to spend more time with the owner. Since the long-term re-engineering goals were connected to cycle time, this was a great opportunity to review cycle-time-related re-engineering team topics with him.

We wrote a twenty-page document outlining the new process design. Executive time constraints were obvious, but we felt this was an important document and wanted them to take time to read it and ask questions. In an attempt to create the need for them to read it, we asked all the key stakeholders to sign the title page to indicate their endorsement. We know of two specific cases where the managers asked us to give them more time to read the document before they signed.

We were not always successful in our attempts to get the right information to the owner and sponsors. It is only fair that we include a couple of examples here:

We mentioned the quarterly process reviews. For the first two or three meetings, the Order Fulfilment team and our two executive advocates spent a significant amount of time working on the meeting content, agendas, preliminary visits with key stakeholders and the value content of the meetings. As the Order Fulfilment team got more involved in that specific project, the preparation for these meetings slacked off considerably. As a result, they were eventually combined with the already existing Total Quality meetings and the meeting control was transferred to the Total Quality Manager, who was not a strong re-engineering advocate. Much of the high-level focus on the core business processes was lost and has not yet been regained.

We asked our process owner to take part in a satellite broadcast to our US Field Sales offices and our European sites. He declined because he thought the timing was premature. We failed to remove the announcement from the satellite bulletin. He saved face for us and did the broadcast. It turned out great. However, our credibility with our process owner was low for quite a while.

Find and use out-of-industry examples

The semiconductor industry is technical and complex. We found that many times we would spend all our time trying to understand the technical themes and variations on a topic and never get to the point where the real problems was discussed. Our team was a mixture of technical and not-so-technical members. A couple of our more technical members began using analogies to explain some of the more difficult technical issues. By using this technique, we could relate tough discussions to a subject everyone could understand. We found we got to the root of the problem more quickly. The solution was much clearer in the everyday example than in the complex world of semiconductor manufacturing. We heard the executives using the analogies repeatedly in different but related conversations.

Our most successful out-of-industry analogy was an airline analogy. Early in our process we benchmarked a major airline. We asked ourselves questions relating our business to the airline's. As an airline customer, would we be willing to call for a reservation and wait up to two weeks for a commitment? That is what we sometimes asked our semiconductor customers to do. If the flight times for the same flight ranged from three hours to five hours, how predictable would commitments be to customers? How efficiently could the airline run? This was the type of variability experienced by some factories.

The airline analogy is built into our vision and people still discuss issues in that context two years later. It was a breakthrough in getting us to forget how complex and technical we were and look for the basic problems that had to be addressed.

Another analogy we used was pizza. We were moving from a commodity business to a custom business. There are standard buffet-type pizzas, then there are special-order pizzas. Everyone at the table wants to be served at the same time regardless of the type of pizza ordered. That is how our customers ordering commodity and custom parts think. They want them all to arrive at the same time to be loaded into the computer board. They did not want to wait for the longer cycle time of the custom-products.

One of our team leader's favourite analogies was made when he visited a Japanese bank to exchange some currency. The lobby was large, with many comfortable chairs. There was a 35-inch, big-screen TV in the lobby. He handed the teller his currency and asked how long it would take. The response was 30–45 minutes. He was curious as to why it would take so long, so he watched the process. It was made up of a series of eight to ten desks or workstations piled high with what looked like church offering plates. The teller took his currency and the instructions and put them in the first offering plate. This was added to the queue of offering plates at the next desk. This person verified the information and put it in the next queue. This went on until about the fifth handoff, when the offering plate was carried into the vault. It eventually appeared, to be handed to another worker who verified the count. There were a couple more handoffs before it was given to the teller who called for the owner of the transaction. Seen in this small condensed form, the process seems ludicrous. However, when we began discussing the handoffs in many of the pieces of our Order Fulfilment Process, they were just as ludicrous. In our case we just had to travel thousands of miles to the next offering plate.

Depending on the situation, we have used Wall Street, hospitals, dry cleaners, farms and countless other out-of-industry examples. This simplifies the discussion, gives everyone a common understanding and is more easily remembered than a complex technical discussion.

Keep communication and education of the stakeholders simple

We determined early on that there was a certain amount of education that needed to occur with the executives. It was difficult to understand at first that one of our responsibilities was to create and deliver educational information to them. After all, who were we to teach the executives? One of the important realizations for us was that we had been given the luxury of time to learn and to explore a problem in depth. It was our responsibility to educate the executives and key stakeholders. We also had the responsibility of creating an environment in which the executives felt comfortable being taught the concepts required to move ahead on the project.

A lesson we learned at an early stage was that, regardless of how clear we thought the message was, not everyone grasped it on the first communication attempt. After

countless presentations and one-on-one conversations, we realized that for our environment, it took, on average, three two-hour communication sessions for people to grasp and understand the importance of business processes and the radical changes implicit in managing by process. After these sessions, in most cases, the stakeholders had a clear understanding of what a business process was, how that could benefit the company and buy-in to the High Level Process Map that was created for SC. Again, this was on average. There were people who never saw the light and others who were ahead of us after our first initial conversation. This knowledge proved very helpful to us as we applied this general communication rule of thumb to other critical messages we needed to communicate.
The following are some of the specific activities and tools we used in communicating and educating key stakeholders and executives:

Our stretch goal was to reduce cycle time radically. We learned that we had a huge mountain to climb because people had different ideas on cycle time, did not use the same words and did not understand some of the very basic principles. We found earlier work that had been done to address this problem. It was done by an operational methods team and was wonderful in its simplicity. It outlined three or four basic principles and definitions, a formula called Little's Law, and a chart showing the Little's Law relationship. These simple pieces were the core of the education and training we did to reduce cycle time by up to 50 per cent and variability by more than 75 per cent in SC over a two-year period.

Because we kept it simple, everyone had the same knowledge base, the same language, and the same goals. We still have to fight to retain the simplicity, but our acid test is 'could a fourth grader understand this?' The executives seem to enjoy the simplicity as a relief from the complexity of the majority of topics they address.

One of our most effective simplicity techniques was to take specific business situations that were occurring and use them as test cases to try out the new vision. The executives could relate to the real-world problem. We could contrast the way the problem would be handled in today's environment with the way it would be handled in the new environment. This was especially effective for us when we were trying to make decisions concerning where new equipment should be located. When the problem was analysed according to handoffs created for the entire process or whether the location caused additional non-value added steps, it highlighted key decision criteria.

Repetition played a big part in keeping communication moving and keeping it simple. In all meetings and encounters (even if they were not directly related to the project) we tried to speak from the process perspective and to use the vocabulary we were trying to teach to the executives and stakeholders. We also used the same slides and presentations repeatedly to get a consistent message across.

We also provided executives with current reading material that addressed the critical issues of the Order Fulfilment Process. We summarized books and key points from articles to make it easy and time-efficient for them to use the material.

Assign communication responsibility for stakeholders to team members with similar or complementary styles

We found early on in the project that there were many ways of communicating. Sometimes we were much more effective than other times. As we began to analyse our successes and our opportunities for improvement, a pattern began to emerge. As a team, some of our training was centred on the different personality traits of the team members. We began to realize these were also affecting the communication with our stakeholders.

- We used several different techniques that helped us categorize the characteristics of the executives and stakeholders for communication and education activities. (For example, are they tactical or visionary? Are they thinkers or feelers? etc.). We also made the distinction between whether they were visual or verbal. These techniques helped us plan and develop the communication and education strategy for the stakeholders. By pairing a person on the team with a stakeholder of similar traits, we made our communications much more successful. We also found we had to prepare presentation material in more than one style if we had a wide recipient base. We could also predict to some degree the reaction to situations and the amount of follow-up or preparation needed, based on our assessment of the stakeholders.
- We used our different skills and backgrounds to approach the executives from different angles. One of our executive advocates had a marketing background, the other a strong business focus. One was very tactical, the other very visionary. By using these different characteristics, we could create a message and delivery plan that would be the most effective for the stakeholder we targeted. If we were not sure which would work best on a stakeholder, we might send several people to the communication session to try several different approaches. We usually found a close match during or after the first session.

We determined that one of our most vocal stakeholders was very crucial to the success of the project. After trying several general communication sessions with him, we had made very little progress moving him toward the new process vision. He could have become a major stumbling block if we had not been able to convince him of the vision. Our team leader was the team member most effective in communicating with him, so he began a constant and time-consuming one-on-one communication effort. After several months the stakeholder became a process advocate and an asset to the project.

Communication should be hands-on

We were no exception to the rule that hands-on learning activities are much more effective and memorable. These also played a critical part in creating a new language and symbolism during the consensus-building needed in the early project steps. Following are some of our successes in creating hands-on experiences for the executives and stakeholders.

Our team leader is very visual and has a knack for taking a complex principle and

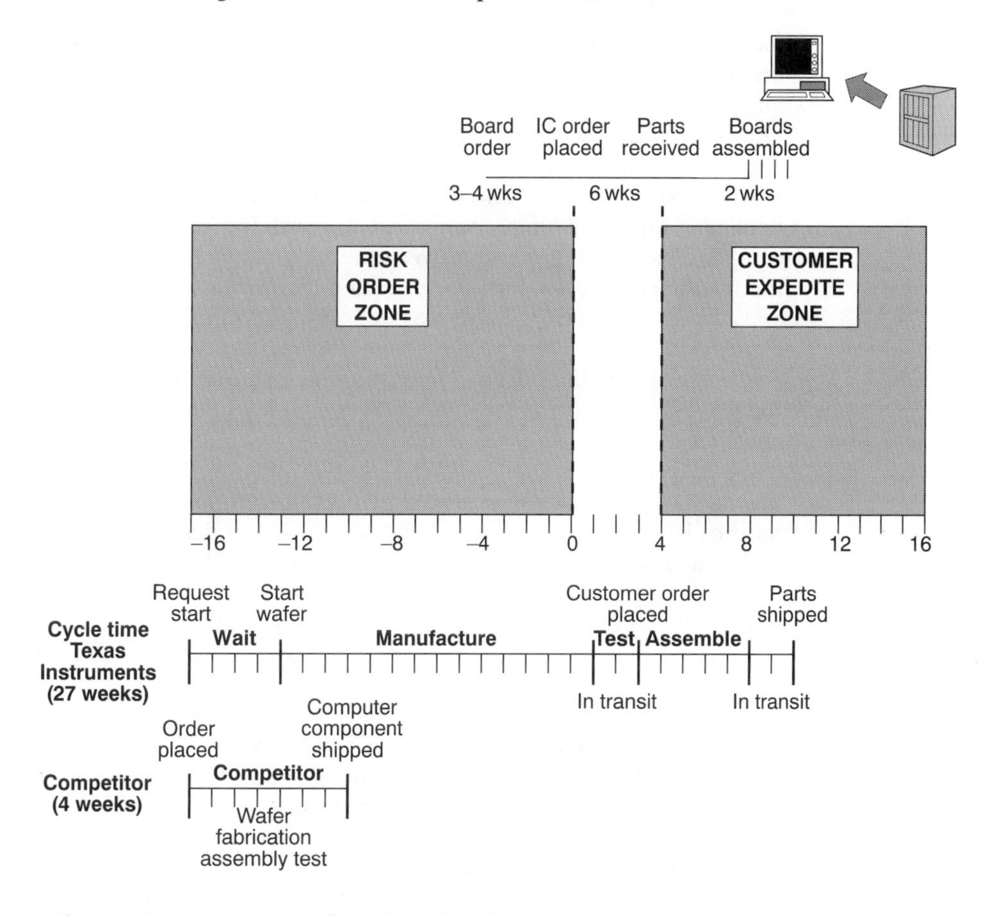

Figure 2.1 Customer timeline (Gameboard).
Source: Developed by Randy Harris (1991).

turning it into a game or puzzle. When developing our Case for Action, we were comparing our cycle time to that of a competitor. The benchmark showed their cycle time was five times better than our own. We were always asked how this is possible. Our leader developed a startlingly effective way of showing this. It is what we call 'The Gameboard' (see Figure 2.1).

The Gameboard consists of a large sheet of paper divided into weeks. It represents the time required to recognize a customer's need and deliver that need to the customer. These weeks are then divided into zones: risk zone, acceptable lead time zone or expedite zone. The zone you are in is a direct result of the cycle time.

The other component consists of strips of paper representing our competitor's cycle times and our cycle time. Taking SC's cycle time strip, you can then fold away the time required to reduce our cycle time to the equivalent of our competitor. Each fold is an explanation of how our competitor was able to reduce cycle time. Each fold is also something major in our process that has to be changed. For example, one fold (or reduction in cycle time) required a change in product strategy. Another fold required the elimination of in-transit steps between factories. It was a compelling way to communicate with both our stakeholders and our customers. It also showed that the change required to accomplish the cycle time objective was composed of many parts. You had to make several major changes to reach the goal. This technique was so successful we videotaped it and use it extensively in our own change management activities and in the Guiding Radical Change courses we offer both internally and externally.

Our most famous slide is one showing all the handoffs required to ship product from one US wafer fabrication site to an overseas assembly/test area. The in-transit time was long and there was sizeable variability in that cycle time. The major components of the cycle time were the movement from building to building and the transportation handoffs. We depicted this process by drawing buildings, trucks and planes. This slide is known as our 'Planes, Trains, and Automobiles' slide (see Figure 2.2).

It was a simple but effective message which showed the executives how complex the process had become for something as simple as moving product from one site to another.

We played games that created a simple but effective vocabulary. To teach the principle of variability in a process, we use a coin and dice game. In the factories months later we still hear 'coin' and 'dice' used to describe certain conditions.

To teach teamwork we play a game using blue and green balls. Blue represents teamwork and green indicates individual gain. The blue balls have come to be a symbol of teamwork. The re-engineering team has presented blue balls to managers and leaders who have displayed teamwork skills. Sometimes even the mention of a green ball gets the discussion back on track.

To communicate to the executives very early in the process perspective, we scheduled expositions, which we referred to as Business Process EXPOs. We held the first EXPO in a large conference room. Positioned around the room were eight different booths, one for each major business process and one for the overall processes and the methodology we were using to manage the processes. The displays consisted of the process and its subprocesses, any metrics developed by the teams to measure the process, and the inputs from and outputs to other processes. Each booth was staffed by the process owner and team members that had been assigned to define the improvement plan for that process. The executives and key stakeholders were escorted from booth to booth (a set time was allowed for each visit). A brief description of the process was given, then executives were free to ask questions, comment on the process, or point out possible conflicts.

After the initial EXPO was held to familiarize the executives and managers, additional EXPOs were held at a central locations that were open to all employees. We held them for two days to allow as many people as possible the opportunity to understand and ask questions. The teams responsible for the work on the processes again staffed the booths. The objectives were to familiarize people with the process perspective and provide them with the opportunity to ask questions and make comments about anything relating to the processes or the plans for the processes. The EXPOs were well received and we are thinking about developing a travelling EXPO to update everyone on the status of the processes and give a boost to the process perspective.

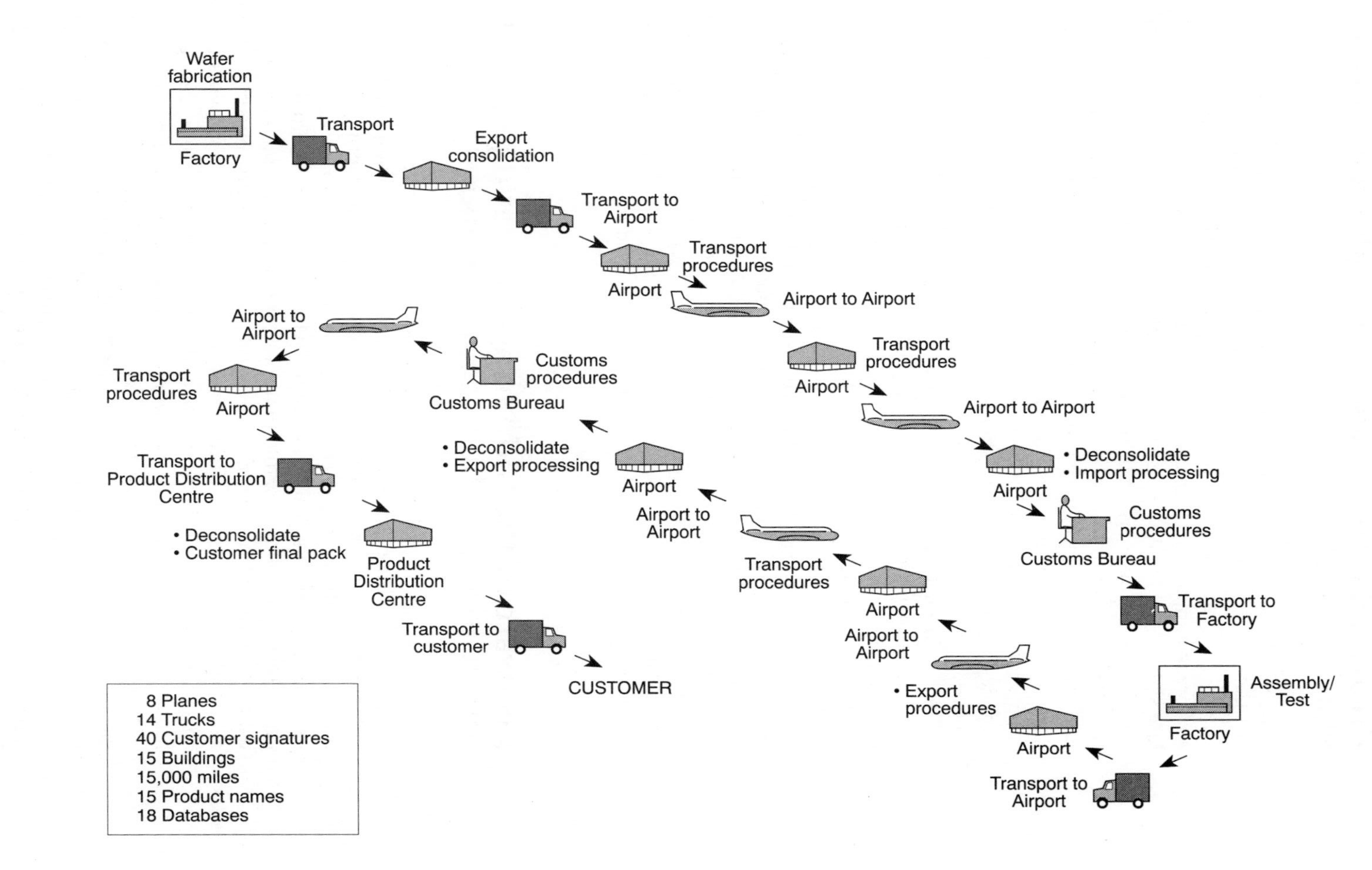

Figure 2.2 Planes, trains and automobiles.

Create a 'bounded vision' but always keep the true vision in tact

The re-engineering methodology we practice is one that says the new process should be designed without any constraints being placed on the design team. This is important because only in this pure environment will the design stretch to the limit and break paradigms. Once constraints are introduced into the design, you begin to lose sight of the breakthrough ideas. If that pure vision is not well documented and accepted as the pure vision, it will be lost. Also, your competitors may not be faced with the same constraints or boundaries and your own boundaries may change over time. Documenting the pure vision captures the true potential of the process.

We were successful in getting our executives and stakeholders to buy the unconstrained vision only when we developed the concept of the 'bounded vision'. The bounded vision is the vision slightly tempered by reality. An example of bounding follows.

The SC Order Fulfilment Vision clearly states that all manufacturing should take place in one geographical location under one roof. This eliminates non-value-added handoffs and material movement and is necessary to meet the design goal of two-week cycle time. In reality, SC has a huge asset base scattered around the world. The wafer fabrication portion of manufacturing is very seldom on the same continent as the assembly and test operations. The cost of moving or shifting these high-dollar assets is out of the question. The vision is bounded by adding what was called a 'virtual factory'. The factory pieces are linked by virtue of process routings, metrics, common practices, shared people and information systems. There will still be transportation steps from one factory area to another, but the factory areas will not operate as stand-alone. The vision still states the need for all factory areas to be under one roof, so future investments can be based on the vision principles.

Be aware of the hidden agendas and political implications in the executive ranks

It would be much easier if all communication was open and the agendas of the individuals and the political implications at the top of the company could be ignored, but these can have significant impacts on the re-engineering of a core business process. Often the re-engineering team does not have enough insight or information to make adjustments. There are times when the re-engineering team just has to accept that they will not be told that some information is 'too sensitive' even for the team. However, awareness of the existence of these factors sometimes helps explain actions that appear counterintuitive to the team. An involved owner and executive advocate can be very helpful when these issues arise. They can get additional information for the team or can work on individual areas of concern.

An example of this in our case was a decision involving a particular factory. The decision made was counter to the Order Fulfilment Vision. The re-engineering team was trying to understand the logic behind the decision to determine whether there was a problem with the vision or whether this was a one-time occurrence. We kept hitting roadblocks when trying to determine why the decision was made. We tried many different avenues, but eventually had to give up on determining the reason.

Our owner assured us the vision was still valid and that we should proceed. We assume there was something involved that we were not aware of and had to move forward without that information.

There were times when things happened that looked very much in line with the vision for our process, but we were not able to confirm the actions. We were told on several occasions that we should not ask too many questions, because there were things happening of which we were not aware. When you need open communication and as much information as possible to make informed decisions, it is difficult to accept these answers. It also causes the team to wonder if the executives are sharing as much as should or could be shared with the team. In our case, we really had no choice. We were pleased with the decisions, so we just continued keeping as much information in front of the Process Owner and other executives as possible.

Find a business process re-engineering advocate/ champion with enough clout and persistence to resolve issues

The role of elevating and working on issues might ordinarily reside with the process owner. In our case, the process owner was at too high a level in the organization to work the more routine problems and issues. And, by his admission, he was more of a process facilitator or mentor than an owner. We have access to an SC Vice-President who has proved very valuable in the role of communicating with executives, discussing issues with them in one-on-one sessions and linking the re-engineering activities to other aspects of running semiconductor. Two specific examples of the areas where this has been key are:

1. Linking compensation to the milestones and deliverables from a process perspective. He had the clout in the organization to make and follow through on recommendations with Human Resources concerning such things as team-based compensation, pay for performance contracts and linking contracts to the re-engineering deliverables and milestones. He was able to facilitate this for both the executives and teams. He continues actively to pursue new, innovative compensation techniques.
2. Making stakeholder assessments on the three SBU managers. All three are critical stakeholders in the process and their positions on issues can greatly affect our progress. We are able to use our advocate to hold one-on-one peer-to-peer sessions with them to determine their position and their concerns.

Position existing programmes with re-engineering or at least define their relationship to the re-engineering effort

If the project is a major high-level business process that involves a lot of resources, it is critical that high-level stakeholders do not think re-engineering is going to throw away all the current efforts or programmes that are underway. Many of the programmes we found were directed at making continuous or incremental improvements or were teaching the people in the Order Fulfilment Process certain skills. We spent a considerable amount of time understanding the existing programmes, understanding how they align with the vision and stretch goals of the re-engineering project, educating the people involved on the work we were doing and providing a vector for improvement from their programme if possible.

A critical programme to understand in relation to the re-engineering effort is the Total Quality Thrust of the company. SC had a strong Total Quality culture that had developed over the last decade. One of our early mistakes was not taking the time to align the re-engineering work with the Total Quality Manager. We never recovered even though we spent a lot of time in the following stages of the project positioning the two efforts. Our choice was to position re-engineering as one of the tools used in the Total Quality effort. It would be used when dramatic change to a high-level business process was required.

In Semiconductor, there is a yearly Policy Deployment cycle which determines the critical areas where improvement is needed for the coming year. During that year, the executives monitor the metrics that will determine progress toward the goals set by Policy Deployment. One of the best boosts to our project was the alignment of the 1992, 1993 and 1994 Policy Deployment objectives with the goals of cycle time and variability reduction we were working on in Order Fulfilment. The advocate mentioned above was critical in making proposals of how the Policy Deployment objectives should align with the Order Fulfilment objectives. The alignment gave credibility to the re-engineering effort, as near-term results from the Policy Deployment objectives were linked back to the re-engineering effort.

Business process management (BPM) was a technique or tool taught to SC employees. It consisted of a twelve-step process that taught how processes were defined, measured and simplified. The approach had been to teach this at the micro process level. These were very valuable skills needed to understand the macro core business processes when we were building the High Level Business Process Map and understanding the existing Order Fulfilment Process. We re-emphasized the skills taught in the earlier BPM courses and applied them to the macro core business processes. The techniques were well received because they built on an existing base.

One activity we have not successfully positioned is the link to the work we are doing towards achieving the Malcolm Baldrige Quality Award. In Semiconductor the decision was made to use the Malcolm Baldrige criteria to define improvement gaps and measure the strengths and weaknesses of the organization. The team had a clear understanding that Malcolm Baldrige was a mechanism to measure how successful we were at defining and implementing business processes. However, we never took the time to position this effort. There is still a lot of confusion, as executives are assigned to each of the Malcolm Baldrige categories. There is a new effort to add a new gap identification effort. If this is not positioned using the existing High Level Business Process Map and to comprehend the current Order Fulfilment Project, this will cause more confusion and frustration.

Spend a lot of time solving issues in other processes because their output is critical to your process

We estimate that only about 30 per cent of the problems we have solved or identified that need to be solved exist in the Order Fulfilment Process. The other 70 per cent are problems caused in other processes. So why did we re-engineer Order Fulfilment instead of the other processes? Remember earlier we said the decision was made to re-engineer the process where we were getting the most customer complaints. Sometimes the symptoms appeared in Order Fulfilment but the problems were actually generated further back in the product life-cycle. We found that we were often the drivers to work through the issues to resolve the other 70 per cent, especially the ones that were in our critical path.

A critical factor in our success was a statement the executives made very early in the re-engineering process. They said:

> We are re-engineering one high level business process, Order Fulfilment. All the other processes will work on continuous improvement programs. If Order Fulfilment highlights something that needs to change in another process, it will be given top priority by that process.

Following are some examples of changes in other processes identified by Order Fulfilment.

- Many of our problems stemmed from the fact that some elements of the business plan were not defined, or if they were defined they were not clearly communicated. In our High Level Process Map, the business plan is developed by the Strategy Development/Business Management Process. Our advocate and our Process Owner spent a lot of time and effort working on the business plan to incorporate and communicate the items needed by Order Fulfilment. Critical was the development of a factory roadmap which defined a map for the transition and construction of factories. Prior to our identifying this as an issue it had not been a clear deliverable.
- A critical problem/issue in Order Fulfilment was that the same factory resources were being used in Product Development and in Order Fulfilment. The different needs of the Product Development activities were introducing significant variability into the time-dependent Order Fulfilment Process. This problem was outside the Order Fulfilment boundary, but we had to address it before we could ensure the stretch goal of the process would be met. A strategy was defined and we are now moving forward with the strategy to remove product development variability from the Order Fulfilment Process. We must ensure that we do not create another problem solving this one, because we are no longer developing and producing on the same equipment. The answers are not always clear choices.
- Another critical problem in Order Fulfilment is that we were accepting orders for new manufacturing processes before we had them production-ready. Our Product Development Process was also delayed waiting for the new manufacturing processes. The development and installation of the new manufacturing processes are in the Manufacturing Capability Development Business Process. We celebrated a major victory when a new organization called Manufacturing Capability Development was announced recently. This new organization owns the business process from the definition of a new manufacturing process until it is production-ready and released to Order Fulfilment. It will focus on its continued improvement to enable faster Product Development and a less variable Order Fulfilment Process.

Several of the activities mentioned above were the clarification or definition of a strategy. The level of strategic changes we needed took top-level executive involvement. Strategic change is slow, so we often wondered whether anything was happening. At this point, the education, understanding and commitment of the process owner took over. He worked on these issues in the executive meetings and one-on-one as needed. The critical changes we needed were made and communicated.

Understand and communicate in the language that fits the culture

Semiconductor has a very strong engineering culture. The way to make an impact on the majority of people in SC is by using facts and logic and supplying the solution in terms that can be expressed in formulae and proven theories.

An example of how this worked was in the development of the algorithms to be used for scheduling starts into the factories. Historically the average projected cycle times were added up and then a 'judgement' or 'pad' was added to determine how far in advance of the due date production should be started in the factories. The judgement number was always a source of concern for managers. They always wanted to know how 'judgement' was calculated. Amazingly, no one ever seemed to have the answer. The new algorithm does two things. It plans the cycle times at a given confidence level (rather than average) and it replaces the 'judgement number' with statistically calculated sigma. The emotion has been removed from numbers, the formulae are verifiable and consistent, and the new algorithm follows logic and facts to satisfy the engineering minds of SC.

An area we still struggle with in this culture is the change management or human side of the change. There are not many statistical formulae that can be applied. However, we have had more success with results of change management assessments when we can show the results empirically or graphically. If we can communicate in terms of percentages or milestones even on the softer change issues, the required activities are easier to get past the data requirements of the culture. Also, if we can communicate and follow a defined procedure or plan (e.g. a clearly documented communication roadmap and time line) the change management activities are better accepted and supported.

An engineering culture does make change management issues very difficult. The culture searches for facts and tries to make everything quantifiable. In change management that is not possible. Be prepared for different types of resistance in this or similar cultures.

Do some very visible, quick-hitting communication

Early in the project, we had difficulty getting some of the mid-level managers and owners to admit that we would make different decisions based on taking the process perspective of Order Fulfilment. No matter how well we thought we were communicating, we still received a significant amount of scepticism. We decided to try some very visible actions to help reinforce the process perspective.

One of our favourite examples is what we called Cycle Time Court. The process owner of Order Fulfilment served as the judge. If there was an Order Fulfilment decision to be made involving two different pieces of the process or functions in the process, and the decision was not black and white, both sides would present their case to the judge. He would make an immediate decision based on what was best for the process. This sent a clear signal to the business that things were changing.

There was a metric in one piece of the Order Fulfilment Process that caused product to be held in the line of a factory if month-end numbers had already been achieved, even if there was still a need for the product by the customer. This caused delays in getting the product to the customer. The Order Fulfilment process owner publicly announced nothing else would be held over the end of the month. The metric used to measure the factory managers was changed to reflect this 'no holding back' philosophy, and cycle time to the customer was reduced. Again, this was a clear signal to the business that things were changing.

Just about the time you get your process owners and sponsors aligned and trained, there will be a major reorganization

This re-engineering activity occurred primarily during one of the most stable organizations we can remember. However, as we are now moving deeply into Business Transition, we have just had a major reorganization that affected our process owner and several of our key executive stakeholders. We are at the point where we can continue Business Transition with little interruption, but we still find ourselves doing additional work and change management as a result of the reorganization. In earlier stages of the project, this could have had a significant impact. All we can add at this point is that you should prepare a contingency plan.

Critical deliverables

Looking back on some of the work done in this project, it appears much more orchestrated than it was. There were honestly times when we just stumbled across what turned out to be critical deliverables as specific problems arose. Listed below are examples of these which we have used again and again. These have also been used to spark even better ideas, and we encourage that as part of the objective in reading this section. The techniques used to formalize most of this work are documented in the classes and methodology, so the focus will primarily be on how these are applied and how the project benefited.

Vision – if you do not have one, get one

We use vision here to mean the statement that defines the destination the corporation or business entity wants to reach in the future. If this is not clearly defined, stated and written down, the other activities down the road in Process Understanding and New Process Design can take the corporation in the wrong direction. The team will spend a lot of time wondering or playing detective trying to determine what the vision and supporting strategies are. If there is not a clear vision, it is well worth spending time to develop and communicate it before assembling a team. The vision and strategies must be perceived as reachable by the corporation. From re-engineering's standpoint, it makes the job of buy-in and commitment much easier if these also motivate the company to do something differently than they currently do. We have debated whether re-engineering is actually the deployment of the vision and supporting strategies of the corporation. The deployment requires definition of the work, the new jobs and organizations, the new metrics, and the change in the belief system and culture required to make the new vision a reality. Those are the components of a successful re-engineering project.

Build a high-level business process map

As mentioned earlier on, the High Level Business Process Map was probably the most critical deliverable developed. The proposal to do this was made in response to some conflicting re-engineering efforts that were being started and aimed to help define the scope of our project. The questions to be answered with this map were:

- What does our customer think we are in business to do?
- What input does our customer give us to trigger our work, and what output can be expected from our work?
- What work do we do to produce these outputs?

By focusing the discussion around the customer and the customer's high-level business processes, we were able to look at the work differently. The Customer Number One motto was on all the conference room walls at TI, but until we put the customer at the centre of the work and asked questions as the customer would, the motto was not really practised. The map allowed us to accomplish some very interesting things from this customer-centred perspective:

- As already discussed, it puts customers and the work they do at the centre of all process definitions and discussions.
- It turned the discussion of a complex technical organization into a simple diagram of boxes and arrows. With a short explanation, anyone could understand Semiconductor activities.
- It removed organizational names and baggage from discussions. The processes defined did not vaguely resemble existing organizations, but they were clearly tied to the customer.
- It clearly set the scope of the SC Order Fulfilment Re-engineering project.
- It elevated the examination of the basic work we do above the complex organizational hierarchy built around the activities.
- It provided a common vocabulary.
- Building the map was an excellent process training tool.
- It took the focus of the executives to the macro business process level rather than the micro level that had been the focus of previous process studies.
- It provided a starting point for benchmarking discussions. Clear understanding of the high-level business processes led to us achieving the most benefit from benchmarking activities.
- It pointed out the difference between a revenue-producing (core) process, a

governing process (a process necessary to support to core process) and the enabling processes. (The enablers will be discussed later.)
- It has proved to be a valuable communication tool when asking suppliers to support our core business processes.
- Finally, it has provided numerous opportunities to review our business approach with our customers and provides a framework to address their current and future interactions with TI.

We believe this deliverable is such a critical element in understanding the process perspective of the business that we recommend that any business build this map whether the plans include large-scale re-engineering or continuous improvement. All the benefits listed above (with the possible exception of the scope) are benefits that apply whether a business is re-engineering or not. We have built process maps for our major business units at TI and the corporate-level map. The important thing to remember here is that the learning experience is as important as the deliverable. The deliverable does serve as a constant reminder of what was learned or a constant opportunity to teach processes and their importance to internal workers, customers and suppliers. But the understanding of the business from the customer's perspective is the best outcome.

The high-level business process map is never finished. There will continue to be debate and discussions regarding the decisions made and the changes that should occur. These discussions are very healthy and continue to promote the process focus in the business units.

We believe all the glowing references above. However, the process map did not solve all the problems. The SC group still fell back into the comfort of functional alignment. The commodity business wanted to define its customers differently from the way the custom business did. But the model did at least bring these debates to the fore-front so that they could be addressed as key decisions or reasons for continued suboptimization. We continue to work on these issues today.

Make sure the case for action is armour-plated

The methodology says that a case for action should be strong, clear, concise and simple. It should also be added that it should be able to stand up to all levels of rationalization and all types of weapons. We were fortunate that our case for action was hammered home every day by our customers and that we had benchmark information from a strong competitor. It was still challenged, especially by the parts of the business that were perceived as world class and were doing well operating in the existing way.

We found that a visual representation of the case for action, which we continued to update and modify, was very valuable. Everyone remembers a long strip of paper with every inch representing a week's worth of time, especially when compared to a much shorter strip of time for the competition. Long lists of facts and data are not so easily remembered.

We found it important to continue to strengthen the case for action with more customer-supported information, more competitor information and more internal experience whenever possible. The 'Gameboard' continues to be an education tool for the stakeholders as new phases or programmes are initiated. For example, we are now adding enabler strips of paper that explain the relationship of an enabling process to the core business process. The 'Planes, Trains and Automobiles' slide mentioned earlier was an addition to the original case for action.

Clearly communicate scope and scale, especially if they change

Outlined here is the history of the scope and scale of the SC project (see Table 2.2). In retrospect, the scope and scale path is traceable. However, during periods of transition from one scope to another it was not always clear or well communicated. Time was lost and lots of energy expended discussing the pros and cons of the scope and scale changes. The discussions were necessary from the change management perspective, but the team and the stakeholders were often confused by the scope during these discussions.

A particularly troublesome spot in the scope and scale discussions was the June 1992 timeframe when the focus was on the one Strategic Business Unit (SBU) producing the majority of the custom-products. Several key stakeholders from the remaining two SBUs were very critical of the project and were casting a lot of doubt among managers, especially the executives of the more commodity-type product lines. The decision was made to form a study team comprised of the members of the remaining two SBUs. The team's charter was to start from scratch and define the Order Fulfilment Process vision for commodity (or Make-to-Market) products. The team spent six months working diligently with the customers and finally reached the conclusion that the visionary process should be the same as the one for custom products. The effort tied up a lot of resources but was absolutely critical for the buy-in of the Make-to-Market stakeholders. Only after this intense effort were we able to increase the scope to all Semiconductor divisions.

At one point there were three teams, the original re-engineering team working on custom or Make-to-Order products, the team working on the remaining commodity or Make-to-Market products described above, and a Pilot Case Team focusing on a specific Make-to-Order product line. For those not involved with the re-engineering effort directly, it was very confusing and difficult to keep the activities straight. For those involved in the effort, the discussion topics of the teams overlapped, making sometimes simple problems much more complex than necessary. It took us a long time to recognize the problem fully and to begin addressing it by defining it as a

Table 2.2 Scope and scale

Date	*Re-engineering scope*	*Scale*
April 1991	Everything custom	Worldwide
August 1991	One custom product line	Worldwide
November 1991	One business unit – focus on product line	Worldwide
June 1992	One business unit – study the remaining two	Worldwide
November 1992	Pilot in one custom product line	Two of four regions
April 1993	All Semiconductor Order Fulfilment	Worldwide
June 1993–1998	All Semiconductor Implementation Order Fulfilment	Worldwide

scope and scale issue. We began prefacing all meetings, presentations and discussions by first clarifying the scope and scale of the topic.

Create a clear picture of the current process with value-added activities easily identified

One of the questions most often asked is how much process understanding should be done. Some team members will be content to do this until they die. Some team members want to document two or three pieces of work and call the work complete. Somewhere there is a compromise. The level of detail in process understanding should be enough to communicate clearly the boundaries of the project and give the stakeholders a common understanding of the work that is included in the process. Those team members who want all the details will have to hang around until Business Transition (Phase 4). The opportunity will arise at that point to understand everything in gory detail. In Business Transition it is critical to understand the current work so as to clearly define a transition path to the new work.

The best tool we found to represent the process is a block and arrow diagram. The blocks represent activities, the arrows show the direction of the work, and these pass through functional organizations that perform the work.

A critical element of our process understanding step was the definition and identification of 'value added'. There is always a lot of curiosity about the definition of value added. The one we use consists of two parts. First, whether the customer would pay us for the work done in that activity; second, whether that activity would bring the product closer to its end state. This is a rigid definition, but it highlights the few activities that must be performed in some way in the new process vision. The ones not classified as value added can be very closely scrutinized for obliteration, simplification or transfer. Highlighting the few activities in the process that fit the rigid definition is very illuminating for the majority of the stakeholders and executives. It forces some very difficult issues onto the table. Either the definition can be diluted or the analysis of the new process can begin with just the customer-critical activities as the new core.

If the current-process documentation is done effectively, it will become a valuable piece of the case for action. It will highlight the non-value-added steps that are not creating revenue for the company and provide a transition to the new process vision.

Have clearly defined metrics for success

In our project, the success metric we measured was cycle time of the entire process. We had not done this before, so it took us over six months to reach the point where we could measure Order Fulfilment cycle time. It was difficult to get a standard acceptable definition. The data was scattered across several databases. Some of the information had to be modelled because we did not have the information to track it. Our project stretch goal was fourteen days for Order Fulfilment Custom Product cycle time. The first time we measured the process, the cycle time was 186 days. Once people realized our customers and competitors were serious about the fourteen days, the difference between the current cycle time and the goal added significant power to our case for dramatic change.

People needed to understand what their contribution to the goal was, so we divided it up into subprocess pieces and assigned yearly goals to these pieces. There was some risk of suboptimizing the pieces, so we made very sure the overall process goal was well publicized and continue to educate people on the fact that meeting their goal without the process meeting the overall goal does not meet the customer's needs.

We had to give people as close to immediate feedback as possible on their progress. We began publishing the cycle time results weekly and recording them officially at the end of every month. The goal is to have them available on a real-time basis, so the process can react immediately.

We spent the first two years measuring cycle time, but understanding that the real culprit to our process was variability. After significant progress on cycle time, the executives are taking the next step this year by adding a yield metric to the process to remove waste and other types of variability from the process. The questions we get asked most often now are: Has the emphasis shifted away from cycle time to yield? Does that mean that we are no longer re-engineering?

We did such a good job associating re-engineering with the metric of cycle time that we now have to spend a lot of our time explaining how metrics interrelate. What we are really working on is reducing all variability in the process cycle time as one good measure of the progress. So be prepared to explain the goal metrics, but also to understand and educate people on the relationships between metrics. A good process performs well on quality, on time delivery, cycle time and waste. Those metrics lead to improved customer satisfaction, flexibility and productivity at the process level.

For the new process vision, have a clear and simple visual representation

It seems the most anticipated deliverable (other than the demise of the re-engineering team) from the SC project was the New Process Vision. We tried several methods of presenting this deliverable, and after trial and error, ended up with two key elements. The first was a simple picture of the new process that would reach the stretch goal of two weeks' cycle time for custom-products. Be prepared for everyone wanting to add their own touch, however.

The second method we used was a twenty- to thirty-page document describing the attributes and objectives of each portion of the new process design. This written document can be absorbed at the reader's own pace and when the time is right. The document we produced has some interesting and sometimes unexpected uses and expectations:

- Communication of the new process design.
- Documentation of the vision so that, when it is bounded, the vision still remains intact.
- Evidence that some thought was put into the simpler visual drawing.
- The logic behind the design.
- Through the process of translation,a chance to educate and ensure understanding in the different cultures. (This has been very illuminating for the original writers.

We thought the document was clear and concise until we realized that Case Manager does not translate to French, the German language does not recognize stakeholder, and Japan does not recognize credit – only a sample of the issues not covered in a global corporation.)

- Source of information systems requirements. This one is included with a word of caution. If the information technology supplier has not yet realized the business interface with the IT organization has changed, it will be looking for detailed requirements from the vision. In reality, all this document provides is a business direction and framework. Now the information technologists must become intimately involved in this new business process and help define the new systems requirements. In our case, we are caught between our IT organization beginning the move to the new environment with the bulk of work still occurring in the old environment. We have since created a supplemental document for the information technology vision.
- Change management tool. For example, it provided a consistent reference to the details of the change. We had the executives sign the document as a sign of their commitment as well as to give the executives added incentive to read the entire document.
- Something to ensure compliance. This one worried us because even though this was the vision, we wanted to be sure people would continue to question and challenge it in the next few years in the event that something better could come along.
- The answer to all Order Fulfilment questions. Any stakeholder with this expectation has been disappointed. The vision document provides only the framework and direction.

Documentation of the new process design is worth the effort. Writing the details forced the discussion on topics the team had taken for granted. It was amazing how much ambiguity and disagreement remained after we thought the design was complete. It was slow and painful, but worth the work.

For Business Transition, create a roadmap

In the project, it was about eighteen to twenty-four months from the time the effort was launched until it was ready to move to full-scale implementation. This is a long time for an organization to wait around to get involved. In our case, even after we began Business Transition the progress seemed slow to us and especially to those who were not so involved in the project as the team. A critical deliverable that was very helpful was the creation of a high-level roadmap. The roadmap shows the projects launched in the initial phases, the current projects and the planned projects as they relate to the move to the new way of doing business.

Behind each project for the current year is a detailed project plan. A member of the Order Fulfilment team is responsible for setting up and maintaining the milestones for the project. The milestones are set according to the involvement level the team feel is necessary for the project. The involvement levels are managing, steering or monitoring.

The culture in SC is very tactical and action-item oriented. The development of the roadmap and the detailed action items and milestones matched that culture and boosted the momentum of the effort. The business can now visualize all the separate projects linked under the Order Fulfilment umbrella. The relationships of the project milestones across projects are documented and managed. As new projects are added to the structure, they are brought into the formal review cycle. The business involvement in the transition to the new process is growing, based on the pull from the current-year projects. Most importantly, with this growing business involvement comes a growing sense of ownership in all levels of the SC organization for the new way of doing Order Fulfilment.

Life as an enabler is rough and getting rougher

In the SC High Level Process Map, there is a box on the right side of the diagram labelled 'enablers'. The members of this box are human resources, information systems, legal, finance, quality, procurement, capital, training, etc. These activities are the ones that allow the core business processes to be the best they can be. The enabling activities do not produce revenue for the enterprise, our customers will not pay us to do them, yet they produce outputs that are necessary to keep the enterprise going. We have found that about the best performance indicator an enabling activity can hope for is to be ignored by the core business processes. Any attention the enabling activities are drawing is probably due to a problem or interference caused in the core process.

The enablers must support business processes, including other enabling activities. The work done may be similar, but the needs of each of the processes they support are different. Since the enablers do not produce revenue, they are always under close scrutiny to add internal value to the organization.

We found that the enabling activities are where most previous improvement efforts have been focused. As discussed later, this is fine, but unless the improvements are done in direct alignment with the work of the core business process improvement activities there is a risk that they will be improving the wrong things.

We are just beginning to understand and work the enabling activities of the Order Fulfilment Process. We know there is room for major improvement in the efficiencies of enablers leading to major improvements in the core business process if breakthroughs can be made. There is a lot of room for advanced study and understanding of enabling activities. Below is what we believe to be the tip of the iceberg.

Be prepared to shift the paradigms of enablers, then prepare for resistance

The people doing enabling activities typically do not think of them as non-value-adding activities (based on the definition the customer will pay for value-adding work). These activities should exist only to serve the core business processes. This is a rather rude and harsh awakening. This tends to make the people, especially the middle and upper levels in those activities, defensive and resistant. Some of the enabling activities are so formal and ingrained in the culture and embedded in the way work is currently done that it takes this type of awakening to see them as support activities for the revenue-producing work. Another risk is that the enablers have convinced themselves they are doing value-added work for the 'internal customers.' By looking at this from the internal customer perspective you may be diminishing the effectiveness to the external customer – the only customer really of importance to the enterprise.

One of the most difficult tasks has been to get the enablers to realize they exist to support the revenue-producing processes. The fact that they may be in the way of some of the revenue-production work today is no one's fault; it just happened as more and more structure was added to the work. If practitioners can get a key manager in an enabling process to recognize these two points, the door opens for major improvement as new, creative ways to manage the enabling activities are found.

Be sure the enablers understand the business processes they serve and how these processes want to interface with them

One of the first things an enabler must do is understand the businesses and the business processes it supports. This can happen only after the core business processes understand if and how they want to interface with the enablers. Any improvement work done prior to this understanding may not be in the best interest of the core business process needs. This must be done with the help of people in the core business processes who are trying to use the enabling activities. The technique used in SC is to map the enabling activities using the high-level mapping techniques described earlier (modified for enablers). The other business processes and their interfaces to the enabler are substituted for the market/customer box that we discussed earlier on the SC High Level Process Map. The work done by the enabler is then documented and boundaries drawn based on the interfaces with the processes. This sounds confusing, but basically the other business processes are reviewed as the customers of the enablers.

Enabling activities are not limited to the activities done in the organization of that name

Enabling activities go on in organizations across the business, not just in the functional organizations that tend to have a similar name. Two examples of this found in Order Fulfilment are:

1. The training activities are typically defined as those done in the training organization (needs analyses, class development, instructor preparation, etc.). These and other training activities are also done in many of the Order Fulfilment activities. For example, training is done on a one-on-one basis when new employees arrive; or, as a skill is learned, it is informally transferred from one person to another. Formal classroom-type training may be conducted without the involvement of the training organization.

2. Information technology activities are typically thought of as being done in our Information Systems and Services factories. In attempting to understand the enabling activities provided by information systems, you must comprehend all the activities.

It is critical to understand all the activities that make up enabling processes, not just those centralized or formalized in an enabling function or organization. This will allow the full scope of the enabling activities to be defined and critical areas for efficiency improvement to be pointed out.

Think of enablers as suppliers to the core business process

If you believe the ideas outlined above about enablers, it becomes apparent that enablers are not the core competency of a business. If they are not the core competency, how much effort should the core business spend on them? That's a question the enabling activities have to be prepared to answer. The paradigm shift we have tried to encourage in SC is for enablers to think of themselves as a suppliers (not necessarily the supplier of choice either). From the supplier perspective they must then try to become the supplier of choice, or, even better, a partner in the work required to make the core processes faster and more efficient. As a partner, the enabler begins to recognize that the very existence of the enabling activity is based on the success of the revenue-producing processes of the business.

The 'in-house' enablers should be prepared to undergo the close scrutiny any external supplier would undergo. An internal enabler may even be asked to provide the industry benchmarking and comparisons. The revenue-generating process has to be willing to select the best enabler supplier for optimizing the revenue-producing processes of the business, even if it means making outsourcing or other such decisions.

Do not let enablers define, change or slow down the flow of work in the core processes

Some enablers have done such an effective job formalizing and standardizing the work they do that it gets in the way of the core business process work. Three examples found in SC were:

1. In the fabrication facility, an outgoing count of chips was performed. The chips then travelled to the assembly area where an incoming count of chips was done. This task was duplicated because of the financial enabling activity of tracking ownership and financial accountability in each factory. Each of the factories wanted to ensure the financial accuracy of the count before transferring or receiving ownership. There was no value in this activity to the customer. It added time and cost to the movement of chips between factories.
2. Paperwork for moving product was needed at a central export consolidation point. The paperwork was attached to the product, so all the product was routed

through this central point, although the only real requirement was that the paperwork be consolidated to meet the export requirement.

3. An enhancement to an information system in a core business process was identified in June and needed as soon as possible. The funding cycle was not until December for the following January. The business was asked to wait or take it up with the steering committee for an exception. The steering committee was meeting in August. A core business process improvement was held up due to an enabling process procedure.

In each case, the enabler was controlling and managing the work it did. However, in each case, it was getting in the way of the work that needed to be done to produce revenue. It should become the enabler's responsibility to recognize these problems for the core processes.

Enablers often serve more than one master

Earlier it was stated that the enabler should redraw the process map with the business processes it serves in place of the customer box. However, enablers often serve corporate or legal requirements as well as the business processes. This is a balancing act the enabler must learn to manage.

An example of this is the project currently underway to understand the enabling finance activities in SC. The core business processes are the customer for this enabler; however, there is work that must be done by these processes for legal and compliance reasons. The challenge of the enabler still remains to do all the work required while not adding overhead or time to the core business processes. In other words, do not interfere with revenue production to carry out compliance or legal activities. The compliance and legal requirements must be met without interfering with the core business process work flow.

Beware of overloading the core processes with requests from enablers

We are finding that the same enabling activities are carried out by multiple functions or organizations. Unless these activities are very well coordinated and aligned, they can cause significant confusion, as different approaches are used for the same problem.

A simple example of this in our project is cycle time training. The factories and other activities involved in Order Fulfilment needed cycle time training. Several organizations became involved in defining and delivering this training to these activities. The re-engineering team, the training organization, functional training activities within the factories, the Operational Methods team and outside consultants were all working on cycle time training. Imagine the confusion caused if one factory was bombarded by all these different activities trying to accomplish the same thing. It is critical that these activities be coordinated and the message consistent. In each case, the coordination of the multiple enabling activities fell to the re-engineering team.

Lessons learned about the team

There are times when a re-engineering team environment closely resembles a bad comedy. However, after working in the team environment for the last several years, it is going to be difficult to be as effective in any other type of work relationship. There are good things, great things, bad things and difficult things about being in a re-engineering team. Hopefully, in sharing some of the lessons learned, the good and great things will come more often to future teams.

Have a very diverse team, not only in skills, but in personality

The re-engineering methodology stresses the importance of teams and outlines the need to select key people from each of the diverse activities. The acid test to identify key people is when their manager fights to keep them or simply refuses to let them go. If the practitioners can get this type of team member with the knowledge and skills needed, the team is one step closer to victory in the re-engineering battle.

Step two is making sure these key people have different what we will call 'ranges of view'. Some people think very tactically. We have found these tactical people typically think in a time horizon of about three to six months – one year if stretched. The other end of the spectrum are those that think only three to ten years in the future. (At TI, the second group is much harder to find.) To balance the continuum, there are those with the mid-range of view. The critical skill here is the ability to translate between the first two groups and continually to recognize the value of those who are different. This third group can use and understand the long-range view of the second group to help define and stretch the new direction and use the tactical skills of the first group to plot a course toward that vision. This third group of mid-range skills seems to be very rare in SC. We have either those that have created the vision and cannot understand why we are not there yet, or the more tactical executors waiting for someone to tell them specifically what must be done.

The point here is to be aware of the need for all three types of contributors in the team. Each of them brings a valuable addition by addressing the entire span of the project time line. If the team can recognize and value the frame of reference of each team member, this greatly lowers the level of frustration when topics are discussed. The team leader or facilitator can point this out as needed to help position discussions. We have one very eye-opening example from our team. We were lucky enough to have a true visionary on our initial team. He thought five to ten years into the future. Many of those of us with shorter time horizons would look puzzled and try to be patient with him. He left the team (and the company) after the New Process Design phase. Only after his departure did we truly recognize his contribution. And we continue to see the influence he had on the team. It is unfortunate we could not have listened and asked him more questions while he was here.

The third factor in the team diversity topic is personality types. We used several personality assessments to determine responses and approaches. When we really started using these to understand other team member responses (e.g. the team leader is a heavy 'thinker' and team member A is a heavy 'feeler'), team discussions became less emotional. Believe it or not, it also helped us to manage time and expectations. We found the team members with heavy emotional needs required many more one-on-one discussions, especially about the softer side of the issues. The 'deciders' ran out of patience long before the 'thinkers' had enough facts to feel comfortable making a decision or moving on. This is over-simplified, but reminding ourselves of the differences helped when discussions became bogged down or when patience ran thin.

The main point here is to understand the differences between team members. If possible, before a team is staffed, look for specific differences. The more balanced mix the team has, the better the end-result of the project, but more facilitation is required to bridge the gaps and find the values.

You must have a strong, humble, open team leader

The methodology we follow states that you should select a team leader in the Project Initiation phase. The team leader should have all the traits listed for a re-engineering team member, plus an extra amount of business respect and credibility. The team leader has also to be a saint – well almost.

In our case, the team leader came from managing a large engineering organization. He had to make the transition from manager to team leader. We had a very strong-willed, diverse team that had a lot of ideas about how to help him with that transition. Our ideas often collided with his. He was used to handling situations as a manager. As he continued to do this, the team resented not being involved in some of the decisions or having access to the same information he did. It is difficult to assess whether the team really needed the information, but it did create some tense times in the team environment.

The re-engineering team members came from positions where they were recognized for individual contributions. These had to be traded in for the good of the team. If you have pulled key people, you are dealing with quite a bit of self-esteem, some might even say ego, trapped for eight hours a day in a conference room. This can become tricky for the team leader to manage.

Be prepared to deal with the team dynamics

The first lesson learned in this section mentions the importance of having a diverse team. That diversity in the same conference room with the egos described earlier can be very complicated. It is up to the team leader, with the help of the practitioner, to manage all these complexities. At this point prayer might be a viable alternative, but there are other techniques that worked when the situation needed to be discharged:

1. Take a break. That seems easy, but not everyone is going to be happy with that decision. Some team members will want to continue discussion. Some people need think time, so to manage diversity honestly, all needs should be considered. The team leader or facilitator has to make the call on whether it will be productive or destructive to continue.
2. Try to structure the discussion by using some problem-solving technique. We

were never able to find one that worked every time, but just adding some structure usually helped us make progress.

3. Break up into subteams. Sometimes the group dynamics were just too much to deal with in the larger group. Subteams with similar ideas could be grouped to address specific problems.
4. Have a 'feelings' session. We would make sure the conference room door was closed, then open the floor for people to share anything that was bothering them. It was in one of our early feeling sessions that we learned no one can tell someone else what to feel, or try to change what they feel. It was an important lesson for all of us. I am not sure these sessions worked for all team members, but they were valuable for others and valuable for team effectiveness.
5. Have a motivation break – pull out some old slides or information that reminds the team of what they need to accomplish. Review the Victory Log (see p. 49).
6. Let the resident 'smoother of ruffled feathers' take the lead in the meeting. This is the person who can always find the positive in the discussion and build on something while other issues are allowed to drop. Every team needs someone to take this role. It is not always easy to find someone willing to play this role.
7. Pull in a team/marriage counsellor. We never found one with the specific team background we needed, but we used several outside consultants. There were seven to nine strong personalities in a room for eight hours a day trying to discuss and reach some agreement on complex issues. Negotiation and compromise are at times difficult in a relationship between *two* people, so the re-engineering environment, with several very diverse individuals, is much more difficult. If the team relationship became too intense, we broke into smaller teams to finish parts of the assignment. We also attended team-building classes and seminars over the life of the re-engineering team.
8. Develop a sense of humour. It will get plenty of exercise over the life of the project.

Beware of the pessimists and opportunists that may be disguised as team members

The importance of team dynamics and the support network the team builds are critical to the success of the project and the quality of its results. There are characteristics in some team members that are well hidden at first, but as the team members get more familiar with each other these not so positive traits tend to emerge. The team should be prepared to deal with these.

One person that can be very draining on the team is the pessimist. This is the team member who always sees the negative side of any situation and continually questions the commitment or wisdom of moving forward or taking action. The team is having to deal with this type of resistance outside the team, so having to face it internally as well adds stress. There is a role of 'devil's advocate' to be played, however. It is better if this role can rotate. It also may call for some role playing.

Another concern is the team member who, in front of the team, appears to be totally supportive, but away from the team works the informal networks to plant seeds of doubt or question the team's direction. This is very dangerous. The re-engineering team is walking a fine line with the organization as it is. If the organization or stakeholders sense a breakdown of the team, the results can be disastrous. At the minimum, it requires a significant amount of effort to reconfirm the team's position. We found this to happen most often when new members were brought into the team. They did not necessarily buy in 100 per cent to the decisions made prior to their arrival.

Another problem is the team member who claims to be full time, but has conflicts and 'more important' activities that do not allow participation in much of the work. If that team member continues to claim team membership, and therefore credit, for the hard work of the rest of the team, there is resentment from the members doing the actual work.

We did not come up with any major breakthroughs on dealing with these situations. We tried a few approaches:

1. We had team reviews where we shared three positive attributes about team members and three areas where they could improve. This allowed for some of the more difficult topics to be brought to the table and discussed. This is a difficult exchange to manage and is very difficult for some team members.
2. We set up a simple fine system where people were fined for things like:

    - late arrival at meetings;
    - unexcused absences;
    - unprofessional statements.

    Monies received from the fines were used for a social activity. Some team members thought this discredited the professional nature of the team. This had only moderate success.
3. We tried to develop formal codes of conduct, but as we had no formal review mechanism or metrics it was not always followed.

    The point here is to be aware that, in the team environment, team commitment to the project and to the team is critical. There will be cases where this commitment is not present. Watch for this if team performance declines and have some ideas ready to try if it becomes a problem.

Be on the lookout for team members sent with the objective to derail the team

Not all stakeholders or organizations will support the work of the re-engineering effort, particularly those that feel they are successful in today's environment and do not see the need to make significant changes. If the work they do will change as a result of the re-engineering effort, however, they need to be involved in the team and the work that is done. We found in several cases that members were assigned to the re-engineering team or the expert teams with the purpose of derailing or slowing down the progress of the effort. This caused tension and a drop in the motivation of the team. Since the purpose was not always evident initially, it was difficult to pinpoint what was causing the team concerns.

The most effective way we found to deal with this was through education. This was a sure sign that the individuals' organizations were prime targets for more intense change management. Often, once the individuals had been through the training necessary to bring them up the re-engineering learning curve, they became proponents and would take the message back to their organizations themselves. There were times we just had to continue with the work, recognizing that not everyone was a believer.

Plan for unpopularity of the re-engineering team

The re-engineering team will quickly come to represent change in the business environment. As we know, change represents pain. The organization tends to place a lot of blame for the change on the re-engineering team. Much of the blame is not out in the open, and this makes it difficult to deal with. It comes in the form of negative comments, backstabbing, sabotage. This is not always the case, but we had to deal with all of these. The most important thing we did was to keep reminding ourselves that the reason for the unpopularity of re-engineering was the resistance to the change itself and that it was not reflective of the re-engineering team's work. The easiest way for us to deal with this was to continue to deal in facts, especially facts about our inability to do what the customer needed if we did not change. We kept customer quotes, competitive statistics and evidence of our executives' support ready to use to move beyond the resistance that was directed at the team.

There is also unpopularity caused by jealousy. The well-publicized fact that re-engineering teams should be made up of the best and brightest can cause considerable problems for those stakeholders who are not on the team. It is critical that these stakeholders understand their valuable contribution to the progress of the team. As a team we repeatedly called in our 'experts' and made sure they knew we did not think we had the answers but that we felt lucky to have been given the time to work on the problem. We tried to make them win whenever possible. It is difficult for the re-engineering team to keep making winners out of the very people that may be trying to put up barriers, but once the sceptics realize they can benefit from what the team is doing, they tend to become some of the most avid supporters.

Another caveat is that much of the existing improvement work stopped when the re-engineering effort was introduced. Everyone would say, 'We don't need to work on that; the re-engineering team is going to take care of it.' It is very important to clarify with the business early in the effort who is responsible for the level of improvement. Progress on many continuous improvement activities cannot stop and wait for re-engineering results. Once re-engineering results are available, they should be communicated to the other teams and plans made on how to adjust the other efforts.

Plan celebration points

One of the things we would do differently if starting over would be to plan for celebration points at close intervals. The deliverables should be clearly definable and about six to twelve months apart. Celebration points can be the completion of key deliverables, a big communication event, hearing something positive from one of the sceptics or even a failure. The purpose is to celebrate learning. The team will need the celebrations because the re-engineering environment tends to be an emotional rollercoaster ride.

We also attempted to keep a 'Victory Log'. Ours was a bulletin board in the re-engineering area where we posted newspaper articles, newsletters, speeches, pictures, messages or anything that represented something positive or progress for the team. We have not maintained the Victory Log as well as we would like, but after three years it is quite a collage of memories and accomplishments. It is also good for morale, posting things to be used in performance reporting and reminding us of what we have done (or not done) lately.

Define the roles of team members

There are a lot of administrative activities surrounding the re-engineering team. If these are not well organized they can take up a lot of time. If this is possible, a team administrative assistant might be a worthwhile investment. We did not have this luxury, so we assigned specific roles to team members. Some of these roles were Librarian, Communications Specialist, Social Coordinator, Motivator, Team Training. The roles should be defined to meet the needs of the team and should be reviewed as the team's needs change or as team members' interests change.

One very helpful role was assigning specific team members the responsibility of bringing particular stakeholders or executives along the change curve. The assignments were based on similarities of personality types, background, knowledge base and existing relationship. This proved very valuable.

The team and its members will move through the change cycle at different rates

In the methodology, a big part of the change management effort is recognizing where stakeholders are in relation to the four stages of business process redesign (also known as the grief) cycle. A critical point is to recognize that the re-engineering team will go through the change cycle both as individuals and the team as a whole. The team members moved through the phases of the cycle at different rates. Also, the cycle recurred for the team and individual team members. The re-engineering team does not escape the effects of the changes happening in the re-engineering environment or their 'home' environments.

In our case, we typically had seven members scattered at various points in the cycle. The team as a whole was at some point in the cycle; the stakeholders, sponsors, and champions were also impacted. It quickly became complex. We did not necessarily determine a tool to make the management of this easier, but recognition of what was occurring and being able to put it in perspective were helpful. These things provided a common communication vehicle for managing team change management issues.

Outsiders can be equal participants or facilitators depending on the situation and the culture

There were initially three 'outsiders' from our Information Technology Group on the team. From the beginning these three outsiders served as equal participants in the team. They shared in the work and were equal contributors in the team meetings. At certain points, because we did not have a direct career link to the organization being changed, we played the facilitator, the objective observer role. However, for buy-in and commitment from SC, we were expected to carry as much weight and responsibility as the other team members. This is something that must be decided by teams by situation.

Be prepared for the natural team transition points in the project

We observed three natural transition points in the re-engineering team. The first occurred after the scope of the project had been set. Our team was put together very early in Project Initiation. After the scope was set, we realized that we had pulled people from areas that were not going to be impacted by the redesign and that other areas that were going to be impacted were not represented. The membership changed to accommodate this before we moved into Process Understanding. This was a relatively easy transition.

The second transition was much more difficult because we were not expecting it. It occurred after New Process Design. After the team defined the new process and did a lot of the validation, there was a letdown. The intensity of the teamwork declined. During this period five team members moved to other positions, returned to their original areas or joined other projects. This occurred over a period of about six months. It appeared gradual at the time, but each time a team member left, the remaining team members struggled to keep up the momentum. It affected the team dynamics and the personality of the team. We brought in other members during this time, but we reached the point where only four members remained.

At that time we took a hard look at the previous few months and discovered that when we moved from New Process Design into Business Transition the team should have undergone a formal transition. The skills and requirements changed. We moved from the high-level understanding and visioning phases to a phase where tactical execution was critical. The informal transition was natural, but took us by surprise because we had not planned for it.

After this hard look, we declared a victory on the first three phases of re-engineering, established a new 'transition team' more in line with the tactical execution and project management skills needed in the next phase, and moved full steam into New Design Implementation. Two members present from the beginning of the project (the team leader and one practitioner) remained on the Transition Team to see the project into implementation.

The third transition is currently underway. The project is in the midst of Business Transition. There is a formal roadmap defining the plan for the next three years. There are numerous subprojects underway, with detailed project plans behind each. These link to the overall project plan. Each of the subprojects has an owner from the business. Increasingly the business is taking ownership of these subprojects and taking ownership of the transition. As this occurs, the role of the Transition Team is changing from spearheading the efforts to monitoring or guiding the efforts. This is a victory and celebration point for the team.

As education continues, the need for monitoring or guiding will become increasingly smaller. Ownership of the roadmap will convert to the business stakeholders. At the point when business ownership is dominant, the Transition Team will need to evaluate its role formally and restaff or redirect resources to support that role. If changes in the business organization or resource assignment are needed, these will be put in place. Just make sure your sponsors and advocates recognize this and then move forward to the next decision.

We discussed bounding of the vision earlier, but here are examples of the impact on the team.

First, our New Process Design said all pieces of the manufacturing activities should be housed under one roof. The semiconductor industry is very capital-intensive, so we knew there was no way we could move the existing asset base. The vision was bounded by creating a virtual factory. Even though pieces of the factory would exist in different locations, the factory would be bound together by common goals, common methodologies and tools, and a common information flow. Many of our stakeholders and some team members felt that since SC would never move all the factories, re-engineering was a failure. It was a large communication and change management challenge to communicate the bounding process and show the results of the bounded activities. The team first had to understand and buy in to the bounding that had occurred.

A second example was the deployment of near-term cycle time goals. We had worked very diligently to teach the importance of the process perspective. The short-term cycle time goals were set from the process perspective (seven times value-added theoretical cycle time for the Order Fulfilment Process in 1993). However, when it came to deploying those goals to portions of the process, they were deployed functionally. Each piece of the process was given its portion of the time allotted. We made significant progress in the reduction of cycle time, but because it was deployed functionally rather than across the process, we did not achieve the strong dependence and link of all pieces of the process in meeting the longer-term goals. We are having to address this separately. We hope to continue working towards process deployment of short-term goals.

If you get 70 per cent achievement of what you set out to achieve, that leaves 30 per cent that is not achieved. The 30 per cent is relished and highly publicized by re-engineering critics. The team should prepare in advance to handle this, because any action that can be viewed as counter to the re-engineering effort will be a change management setback. We published the 70/30 rule early in the process and have not hesitated to point out a decision that falls in the 30 per cent side of the rule.

Celebrate and capitalize on failures

There will be failures. Make sure the team is prepared and ready to handle them. Make sure they are fully understood and the lessons captured and documented. Often we learned more from our mistakes than from our successes. An example of this was when we did not prepare our process owner adequately to respond to questions after a presentation. What we learned from this was that such an approach was risky, but we also got to hear some.

We found that with each transition the team hit a period that was not productive. Once we were able to define the problem and put a plan together to attack it, we were able to move forward again.

The business, not the team, must get the credit for all the victories

Earlier, it was mentioned that the individuals on the team had to give up their individual accomplishments for the sake of the team. Well, the team now has to give up the credit for its accomplishments to the business. The true measure of the team's success is the business taking ownership of the change. The business will not take ownership unless it is first given credit for the change.

This has been one of the most difficult skills to acquire in the re-engineering journey. The re-engineering team members have left their classical career path at a big risk. They have been asked to solve a problem and achieve dramatic results. There is significant pressure to get results as quickly as possible because, in our case, the business was in pain. When the results start rolling in, if the team has been successful the business stakeholders will claim the ideas as their own, take credit for the early success and build on the success for future gains.

In our case we were lucky to have an executive sponsor and re-engineering advocate who understood the work the team was doing and recognized that the results the business was seeing were the results of the re-engineering activities. They walked a fine line, however. They could not publicly give the team too much credit because it would discount the effort of the business to take charge of the project and move it further into implementation.

We have not been able to come up with a remedy for this situation. Strong, understanding sponsors are critical. Awareness is very important so that expectations can be set early. Our advice here is to be aware that this is a requirement of the re-engineering effort and plan for it throughout the project. The team has to provide its own internal support network to handle this during the course of the project. The celebration points mentioned earlier can help make this easier.

Follow the 70/30 rule

On our project, we developed a new process design with no constraints. So much work, effort and soul are devoted to creating the vision that it is difficult to let any part of it go. However, when you apply realism to the vision, there must be some bounding that occurs. The bounding that happened in our case was not always our choice. Luckily, we recognized early in the project that this was going to happen and we were prepared to compromise to keep the momentum directed along the right vector.

Failures are not often easy to spot. Sometimes it takes the wisdom of hindsight to recognize a failure. For example, there is one portion of our process where we have had difficulty getting adequate marketing representation to define what the pilot needs to accomplish. This has been dragging on for months with promises of resources but, until recently, no delivery. We knew there was resistance, but did not take a proactive stance against it. It has greatly slowed progress in defining a critical customer interface portion of the project.

Summary and conclusions

The information provided in the earlier sections is aimed at helping managers in current or planned re-engineering projects. We believe re-engineering, or dramatic improvement, in business processes is a tool in the process improvement toolbox that is here to stay. The pace of change and competition in the work environment is not going to get easier, but rather faster and stiffer, so dramatic change cycles will become common.

The areas we think are ripe for major enhancements and progress are enabling activities and strengthening of the strategy development and deployment processes. We will be continuing our work in those areas as well as continuing to refine the tools and techniques used in specific re-engineering projects.

Since this is an art rather than a science at this point, much of the excitement comes from the creativity and from sharing that creativity. Business process engineering is an area where we can apply many of the elements from our academic and professional careers. Many of the scientific, statistical and behavioural elements come together. The creativity of the team and sponsors in combining the different elements of these capabilities is the resulting power of the project.

Rank Xerox (UK)
Cedric Williams

3

Balancing incremental and radical change initiatives

Introduction

Rank Xerox is dedicated to providing document solutions to businesses of all sizes and for each stage of the document life-cycle.

Documents connect a business with its customers, help people work with others, perform linkages in the business value chain, record ideas and actions, and communicate knowledge. There is one activity that virtually everyone within every office has in common – all of them spend a proportion of their time handling documents, whether text, graphic, data, image, voice or in embedded information (glyph) forms. Simply, documents represent a significant, often underestimated, proportion of the costs of doing business. By comprehending customer document needs and by enabling the creation and production of superior documents, Rank Xerox is branding itself 'The Document Company' – the company that markets and sells products and services that improve business efficiency and effectiveness through the understanding of the document.

The Rank Xerox story

The Xerox Corporation, with its world headquarters located in Stamford, Connecticut, USA, has an annual turnover exceeding US$18 billion. The corporation and its subsidiaries employ over 90,000 people in a hundred countries. It spends over US$1 billion per year in research and development, all focused on document management and document processing technologies.

Formed in 1956, Rank Xerox is jointly owned by the Xerox Corporation and the Rank Organization Plc. The Xerox Corporation has majority voting rights in all parent companies. Rank Xerox, one of four parent companies within the Rank Xerox Group, manufactures, markets and leases Xerox document processing products and services throughout Europe, Asia and Africa.

In January 1995, the Xerox Corporation and the Rank Organization Plc announced the signing of a letter of intent for Xerox to acquire 40 per cent of the Rank Organization's financial interest in Rank Xerox. The overall effect of this transaction has been to increase the Corporation's financial interest from 67 per cent to about 80 per cent.

Rank Xerox has its headquarters in Marlow, Buckinghamshire, and controls the activities of more than 24,000 employees in over eighty countries, with an annual turnover exceeding US$4.9 billion

During 1994 Rank Xerox transferred two of its internal service operations to specialist external companies. Xerox Corporation awarded a ten-year contract to EDS (Electronic Data Systems) to provide a worldwide computer and telecommunications service, including infrastructure, support and applications systems maintenance. A five-year contract was awarded to CBX to provide a real estate and facilities management service to Rank Xerox within the United Kingdom. In addition, Rank Xerox (UK) transferred its warehousing and distribution operations to TNT in 1995.

A background to Rank Xerox (UK)

Established in 1972, Rank Xerox (UK) is one of the principal subsidiaries of Rank Xerox. This company's major activities are in the marketing, selling and support of Xerox products and services.

Rank Xerox (UK) has its headquarters in Uxbridge, Middlesex, employs over 4,200 people and has annual revenues of some US$740 million. Rank Xerox (UK) generates most of its revenues through a direct sales force and a network of resellers. In addition, there is a growing business services operation (Xerox Business Services), which manages Xerox Copy Centres and facilities maintenance contracts, as well as an office stationery and paper business (Xerox Office Supplies), whilst Xsoft provides specialist document software and Xerox Engineering Systems supplies specialist products and services to industry. The company has 1,600 people dedicated to customer service engineering providing a full range of technical, training and other after-sales customer services.

The new structure of the organization

The corporation, like others, is in the midst of an organizational design revolution, driven by continuous technological innovation, rapidly changing markets, developing customer requirements and values, and the necessity of operating on a global scale. In 1993 Xerox launched a new corporate structure aimed at enhancing customer satisfaction, improving productivity and increasing return on assets.

The traditional hierarchical corporate structure has been replaced by a flatter, simpler structure. The corporation has reorganized around worldwide business divisions, each developing and producing one broad product range. These US-based Business Divisions have responsibility for product marketing, design, engineering and manufacturing. The Business Divisions have line of sight to the end-customer through Business Division Units (BDUs) in each company, or Xerox Entity (see Figure 3.1), then through territory-based Customer Business Units (CBUs), which provide local customer sales, service and administration operations. Separately, an integrated supply chain provides a logistics service, moving Xerox products and parts throughout the worldwide organization.

Rank Xerox (UK) is a Xerox entity that consists of three basic components and associated businesses (as seen in Figure 3.1):

- a group of four Business Division Units, each having the primary marketing role for a group of products and headed by a general manager;
- a set of seven regionally based Customer Business Units (CBUs), each having a general manager accountable for the profit and loss of its operation – CBUs are the primary interface with the customers and are responsible for the implementation of revenue and service plans through its sales, service and finance teams;
- a headquarters-based core group providing infrastructure services to the organi-

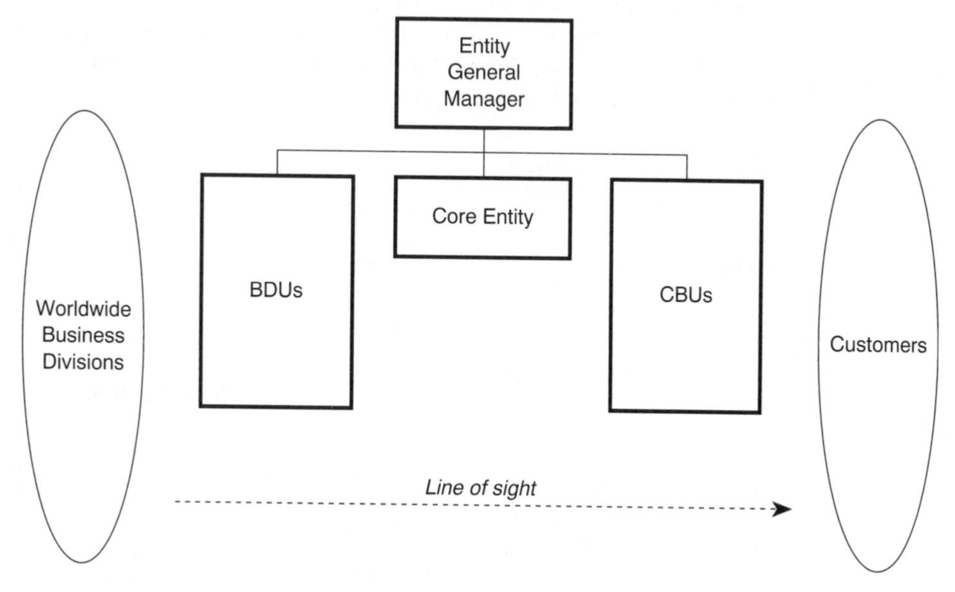

Figure 3.1 Rank Xerox organization structure.
Note: BDU = Business Division Unit, CBU = Customer Business Unit.

zation, including human resource management, financial management and legal services.

In addition, there are other stand-alone businesses, including paper and office stationery, each under the direction of a general manager.

Setting the goals for business

In general, as business investment increases in the substitution of computing capital for human labour, the overall volume of office information will continue its ceaseless growth. The relentless drive to increase office worker productivity requires that larger volumes of information will have to be managed. This market of information and document management has many global suppliers. Xerox has entered this new global market with a growing number of strategic alliances and partners, including MicroSoft, Novell, Adobe, Compaq and EDS.

Xerox intends to lead the global document market by providing document services that enhance customer business productivity. Leadership will be based on superior document technologies, linked to a complete understanding of the document, the document life-cycle (see Figure 3.2) and the role of the document in increasing productivity in customers' business processes.

This Xerox intent has been translated into a mission for Rank Xerox (UK) that is to deliver quality document products, services and solutions throughout the United Kingdom by:

- ensuring all customers are very satisfied and continue to purchase and recommend Rank Xerox products and services to others as their vendor of choice;
- creating an environment where all employees can take pride in the organization and feel responsible for its success so that there is continued improvement in employee motivation and satisfaction;
- reinforcing Rank Xerox as 'The Document Company', achieving and continuously improving its leadership position in market share in all segments;
- exceeding and striving to improve return on assets.

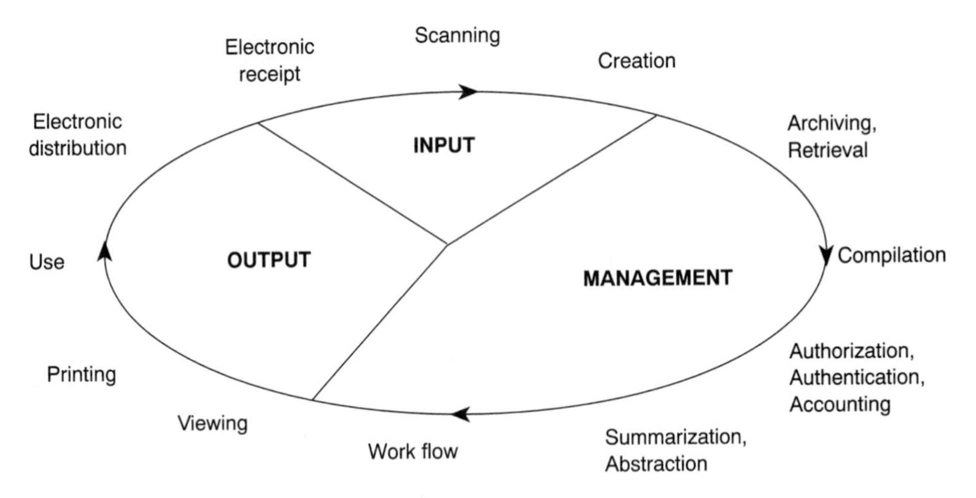

Figure 3.2 The document life-cycle.

Table 3.1 Information and document management industry layering

Layer	*Key suppliers and product examples*
Applications	IBM, HP, Digital, SUN, UNISYS
Groupware	MicroSoft Office, Lotus Notes
Printers	HP, Canon, Xerox, IBM, Siemens, Brother, Lexmark
Networks	Novell, MicroSoft, UNIX, TOKEN ring
Operating systems	MicroSoft DOS, Windows, NT, Apple, UNIX, OS2/WARP
Computers	Compaq, IBM, other PC clones, SUN, workstations, servers
Processors	INTEL, RISC

Development of a product portfolio

Whilst innovation has been the driving force behind the corporation's portfolio of products, the aim is to provide customers with the means of improving their productivity and efficiency through the implementation of document-based solutions. Xerox is building the capability to operate in all the layers within the information and document management industry (see Table 3.1).

Xerox hardware products fall into a number of categories – electronic and printing reprographics, office systems, electronic publishing and facsimile. The range of digital technology photocopiers covers all segments of the market. Compact convenience copiers support small and medium-sized businesses. Work group copiers meet the demand of many businesses, incorporating optional finishing capabilities such as spot colour, on-line stapling and a range of sorting features. The advanced departmental range of copiers is designed to tackle heavy duty tasks with many automated features. The company markets a range of printers covering desktop, work group and network requirements, as well as office colour printers and plain paper facsimile products. The latest products link computer networks with a device that combines the functions of a fax, copier and printer. Using highly sophisticated software for standard computing environments, mid-range and high-volume system-printing products are designed for the laser printing market. Document production systems are aimed at the in-plant reprographics facilities, commercial printing companies and teams on a network needing access to high-quality, high-speed printers.

The organization's characteristics before the change initiative

This section describes some of the characteristics of Rank Xerox (UK) before the current series of changes began, and it begins with a view of the corporation as a whole.

Innovation, invention and ingenuity were the hallmarks of the success of the Xerox Corporation during the 1960s and 1970s. However, the marketplace changed in the late 1970s – the traditional copier markets were under threat by IBM in the high-volume sector and by a group of Japanese companies at the low-volume end. Xerox had not anticipated the need to change, nor did it change rapidly enough, and the earlier sources of success became the seeds of failure. The impact was immediate – the organization was locked into a battle for survival. The reaction was typical of the time, with reductions in the number of employees and operating costs accompanied by a withdrawal from businesses, a concentration on fewer core activities and diversification into financial services.

The power of Xerox sales and service operations, the launch of the 10 series copiers and the performance of financial services enabled corporate survival. However, there were other factors that were fundamental to the organization's turnaround:

- the continued investment in research and development;
- the implementation of a Quality strategy.

A number of Quality programmes had been launched during the early 1980s, providing basic tools including problem solving, the quality improvement process and benchmarking. In late 1983 a group of senior staff met with the Chief Executive Officer (CEO) to design and plan the implementation of a strategy for Quality. This was more than a strategy; it was a plan to revolutionize the organization and its culture. The basic Quality policy developed at this time remains unchanged today. It states:

> Xerox is a Quality Company. Quality is the basic business principle for Xerox. Quality means providing our external and internal customers with innovative products and services that fully satisfy their requirements. Quality improvement is the job of every Xerox employee.

The implementation of the Quality strategy put in place forces that have fundamentally changed Xerox. The common language of Quality today enables any employee, from any part of the organization, to work with others using a shared language and a set of work tools and methods. Retrospectively, the implementation of the Quality strategy has been likened to a never-ending journey that can be viewed as a series of stages of change.

The first stage began in 1984 with the launch of the Leadership Through Quality programme and ended in 1989 when Xerox won the US National Quality Award. This was external proof that Xerox had embedded quality into its business.

By focusing on quality during the 1980s, the Corporation was both strengthened and saved. Improvements were reported in customer satisfaction, product quality and reliability, return on assets, shareholder value and the infrastructure of the whole organization. The Leadership Through Quality strategy and the way it developed have become the foundation for global competition and the single most important initiative that has enabled Xerox and Rank Xerox to win back market share.

The second stage, opening in 1990, continued with the emphasis on quality. However, it was recognized that continuous improvement would not be enough to survive the decade and more radical forces were needed. A rigorous self-examination produced a further strategy document that set out clear direction for the whole of the corporation – Xerox 2000. Taking stock of global trends in technologies and markets, the strategy introduced 'The Document Company' intent and set a course for significant change (see Table 3.2).

The development of Xerox 2000 and the positioning of the corporation around 'The Document Company' made it clear that there was a significant market opportunity. However, the organization was not in a situation to capture this opportunity

Table 3.2 Summary of recent changes in marketing, selling and technology

Changing from	*Changing to*
Narrow product marketing	Customer-driven marketing
Direct salesforce	Combination of direct and indirect
Task-driven sales managers	People-focused sales team leaders
Stand-alone boxes	Networked devices
Sales activity with strong product orientation	Customer relationship account management – customer solution oriented

and a third stage would be necessary. In 1992 the Xerox CEO remarked that the Corporation had to change more in the next five years than it had in the previous ten! Dramatic change, rather than incremental change, was recognized as the most appropriate course of action; specifically, the corporation needed to:

- focus all efforts on the customer, the marketplace and competition;
- provide employees with more end-to-end accountability with clear line of sight to the customer;
- give people the capacity to act, clearly reward, counsel or penalize individuals based on performance;
- enable people to manage quality, customer satisfaction, employee satisfaction, market share and growth for their piece of the business;
- simplify the way the business was run;
- radically increase the speed of the whole operation by reducing the time taken to deliver new products to the market, ahead of the competition, with offerings that meet or exceed customer requirements.

This third leg of the Quality journey began in 1993 and is still in progress. It has the goal of achieving an organization that is more market-responsive, faster in overall operation and more empowering of people at all levels.

The pace of change is accelerating – the challenge is to succeed, rather than survive!

Working relationships and the structure within Rank Xerox (UK)

Before 1992 there were still traits of the classical bureaucracy in the organization, particularly a functionally driven hierarchy, with deep layers of management. There were between six and nine layers in the functional hierarchy.

At the heart of the organization lay the management philosophy characterized by hierarchical command and control. The structure consisted of a series of separate functions, each headed by a director, including marketing, sales, finance (including administration and leasing), customer service engineering, human resources, legal, and information management and quality. This arrangement delivered some special characteristics:

- *functional myopia* constrained the organization's ability to adapt to change;
- cross-functional integration was still limited, despite the implementation of

Quality, which fettered the organization's ability to deliver customer requirements in a timely and orderly way;
- overall, the organization had a complex set of working practices that slowed down decision-making and constrained the organization's ability to change.

In 1991 an internal study described Rank Xerox (UK) as in need of change. The report demonstrated that a functionally aligned organizational structure was sub-optimal when viewed by the customer because it had built-in time delays. Indeed, the very fabric of the organizational structure was defined as the primary cause of the costs of non-conformance in the business.

Goal setting, adaptation and work process improvement

The relationships between employees and managers and between operational line managers and senior management provide a clear picture of the culture of the organization during the late 1980s and early 1990s.

Goal setting primarily lay with functional directors. The communication and cascade of annual objectives was not uniform and coherent across the organization, depending heavily on adherence to preset guidelines.

Line managers drove goal setting within departments using variable levels of input from individuals on objectives and the methods for achieving targets. Cross-functional and interdepartmental goal setting was often informal and relied on detailed functional guidelines. Occasionally, different functions had conflicting goals, leaving individuals to satisfy either the customer or the internal requirements of the organization.

Goal achievement was conditioned by internal control documents, the application of policies and procedures and the apparent work process needs of downstream functions. All these had the impact of appearing to delay ultimate customer satisfaction.

The introduction of a method known as policy deployment improved the situation significantly, removing many of these problems.

Historically, the company had been slow to adapt many of its internal processes to suit new business needs or changes in customer requirements. Change tended to be reactive and hurried, implementation not well planned and often without sufficient reference to downstream functions. Individuals within departments were often not involved in change, receiving communication, then being asked to comply. Sometimes this created confusion and frustration, resulting in the frequent appearance of work-around methods.

Functional groups were separated by rigorous procedures and policies to protect themselves from undefined upstream changes. As they were often in separate buildings, there was little cross-functional understanding or awareness of the pressures for change. As a result, there was little understanding of the reasons behind requests for change from external groups. In contrast, employees within departments integrated and worked well together on changes to defined functional procedures.

The *improvement of a work process* was sometimes handed over to quality improvement teams. These teams were agreed by managers and involved individuals in short projects to find solutions to specific work problems within departments. However, the results of these studies were often inconclusive or poorly implemented.

These localized and introspective actions were frequently ineffective in solving the root causes of problems, which often lay outside the department.

Setting standards for role model managers

The standards and criteria for a role model manager were described through the Leadership Through Quality Programme. Team surveys of management practices applied the criteria, while the appraisal process verified the ability of the manager to meet the standards. These standards became mandatory criteria for management positions and included:

- the visible support of a customer focus in all business transactions;
- demonstrable use of Quality tools and techniques;
- encouragement and use of feedback from peers, superiors and customers to modify behaviour and personal style;
- the application of recognition and reward for teams and individuals using Leadership Through Quality;
- the inspection and coaching of employees.

The regular use of these standards and criteria began to influence the culture of the organization.

Investment in information systems

By 1991 Rank Xerox had a substantial investment in application systems running in an IBM MVS host computer environment. Some Rank Xerox (UK) applications systems had been delivered by Rank Xerox headquarters, but the majority were of a local design. These local systems had been specified and developed by functions and were not the basis for supporting the cross-functional business processes that operated through the organization. At the core of the information systems development plan lay a transition to a set of eleven integrated subject databases.

There was a complex web of batch file processing to support the organization's information requirements. Although there were a number of major on-line systems in place to support sales-order processing, customer service and leasing, for example, there was still a heavy reliance on background batch processing.

Application systems had partially automated the many inherited paper-driven processes of the 1970s and 1980s. As a result there was some duplication of effort at data entry and complex codes were used to enable interface programs to reconcile data. Management information had to be gathered and collated from different systems and manual files. Information reconciliation between information systems and paper documents was still a feature in administration functions.

From personnel to human resource management

During the early 1990s the Personnel function began to take on its human resource management role, moving from a mechanistic, passive operation towards making a strategic contribution through the improvement of motivation and satisfaction of employees. The traditional tasks of Personnel were in hiring staff to fit line management specification and administering employee performance reviews, salaries and job training. This task-list approach was reflected in the design of the employee grading, job specification and compensation schemes.

A formal grading scheme supported the functional organization. During the late 1980s an old fifteen-level employee grading system began to be dismantled and slowly replaced by a broad banding structure. Management grades were reduced from six levels to three bands. Below the management bands, employees also experienced the introduction of career mapping. This enabled broad job roles to be defined in most areas of the company. Three levels of achievement for each role were associated with the development of employee skill and knowledge. Progress through these levels was assessed twice yearly through a well-defined and organized appraisal process.

The late 1980s grading system, with its associated points scheme, dictated compensation policy. Each job in the organization had a grade allocated and each grade had a salary band connected with it. The salary band had upper and lower limits and was further broken into quartiles to enable monitoring of overall changes within the organization. In addition, the sales force was supported by a comprehensive commission scheme.

The Quality programme began to have an effect; the importance of customer satisfaction was reflected in a new bonus scheme for all employees. Managers were also paid on the performance of return on assets.

Drivers for change

Xerox is now in the midst of a technological transformation that is changing the very nature of the business itself. The corporation is also in the middle of an organizational design revolution driven by continuous technological innovation, fast changing markets and inconstant customer requirements and values.

The entire organization is engaged in change. The goal is to make the challenge of change inescapable for all employees by allowing them to see the implications of change through a series of active interventions:

- an internal pace of change has been set;
- a sense of urgency and pressure has been created;
- a comprehensive vision has been communicated;
- a competitor focus has been introduced at all levels of the organization through benchmarking;
- employees have been provided with the techniques to work effectively, including statistical tools, problem-solving methods, process value analysis, and team-building;
- clear milestones and inspection mechanisms to track progress and reinforce change have been introduced: the Xerox Business Architecture (see Figure 3.3) enables all employees to understand *what* work will be required in the future while the Xerox Management Model (see Figure 3.4) details the desired state for the business and *how* the business will be inspected – these models are described in the section dealing with the change initiatives (see pp. 69–78).

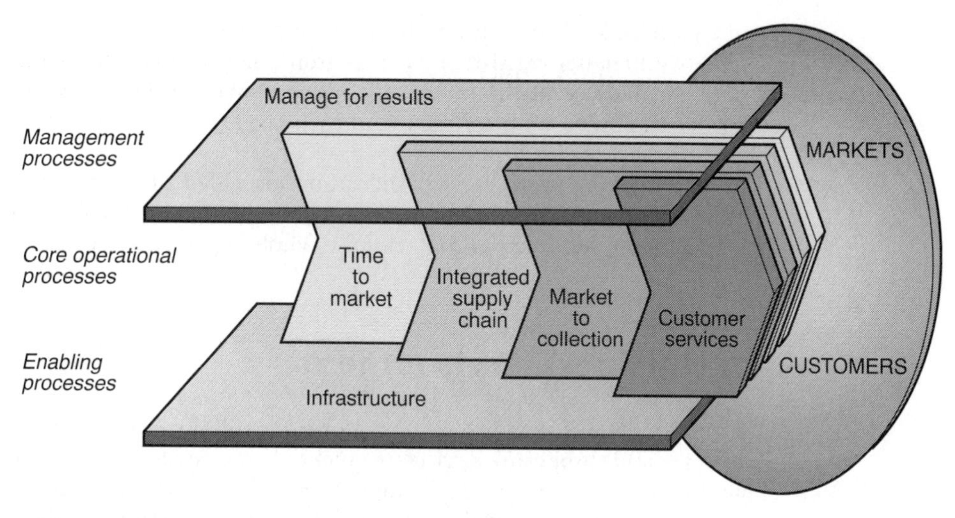

Figure 3.3 Xerox Business Architecture Model.

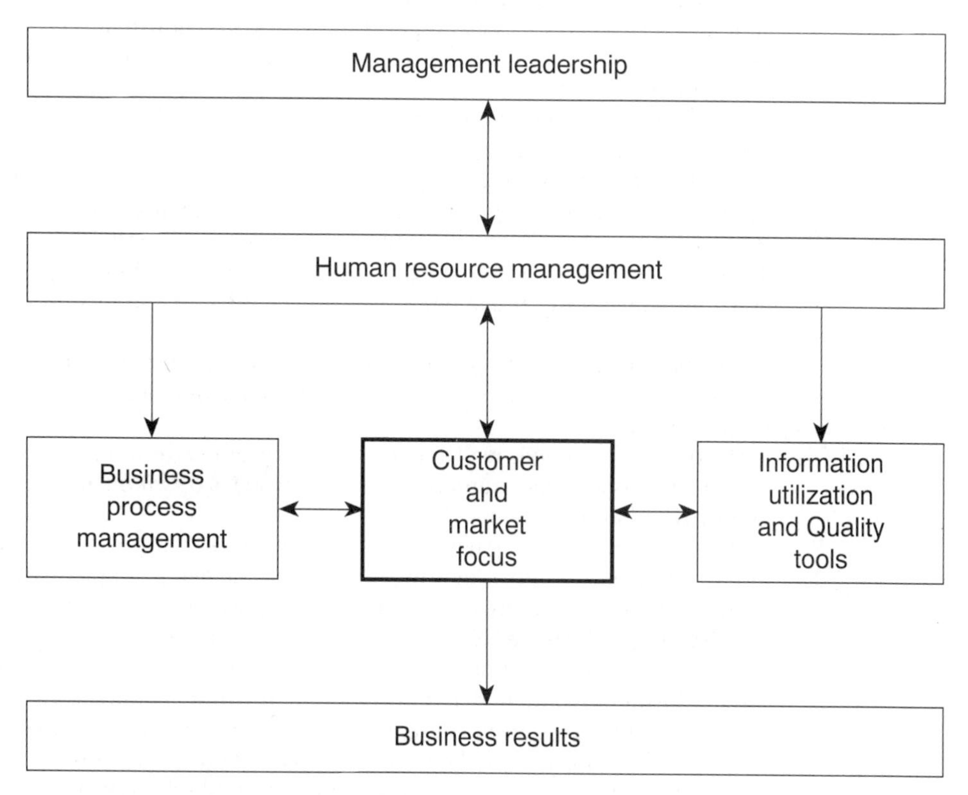

Figure 3.4 Xerox Management Model.

Rank Xerox is being driven both to search for competitive advantages that are inherently sustainable and to accelerate organizational learning to outpace competitors. The organization (with its BDU–CBU structure) has resources that are allocated to product-market units in which relatedness is defined by common products and channels. With investment in the core competencies of this new organization, business functional consistency comes from allegiances to the strategic intent and through active use of the models identified above (in Figures 3.3 and 3.4), which provide employees with a framework to encourage new ideas on how these goals may be achieved.

The new company structure in the UK has provided a frontline unit, the Customer Business Unit (CBU), which is a relatively small, tightly devolved and empowered team, designed to bring the power of the whole organization closer to the customer.

The business environment

The traditional business of the sophisticated stand-alone, light lens electromechanical copier and duplicator devices is quickly being replaced. The rapid evolution of digital and colour technology, coupled with the reduction in unit manufacturing costs, is replacing the traditional electromechanical machines with scanning devices that digitize information. Once captured, the digital image can be manipulated and edited in many ways and can enter the highways of information technology. These new devices are becoming one of the many components of complex digital document systems.

The company is operating in a more complex and volatile business environment and must have the capacity to cope with change at a very rapid pace. The business lies at the intersection of the two worlds of paper-based and electronic information. As the marketplace and technology change, the company must be able to demonstrate its own application of better ways of working and have an organization flexible enough to adapt to change. The requirement is to have in place an organization that can evolve and modify itself as technology, competitors and the entire business change.

Changing from 'The Copier Company' to 'The Document Company' is a visible signal, both internally and externally, of a totally new approach to the document services business.

The organization does well at explaining its products and services to its customers, but now needs to explore and implement new ways of talking to its customers about tomorrow's solutions.

The company is looking beyond the simple device that provides a single output or service for its customers. The range of products is being coupled with services that enable customers to improve their own businesses. The company can no longer just sell discrete products, rather it needs to offer customers distinctive capabilities that will have a major impact on the way *they* do business. As the technologies of paper-based information and digital information merge, the overall direction is to focus on the 'document'. By concentrating on managing documents of all types (paper and electronic) the aim is to make customer organizations more efficient and effective. Rank Xerox (UK) is changing the way it markets and sells its products and services to its customers to enable the delivery of this 'Document Company' intent. The approach has to be more consultative to enable customers to appreciate the capabilities of products that will alter the way they work by changing the way people see and use documents.

In response to this new direction, the organization has to understand the new digital and network systems technologies. This understanding must then be applied to enable salespeople to work with customers to redesign their client's basic business processes. The future of the company lies in selling innovative solutions for performing work that enhance productivity. The challenge is not only for sales to understand the customer's business and how the customer will use Rank Xerox products, but also to apply a consultative approach.

The imperatives for organizational change

Until 1992 Rank Xerox (UK) had the structure, practices and values of a classic large company. A highly functional organization that was striving to improve internally its separate parts, rather than to deliver customer requirements and value in an integrated way.

The imperatives of quality, speed and customer-responsiveness are now replacing the traditional emphasis on bureaucratic control methods of the traditional hierarchy. All these changes place renewed emphasis on learning as the essential characteristic to ensure business success. New information technologies, coupled with new internal business processes, are making profound changes in how the company organizes and manages work.

The goal is to be more entrepreneurial, more innovative and more responsive to the marketplace. Xerox aims to combine the advantages of large organizations (access to resources and the strategic vision) with the advantages of small companies (speed, creativity, flexibility, accountability and creativity).

This goal will be partially fulfilled by organizing into self-managed work teams. Each team will be tied directly to the customer, having the technical expertise, business knowledge and information tools to design its own detailed work processes, and objectives to improve and adapt continuously as business changes.

Forces acting inside the new organizational structure

The new organization design (shown in Figure 3.1 above) forces managers to confront and manage the tensions between autonomy and integration. The design has turned the organization on its side, with technology at one end and the customer at the other. It has established a set of relatively independent business divisions, organized around families of products and markets and having profit and loss responsibility.

In comparison, each core entity team is expected to integrate its CBUs and BDUs. The entity as a whole has a set of business performance targets that are met from the consolidation of all its businesses, including those of the Business Divisions.

One of the challenges faced by Xerox, as it moves into a technological environment founded on integrated product systems, is to create a common design architecture for products across business divisions. Xerox wants the *customer* to integrate the organization. The job of the Customer Business Unit is to build relationships with customers and then decide with Business Divisions how to integrate the products for the customers. In this way the Customer Business Units understand the strategies and directions of the Business Divisions.

Forces acting on the people within the organization

Rank Xerox UK has defined three interrelated components in its organizational design: hardware, people skills and attributes, and software.

1. The *organizational hardware* features include structure, the formal business processes by which work gets done, reporting relationships, compensation, reward and recognition systems, and control mechanisms.
2. The second element in the design covers the *skills* the organization will need as well as the *personal attributes* required to operate effectively in the future. A functional organization will recruit and maintain a number of staff to hold a function together, but in the decentralized, more entrepreneurial organization a completely different person is required.
3. The *software* of the organizational design is the most important and most difficult aspect to change. It involves the informal organization, the networks of relationships that give an organization its values and attitudes – in short, its culture! (In successful companies the informal and formal organizations are aligned and fit together. Where these two elements do not work together, too much energy is wasted in making the organization operate effectively; it becomes an inwardly focused operation rather than one which is externally focused on the customer and the marketplace.) The aim is to lock the formal and informal organizations together on a common track focused on the customer.

Forces acting on the individual in the organization

The central theme in the operation of the new organization is the requirement for all employees to contribute to the company as a whole rather than to a part of it. In future all employees will have a wide understanding of the business and will work closely together – something that was uncharacteristic of the narrow functional organization. Formal individual reporting relationships will be of less importance than the team in which a person works. The team will be the organizational building block.

The type of person needed to manage within the new organization has been defined and set out in twenty-three characteristics, seven of which are described as critical. These criteria include strategic thinking as an important element, as well as the implementation of strategy. In terms of *software*, the criteria include teamwork, the ability to delegate, the ability to empower subordinates; in addition, personal criteria include integrity and personal courage.

It is accepted that if the compensation, reward and recognition systems are not aligned with the new design nothing will change. Alignment will encourage the kinds of behaviour essential to making the new organization work. New reward and recognition and appraisal systems align individual compensation with the strategic objectives of the company and reward good performance and penalize poor performance. The appraisal system has been changed to reflect the new values found in the cultural dimensions and personal attributes.

The internal forces of quality

Total quality management is built on implicit value assumptions that emphasize discipline, uniformity, sense of obligation and duty to others, identification with the total enterprise and conformity. Whilst Quality remains the foundation of the company's business practices, it cannot better its Japanese rivals on quality alone; therefore Rank Xerox has examined other initiatives for competitive advantage.

Rather than mimicking others, Rank Xerox is trying to find the balance between the individual and the value of the group – termed 'rugged groupism'. The focus on work groups engages employees, using their creativity and levering their energies. The company is linking together work, quality and a sense of worth for the individual that should result in higher levels of customer satisfaction and employee satisfaction – a person-centred solution based on the belief that employees and their ability to create value are the unique assets of the organization.

The drivers for change

The aim was to become a very productive organization by employing a variety of means and methods, rethinking the basic concepts of how work is organized and managed and how better to use the capabilities and strengths of employees.

The basic organization design requires the continuous fit between the broad systemic elements of work, people, information and technology. The objective is to use teams organized around units of work, which develop as work communities – communities of practice, work and learning. These work teams are developing around business processes which connect customer values and requirements with the delivery processes of the organization. This allows for both continuous improvement and breakthrough thinking in work processes – a total rethink often from different perspectives. The approach is based on empowered people working together in a collaborative effort, developing from each other's creativity and the experiences they bring.

The change initiatives: balancing incremental and radical change

The changes Rank Xerox (UK) is making are aligned with strategic direction and thinking. The Leadership Through Quality programme provided not only a foundation of business principles, but also a positive attitude towards continuous change. Working within the corporate strategic umbrella, Rank Xerox (UK) has improved its operating performance by introducing a series of change programmes. Whilst there has been no one single change programme in operation over the last three years, a

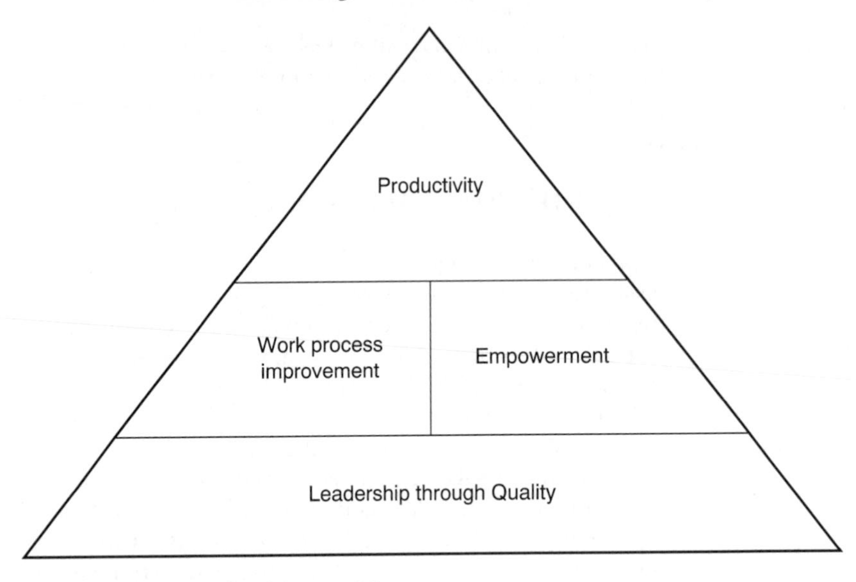

Figure 3.5 Rank Xerox Productivity Model.

number of waves of effective changes have been introduced covering all aspects of the business. Some of these change initiatives have been radical in their nature and approach, balanced with others that have introduced increment improvement.

In general, major change projects are managed by a sponsor, normally a director or general manager, who will chair a steering committee consisting of key project team members.

Productive growth is considered to be the key to competitiveness, profitability and reinvestment in Rank Xerox. Productive growth has its foundations in the linked initiatives of business process improvement and empowerment, both built on the foundations of Quality.

Figure 3.5 shows how Rank Xerox (UK) is looking at productivity in a different way. There are two major internal pathways in place to achieve the goals of productive growth. The first is through business process improvement. A series of change initiatives are in place that incorporate both incremental and breakthrough thinking. The second pathway is to implement continuous improvement and breakthrough thinking in the empowerment of employees. Both pathways are necessary, neither is sufficient by itself, and both have a foundation in the tools, language and processes of Quality.

The business processes of Rank Xerox (UK)

The business process is the integrating theme for the organization of work. The focal point of the core business process is the customer, and the activities that make up the process should add value for the customer. Figure 3.6 compares three groups of methods that Rank Xerox (UK) is using to introduce change in the organization of work. This integrated set of techniques and methods is helping to reshape the company and deliver business benefits.

The *business-as-usual methods* that all Xerox employees are expected to be able to

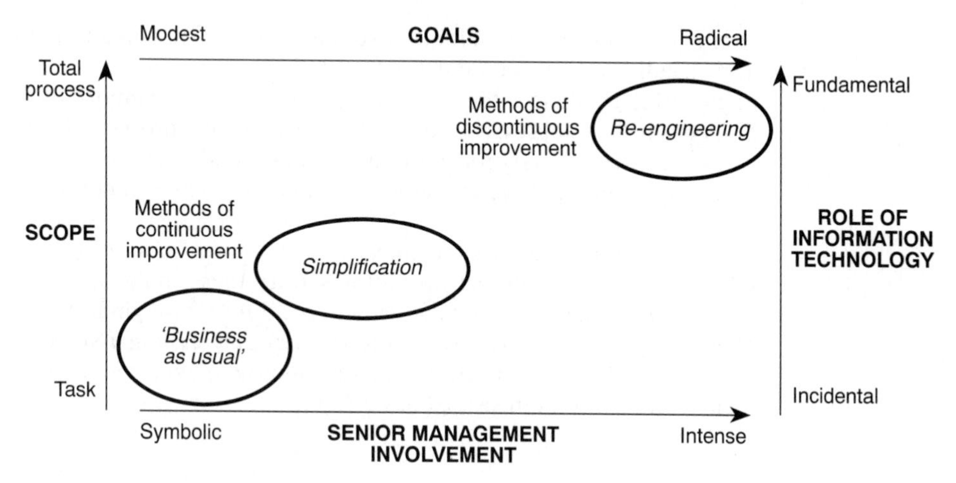

Figure 3.6 Methods of business process improvement.

use are derived from the standard Leadership Through Quality techniques for simple process improvement. These techniques provide a vehicle for incremental change and are capable of introducing efficiency and effectiveness improvements in small areas of the business by between 10 per cent and 15 per cent.

Second, there are the tools and methods described under the group heading of business *process simplification,* capable of delivering 15 per cent to 20 per cent improvement in efficiency and effectiveness. These techniques are again built on the foundation of Quality principles. Process simplification is usually applied to subprocesses – areas of work much broader in scope than those improved using the standard Quality techniques. Process simplification concentrates on improving the process value chain, cycle time and internal resource utilization by working within the existing business 'rule book', information systems and technology facilities. Generally, process simplification project objectives are defined in terms of:

- assessing and documenting a business process, defining its value-adding and non-value-adding activities, estimating how time is used in the process, reviewing decision-making effectiveness and, overall, examining the primary business problems, root causes and opportunities;
- gaining support for recommended changes through negotiated costs of quality;
- describing an implementation plan that specifies how the benefits of change will be captured and sustained.

In contrast, *business process re-engineering* is the most radical aspect of change within the Rank Xerox (UK) application of total quality management. Re-engineering is supported by a structured method that enables the redesign and rebuilding of a whole business process from its basic components affecting the people who work in the affected areas, the way they work, the technology they use and the information they need. The method is centred on delivering benefits described by the company goals, particularly customer satisfaction, employee satisfaction, return on assets and business results.

Rank Xerox (UK) has re-engineered two business processes, affecting some 2,500 people. The scope of these projects is very broad, each having boundaries that encapsulate a basic business customer requirement and how it is satisfied, for example the process of taking a customer order, then converting it into deliverable and installable products and services to satisfy or exceed the initial needs. Re-engineering challenges the underlying values and assumptions of the organization. The approach is holistic, as the component parts of a process – people (including all aspects of a social system), work, information and technology – are redesigned so that all parts fit and fasten together to enable the achievement of steplike change in performance.

Re-engineering projects are sponsored by two or more directors. Steering committees review and inspect the outputs from these major change programmes to ensure senior management involvement continues throughout the project life-cycle. These projects are considered strategic, typically lasting two to three years and affecting significant parts of the organization, with expected performance improvement in key process measures of up to ten times.

Developing the business process model

Having completed the first re-engineering design in 1991, Rank Xerox (UK) faced the challenge of understanding how all work was undertaken in the entire company.

The early years of Leadership Through Quality had brought successful use of process identification and improvement methods at family group level. Gradually, these methods were progressively used on larger-scale cross-functional processes.

In a manufacturing company the concept of work flow is relatively straight forward, but office work is often complicated by organization, terminology, the changes introduced by the market, and a combination of formal and informal means of how work is flow achieved. Leadership Through Quality had provided a common language for this flowcharting work where internal customers of business processes could be linked to the chains of inputs, processes and outputs that make up the infrastructure of the company. High-level flowcharting brought to life the complexity of doing business. A current-state process model provided the means of viewing all Rank Xerox (UK) functional process relationships and boundaries. As business processes communicate with adjacent processes, each passing outputs and value onwards, the chains of value-adding business processes were revealed.

Since early 1994 a Xerox-wide process model (the Xerox Business Architecture (shown in Figure 3.3 above) has described how the corporation will operate to support an overall corporate direction of business process convergence. The process model provides a template for all changes in business and management processes.

Xerox Business Architecture model

The Xerox Business Architecture model is a hierarchical data-flow diagram which provides a vehicle for communicating an understanding of the agreed corporate processes. The model defines what work needs to be done in order to deliver the agreed internal and external customer needs. The model records three types of business processes:

1. Management processes set goals and direction, deploy strategies and objectives, provide decision frameworks, and assess and inspect business processes, typically consisting of a formal series of interrelated meetings and documents.
2. Core business processes are the critical means of delivering value to the customer. There are four core business processes in the model:

   - *time to market* – product concept through to product launch;
   - the *integrated supply chain* – the logistics of moving parts and equipment around the corporation and to the end-customer;
   - *market to collect* – the assessment of the market potential through to selling, invoicing and collection of revenues;
   - *customer services* – the provision of post-sales services, including field service engineering and customer education.

3. Infrastructural processes support the core business process by supplying specific services and competencies; these include finance, information management, audit and legal services, and human resource management.

Each type of process is broken down into four hierarchical levels of detail. At each level, the process is connected with labelled lines to its associated primary inputs and outputs, including the external factors of the market and the customer. The model software provides the means of adding attributes to each process and the lines that link them.

The sponsors and owners of the Rank Xerox (UK) processes

The company is in transition towards the desired state defined in the Xerox Business Architecture model. This model provides the boundaries between business processes and therefore defines natural work management packages. Rank Xerox (UK) has had part-time process sponsors and process owners in place for four years to improve these work packages which define how work gets done. The core business and infrastructural processes have been divided into their constituent subprocesses and allocated to process owners for continuous improvement.

There are four process sponsors, all members of the senior management team, who each set the vision, strategy and the plans for a group of business processes. Process sponsors help spearhead the drive to manage through processes. These sponsor and owner teams provide the communication networks for process change.

In general, the process owner is expected to deliver a business process that is effective, efficient, stable, flexible and measurable. The primary role of the owner is to ensure that a business process is capable of delivering target performance within agreed costs. Performance is usually measured in terms of a general structure of customer satisfaction, employee satisfaction and business results. Detail measures are taken in terms of in-process, output and outcome measures, expressed in terms of quality, service, cost, delivery and cycle time. These dimensions enable the measurement of change, as well as providing a basis for internal and external benchmarking and a means of target-setting.

The measurement systems

Rank Xerox has redesigned its performance measurement system to reinforce cross-functional collaboration and continuously improve its customer-responsiveness. The primary measures listed below are considered to be the *outcomes* of the operation of core business processes:

- *Customer satisfaction* is measured at the entity level, by CBU and BDU. Customer reactions are measured, for example, after ninety days have elapsed since installation to understand satisfaction with product quality, reliability, performance and features. In addition, administration, sales service and logistics are provided with customer satisfaction statistics. The key measures for sales teams include timeliness, management of the order, attitude and helpfulness. Service teams are measured on their responsiveness to requests for support as well as their courtesy and professionalism. Logistics and distribution services are measured on responsiveness, installation work, and the courtesy and professionalism of the delivery crew.

  In addition, Rank Xerox (UK) has other approaches to assessing what customers are thinking about the company's performance – all service calls are surveyed each month, an annual independent sample survey enables intercompany comparison, and customer relationship appraisals provide detailed interview assessments of how business processes are affecting customers.
- *Employee motivation and satisfaction* is measured at least once per year and involves every employee. The company employees use an external agency to survey the workforce and benchmark against other organizations. The survey assesses the changes in employees' perceptions and attitudes to the impact of the implementation of the twenty-three characteristics and other cultural dimensions described in the previous section ('Drivers for change', pp. 64–9).
- *Business result measures* cover many different aspects of the business operation, but focus is usually placed on return on assets, market share, productivity, revenue and profit.

An empowerment objective

The strategy for empowerment is to devolve responsibility and accountability to those teams closest to the customer. This will enable a more responsive operation, with any problems fixed speedily without authorization through a chain of command. The overall effect is to reduce the layers of management necessary and to reduce cycle time. (The company now has, on average, four layers in the operational hierarchy.) The empowerment programme is also modifying the software of the organization.

There are two aspects of empowerment which are fundamental to the Rank Xerox (UK) change agenda:

- structural empowerment, which is related to the new organization of Customer Business Units and Business Division Units within the entity of Rank Xerox (UK), which has an overall goal of having an organization populated with high-performing self-managed work teams;

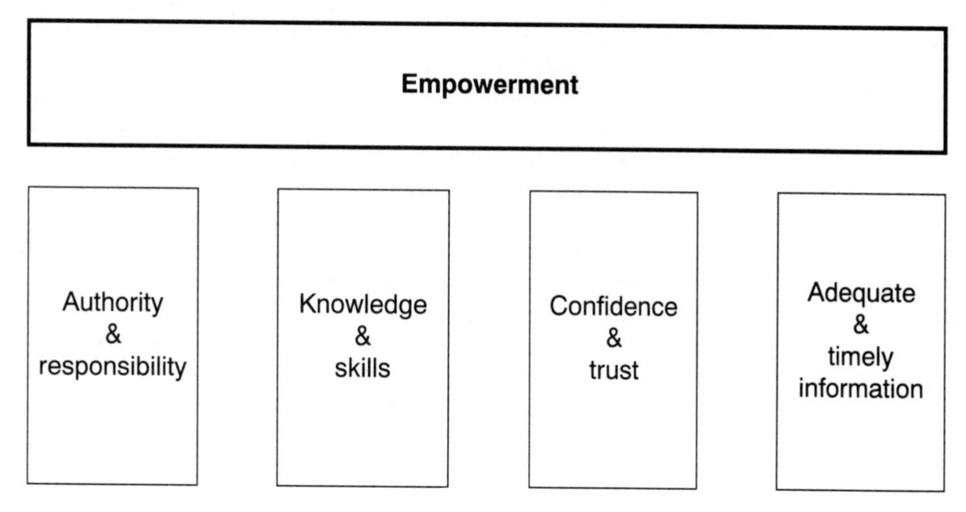

Figure 3.7 Empowerment factors.

- managerial empowerment, where employees have broader authority defined within a business framework, and the manager becomes a coach, facilitator of change and mentor.

There are a network of factors (see Figure 3.7) that provide the basis for the implementation of empowerment and which have been linked together to provide a comprehensive change package. The critical elements of responsibility and authority have been connected with:

- the need of the individual to increase knowledge and skills through active and continuous education, learning and coaching;
- the necessity to increase confidence and trust through active and positive feedback, relationship building, overt and covert motivation, and the application of changes in reward and recognition;
- the provision of adequate and timely information to enable the best decisions to be made.

The Rank Xerox (UK) service force is entirely composed of self-managed work teams. These self-managed teams use the tools of problem-solving process and root-cause analysis to increase their productivity by continuously analysing workload and availability planning. Progress in team development is plotted on a capability staircase, which shows some teams are able, for example, to develop their own business plan and conduct team appraisals. The quality of the products and services delivered by these teams is subject to a standard quality management system. All service engineering, software font services, customer education and spares logistics processes are certified and regularly inspected under BSEN ISO9000 1994 (BS5750) standards.

The changing role of the manager

The fundamental impacts accompanying the new organization can be summarized as moving from hierarchical, functional command and control to an organizational design described as cross-functional, team-orientated and composed of self-managed work teams. With a desired state which embraces the values of teamwork, empowerment, diversity and continuous learning, Rank Xerox (UK) is modifying the role of the manager. The role is changing from one which actively involved supervising, telling, planning and controlling. The role is in transition and continues to change as the impact of job and structural empowerment begins to bite and the focus moves to one of team leader, coach, mentor and facilitator.

More recently, management networks have been built across the organization. Networks are reshaping who makes decisions and how, and they have become a means of integrating the organization. Senior managers have established networks by breaking through the traditional functional barriers, emphasizing the horizontal collaboration required across the organization. With time, these networks will influence the values and behaviour of the whole company.

The Customer Business Unit information systems

Within Customer Business Uuits, the mainstream systems have been continuously upgraded or replaced. Each sales team has on-line access to an order processing system which links with downstream processes of the integrated supply chain, customer service and revenue collection. Recently sales employees have been able to capture order documents on laptop computers for release to the order management system. The service force is supported through laptop devices connected through radio modems to a support system that handles overall work coordination. This support system is linked with the parts logistics process.

Compensation, reward and appraisal

The company is seeking higher levels of performance through the involvement and participation of its people. Employees share in the financial gains that the company generates through improved business results. This reinforces the involvement, enthusiasm and creativity of employees.

The new organizational design has extended the use of performance-related pay schemes. Team-based pay has been expanded into the whole of sales, service and some administrative operations. The re-engineering of the sales management process enabled teams of sales and administrative employees to work together and cover an end-to-end process. These teams have a bonus payment opportunity based on the performance of the whole team in terms of revenue generation, reported customer satisfaction and the cycle time of their process.

Service teams are able to review their own pay. This empowerment decision covering the more developed teams has been reflected in improved employee satisfaction results, and this has enabled further more specific actions to be employed to improve overall satisfaction for these teams.

Management bonus is based on profit performance, sales general and administrative costs, and these costs as a percentage of revenue, as well as customer and employee satisfaction survey results.

Formal appraisals occur every six months and provide a balance of focus between performance review and performance planning. With the introduction of empowerment and self-managed work teams, the appraisal method has been modified. A number of team colleagues prepare documents on another team member which are then used as input to a formal one-to-one appraisal. This meeting is conducted by a team member trained in team development and personal appraisals.

Changing the culture

The culture is demonstrated openly through the management styles and behaviours of the organization, and the way in which change is managed and communicated. It is being driven by modifications in personnel policies and procedures which are designed to manage the employment relationship (involving the contract of employment, job design, performance management, appraisal, reward and compensation system, succession planning, education and learning, and employee relations policies). The culture is also being driven by the employees' perceived level of fit with the organization's requirements, together with their motivation, morale and loyalty. This complex mix of factors is in transition as change is implemented.

The vocabulary to define the organizational software is expressed in nine *cultural dimensions*, described in three sets of core values and behaviours (awareness, values and clarification) which epitomize how the organization will be run. These dimensions are a set of guiding principles behind the company's approach to the business and define the nature of working relationships, empowerment, team-work, all based on a foundation of openness and trust. These dimensions form the backbone to the management appraisal process.

Implementing change through continuous business assessment

The Xerox Management Model (shown in Figure 3.4 above), and its associated business assessment process, is an inspection mechanism used to track progress and reinforce change toward the strategic vision. The common language of business assessment shows that Rank Xerox business results can only be realized through a market focus and an understanding of customers' values and needs.

The model is organized into six categories covering forty-two detailed desired states and measurement criteria. These forty-two statements set out clearly the critical factors for success in meeting Rank Xerox's annual objectives, mid-term goals and longer-term vision. Five categories of the model describe the *enabling* factors that drive the performance of the company; the business results are found in the sixth category. The five enabling categories are:

- management leadership;
- human resource management;
- business process management;
- customer and market focus;
- information utilization and quality tools.

Associated with the model is a business assessment method which ensures the continuous and systematic improvement of the organization. Business assessment has been implemented throughout the Rank Xerox (UK) organization. The business assessment method provides a common framework for organizational self-assessment and links employees, business processes and results. Business assessment defines the gap between the current and desired states and the actions required to close these gaps, to enable ever-increasing targets and business thresholds of success. It examines the critical success factors that drive the performance of the business and enables the setting of business priorities for change.

Each of the forty-two items in the model has a sponsoring senior manager and an owner who manage the associated improvement plans on behalf of the entity as a whole. The role of the owner is to manage and facilitate the movement of the organization towards the achievement of the item's desired state. The owner may engage a networked team to bring input to a self-assessment and to ensure change is managed successfully. Using the criteria above, self-assessment is completed and a final score is allocated at the end of a period. The rating scheme has a seven-point scale and is derived from a matrix of the results achieved to date, the approach taken and the pervasiveness of the desired state.

External validation of the 42-item portfolio occurs annually on selected items. This usually involves two senior Xerox managers from outside the entity, who assess the portfolio and seek evidence and clarification on the performance described. The entity is given a final overall rating on a seven-point scale.

The impact on the organization

The initiative has impacted in a number of ways, namely on the customer, productivity, empowerment, information systems management and the culture of the organization (see Table 3.3).

What was the impact on the customer?

The customer-focused culture continues to develop and progress through a number of initiatives. An extensive set of customer satisfaction measurement systems provide feedback on these changes.

The Sales-Order Management Process Re-engineering Programme significantly

Table 3.3 Rank Xerox (UK) – key performance measures

	1992	*1993*	*1994*	*1995*
Total revenue US$ million	595	615	677	709
Sales general and admin costs as % of revenue	30	29	27	24
Customer satisfaction % overall satisfied	89	92	95	98
Employee satisfaction % overall satisfied	54	52	55	63

affected the reported level of customer satisfaction results during the period 1993 and 1994. The process design concentrated on delivering customer requirements through teams of sales and administrative support staff. These new teams have a simplified work process and modified information systems that are aligned with the way work gets done rather than with old functional departments. These teams will have increasing levels of authority as development occurs. The powerful reward and recognition systems focus attention on the outputs and outcomes of the process including customer satisfaction, cycle time, costs of non-conformance and business results. Team members have a definite view of how their work affects the performance of the organization, its customers and those aspects of process performance important to its success.

As customer satisfaction survey results continue to improve, the performance bar is raised! The organization now formally reports the percentage of customers overall who are very satisfied and satisfied. In addition, emphasis is now on the customer relationship appraisal subprocess, which takes the company beyond the simple survey and into an analysis of the impact of our business processes on the customer. This face-to-face review method assesses the relationship the company has with its customers across a number of criteria, including inward and outward communication, professionalism of the approach by employees, contractual arrangements and product performance. This data, together with post-sales ninety-day survey information, is reviewed by sales and service teams using root-cause analysis techniques from the Quality programme to initiate actions to minimize or remove problems.

The integration of the inspection of the company's business processes through the Xerox Management Model (see Figure 3.4) is driving further emphasis on the customer through reinforcement of the detailed desired states of the operation. A whole category is devoted to the way Rank Xerox (UK) works with its customers, including requirements analysis, translation of needs into products and services, and customer communications. The assessment examines not only the performance against each desired state, but also the contributing factors that are helping or hindering the move towards this objective and the actions in place to improve performance. As the supporting internal networks develop and detail further the requirements for change to get to the desired states, so more employees are engaged. The management team therefore get a wider view of the more important factors requiring attention.

The issue of productivity in terms of its measurement and management

Process management has delivered a series of metrics to the business, and this has enabled it to focus on productivity and the costs of quality. A comprehensive hierarchy of process measures is in place across Rank Xerox.

The Customer Service Process Re-engineering Programme has provided, for example, a detailed set of integrated process measures. This programme has completed its implementation and has engaged more than 100 teams, which make up the entire Rank Xerox (UK) service force. The new six-stage business process (see Figure 3.8) is supported by a series of in-process, output and outcome measures that enable the examination of the impacts of the process on the customer and employee,

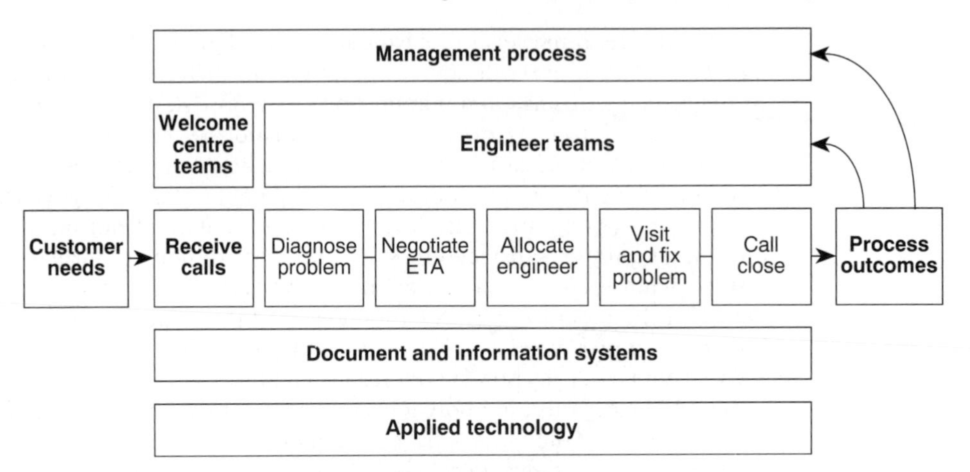

Figure 3.8 Customer service engineer process.
Note: ETA = estimated time of arrival.

its operating costs, quality, efficiency and effectiveness. A monthly customer service experience survey report provides additional feedback on the quality of service provided to Rank Xerox (UK) customers. Process owners are aligned to the six stages of the process, with access to all key process measures through a graphical user interface application built on a service management system.

Service productivity is measured, for example in terms of how telephone calls from customers are handled at the start of the process, not only in terms of costs and average number of calls processed, but also in terms of response time, call duration and the number of customer repeat calls. The level of call assistance provided by a service engineer through diagnosis provides a means of monitoring and improving overall process efficiency and effectiveness. Laptop devices with radio modems enable remote service engineers to communicate with a team member in a fixed location to take new call details and report service call achievements. Comprehensive statistics are gathered on service engineer effectiveness within a given geography of products as well as on overall activity accomplished in a given time period.

The development of self-managed work groups within the service force has supported changes in business process redesign and productivity improvements. An empowerment continuum has been set out for teams to work along to show how they are developing their performance. Teams appraise their own performance, assess their workload and plan their activity. Team awards and bonus schemes support this new organizational structure.

The re-engineered sales-order management process has been effective in delivering improvements in customer satisfaction, employee satisfaction, cycle time and some 40 per cent process cost reduction. Process redesign has enabled an 11 per cent increase in the time available for sales to spend with their customers rather than in the administration of orders. This increase has been translated into revenue improvement. In addition, new information systems, now in pilot testing, will refine the overall sales process and provide further productivity opportunity by reducing the amount of paper used by sales to record sales activity and customer requirements.

The impact of empowerment

The detail results to questions from the annual employee satisfaction survey provide feedback on how people feel about empowerment. The positive trends of satisfaction in 1995 (with 63 per cent overall satisfied) are significant in evaluating the impact of empowerment within the organization. However, there are other aspects to the impact of empowerment within the organization.

The new organization (shown in Figure 3.1) delivered structural empowerment changes that have focused attention on the purpose and objectives of the core entity organization (or local headquarters). The Xerox Business Architecture model (depicted in Figure 3.3) describes the management and infrastructure processes that operate in the core entity as those involved in delivering services to the rest of the organization (including business planning, human resource management, legal services, information management and financial management). This changing role for centrally based groups has had the effect of reducing costs, improving productivity and modifying the way managers see their internal customers, particularly as the costs of the core entity are now shared by the Business Division Units. More of the traditional support staff, especially human resources and administration, are moving out of the central teams to the Customer Business Units and Business Division Units. Core entity service provision is now much more tightly linked to and aligned with the requirements of the Customer Business Units and Business Division Units and to the entity as a whole.

In contrast, the implementation of self-managed work groups in customer service was accompanied by the removal of a whole management layer. In a typical Customer Business Unit two service managers are responsible for all service teams, delivering a ratio of one manager to 100 employees. The overall impact has been to improve employee satisfaction, increase productivity and reduce costs. The ability of a service team to respond to a customer call in a timely manner is a critical measure; if it takes more than one and a half times longer than agreed to respond to a customer, this is known as a *tail*. The work of a service team requires careful planning and coordinated action to ensure their tails measure is under control. These teams are able to examine independently all aspects of response management, planning and coordination, both within and beyond the team.

The Customer Business Unit general managers have taken local initiatives to improve their operations. This level of decision-making close to the customer has enabled more timely resolution of customer questions and problems. More of the decision-making in customer contractual pricing has shifted to these units over the last two years, improving customer satisfaction through reduced process cycle times.

Managing information systems

Rank Xerox (UK) information management application system strategies, development plans and performance review are now organized around the major business processes of the organization. This systems alignment has provided a clearer relationship between the costs of information systems development and operations and the business performance of the organization through the array of processes that operate.

Most of the new Xerox investment in information systems is in multinational systems which will support the convergent processes direction. These initiatives are driven from the foundation of common business processes found in the Xerox Business Architecture.

Impacts of change on the culture of the organization

The individual impacts of the new structure, implementing an empowerment strategy, managing through business processes, introducing changes in compensation and reward systems, establishing inspection through the business assessment method are all coalescing to set changes in the values, beliefs, attitudes and working assumptions of the managers and employees.

Lessons learned

The successful implementation of strategic change is essential for an organization intent on transformation. The strength of the organization will be measured by its ability to change.

Create and deploy a unified vision

Xerox strategies were initially deployed and communicated to engage the worforce. However, continuous communication and reinforcement are required to show how the organization is progressing and how all the implementations of detailed changes fit together. In short, there is a requirement continuously to market and revitalize change to ensure everyone understands the pathway to the desired state.

Constantly review the management process

The management process of the organization needs constant review and frequent redesign. The forces involved in the transition to the new organizational structure, the impact of a modified empowerment framework and the dynamic effects of re-engineering programmes have not been adequately supported by an up-to-date management process. The organization and framework for formal decision-making have not been regularly upgraded and should have been linked with a continuous review and improvement programme.

Handle the change management process well

Fundamentally, there is a paradox to managing change – there is an expectation that the business can continue to be run, with ever increasing targets, while major changes are implemented. It is like changing the fan belt while the engine is running!

The pressure to achieve business results fogs the decision-making process when longer-term changes are under discussion. It is sometimes forgotten that sustainable change is often achieved only when a series of iterative and cumulative actions are implemented rather than a single short-lived project. Some projects have been closed down too soon after the initial significant benefits were achieved without ensuring the infrastructure for continuous improvement was in place and working. Management expectation that change programmes are always serial events sometimes resulted in impatience and frustration when all the business benefits could not be achieved in a single project.

The holistic nature of change is not consistently understood across the company, so that the implementation of some programmes is not always synchronized for maximum benefit; rather the earliest possible completion date is sought.

Some change management issues involve the social, cultural and political systems, which are subtle and delicate to handle. Cultural change takes a long time to achieve and requires a committed and coordinated approach.

Early development and communication of structured change management methods are important elements to overall success. Tactically, the planning and creation of short term wins through change is another vital ingredient. As stretch targets have been set, selecting and designing critical and visible performance measures are important steps in the internal marketing of change. As successful programmes are completed the organization should celebrate, recognize and reward the achievement of those involved in the improvement. The progressive consolidation of improvements offers a springboard for further change.

Another success factor is the hiring, promotion and development of managers who can articulate and implement the vision, reinvigorate the processes of change, communicate new change themes and act as the new change agents.

Continuous communication is a success criterion; imaginative metaphors, images and models reinvigorate thinking and action. The purpose of change communication should be clear, including sharing a vision through persuasive techniques, ensuring integration of all the change components through simple descriptive connections and displays, and providing a workplace where trust is a prominent feature and frameworks for decision-making are defined.

Apply process change methods

The organization has many tools and techniques available for teams to use and balances the application of these different types of change methods. The portfolio of methods includes incremental improvement techniques and re-engineering methods that introduce radical change. Rank Xerox (UK) has to date implemented two radical programmes over a four-year period, as the organization cannot manage too many radical changes and grow the business at the same time.

The re-engineering method delivered process designs which ensured the continuous fit amongst the systems of work, people, information and technology. The application of continuous improvement through process simplification has provided business benefits. Sophisticated workflow tools are useful, but there is still a lot that can be achieved by simply challenging a team and asking why work is done in a particular way, using a detailed hand-drawn flowchart as the medium.

Implement quality initiatives

The Xerox journey through Quality began by recognizing the need for change. The company has progressed rapidly and learned from each stage of the journey. The basics of Quality provided the foundations of process management and process re-engineering.

Total quality management (TQM) requires a revolution that must encompass the whole organization. Initially, Quality was a programme to be managed, something to be controlled, planned, and something that had to have a progress report attached to it. This mechanical approach only addressed certain aspects of change. A systemic company-wide approach to the launch of Quality was essential, covering the hardware, software and people of the organization.

In particular, the approach did not initially address the critical elements of culture change, including attitudes, beliefs, style, norms and basic operating assumptions inside the organization. The company's perception of TQM has changed; it is now viewed as total quality *of* management. Specifically, senior management's approach to change, illustrated by everyday application of Quality principles in operations, is a critical factor. Senior managers should act as role models to reinforce change and be patient, as implementation takes time.

The experience of total quality management has provided a foundation for the change initiatives – the tools and methods of change have their basis in Quality principles, and the programmes for work process improvement and empowerment are built on Quality practices. The Quality programme delivered the foundation for process thinking, as it provided the language to describe the requirements of the internal customer and supplier. It has provided a common language for change and the skills for work improvement. Quality also connects change with the business, as it has enabled senior management to provide employees with a sense of continuity and understanding of the overall direction the company is taking.

Empowerment is a force for a change

The many different facets and scales of empowerment have been difficult to communicate. Used appropriately, empowerment is a powerful force for change. It has sometimes been incorrectly perceived by managers as involving additional work or the loss of personal control, as the organization has not consistently communicated either its plan for empowerment or the link between work process change and empowerment.

Whilst pushing decision-making to the lowest level is the simplest strategic statement around empowerment, devolving decision-making is sometimes not linked with the requirement for self-managed and empowered teams to improve their connecting business processes. The objective is to see teams as customers and suppliers in the whole context of the entity's business processes and to improve all linkages.

Process performance measurement is essential

Performance measurement is essential for effective process management. Simple, visible process measures are an ingredient of a successful work team. However, effective process measurement depends upon having integrated process information systems that are able to supply the values of the required measures. Process owners can define the in-process and other process capability measures, but there is always a time lag in being able to support the actual collection of data through information systems. Paper-based systems used for measurement are only partially effective.

The Rank Xerox group of companies has provided a valuable source of comparative performance data. Process and productivity measurement, coupled with the Business Architecture Model (see Figure 3.3), has provided a basis for understanding alternative practices that can deliver performance improvement. The gap analysis on the companies' performance provided a powerful method that further underlined the fact that quality and productivity go hand in hand with customer and employee satisfaction.

Measurement acts as a basis for monitoring change

There is significant benefit in having comprehensive measures for monitoring all key change programmes. Monitoring performance of the new process design in pilot tests provides a sound basis for problem analysis, and for successes and failures to be identified and appropriate actions taken. The performance measures of a new process render a foundation for design refinement prior to full rollout. During re-engineering programmes significant time is spent creating a hierarchical set of measures which connect the outcomes of a process (customer satisfaction, employee satisfaction and business results) with the process activity steps that deliver the results (through input, in-process and output measures).

Overall, a well-constructed and integrated set of measures can demonstrate progress, give confidence in the programme and generate acceptance for change.

Summary and conclusions

Rank Xerox (UK) has put in place foundations and direction for strategic change that have some years to run. Implementation of the Xerox strategy continues through many change initiatives affecting all employees. Linked holistically, each initiative is building a new business from the foundation of Quality.

The launch of the 1983 Leadership Through Quality strategy set forces in motion that have fundamentally changed the Xerox Corporation. Retrospectively, this implementation programme can be seen as a series of stages of change. The Xerox organization is in stage three, with the challenge of succeeding rather than surviving the 1990s. A comprehensive and unifying strategy is in place that combines and balances the approaches of radical and incremental change.

Before 1992, Rank Xerox (UK) still had the traits of a classical bureaucracy with a functionally driven hierarchy and deep layers of management. This situation resulted in an inability to adapt easily to change; the company was slow to react to customer requirements and had a complex set of working practices which slowed down decision-making.

The implementation of the Quality programme introduced a common language that enables any employee to work with others from any part of the organization using techniques and methods for delivering and managing change. The principles and values of Quality form the foundation of the business of all Xerox companies. They are the bedrock of process development and empowerment programmes focused on delivering productivity improvements.

Rank Xerox (UK) is being driven by a myriad complex forces for change. The strongest external stimuli come from the volatile business environment of continuous technological innovation, fast-changing markets, and inconstant customer requirements and values. The company must respond to these changes through a new organizational structure, accelerate organizational learning to outpace competitors and search for sustainable competitive advantages.

The business lies at the intersection of the two overlapping worlds of paper and electronic information. 'The Document Company' branding now used by Rank Xerox (UK) is a visible signal, internally and externally, of a totally new approach to the marketing of document services. The organization has aligned its perspective and intent as a document services provider with a central tenet of helping customers serve their own internal and external clients more effectively and efficiently.

Internally, all Rank Xerox (UK)'s core business processes are being designed to focus on the customer and to deliver products and services that enable customers' businesses to be more efficient and effective. The company is changing the way it markets and sells its products and services, taking a more consultative approach with customers.

A new structure has turned the organization of Xerox on its side, with technology on one side and customers on the other, connected primarily through a network of business divisions. The products of the Business Divisions are integrated together through an entity, a Xerox company – Rank Xerox (UK) as an example – where Business Divisions are represented by marketing teams who work with the Customer Business Units. Rank Xerox (UK) has been restructured to become more productive, entrepreneurial and innovative. It has created six small Customer Business Units that combine the skills and competences of sales, service engineering and financial administration.

Alongside restructuring is another programme singularly aimed at improving internal productivity through the pathways of business process improvement and empowerment. Both of these pathways are considered necessary and should be engaged at the same time. Productive growth is considered the key to competitiveness, profitability and reinvestment.

A comprehensive set of methods for analysing and changing business processes is available and is supported by a Xerox framework for understanding the desired state for all processes. This process model provides the framework for further definition of business processes into the categories of management, core and infrastructure. Until recently, more attention was paid to the core business processes than the other types, limiting the ability of Rank Xerox (UK) to manage change.

Rather than mimicking others, Rank Xerox (UK) is employing a variety of measures to rethink how work is organized and managed and how better to use the capabilities and strengths of its employees. The basic organizational building block will be the team, which will develop as a work community of learning. Underlying this design principle is the intent to ensure the fit amongst the elements of the work system of work tasks, people, information and technology.

The entire organization is engaged in change through a series of intervention programmes aimed at making change inescapable for all employees. These programmes are creating internal forces that can be categorized into three organizational design features: hardware, software, and people skills and attributes. The software of the organization is the most important and the most difficult to change. It involves the informal organization that holds the values, beliefs, attitudes and basic working assumptions – in short, the culture. Rank Xerox must ensure that formal and informal organizations are continuously aligned to operate effectively. Nine cultural dimensions have been defined as guiding principles for the conduct of business and linked to the management appraisal process.

Compensation, reward and recognition systems are aligned with the new structure and internal change programmes. Employees share in the financial gains the company generates through improved business results. The impacts of implementing an empowerment strategy, managing through business processes, introducing changes in compensation and reward systems, and establishing inspection through the business assessment method are all coalescing to set changes in the culture.

The powerful and complex forces that make up the culture have been analysed from three perspectives:

- management styles and behaviours, together with the way change is communicated;
- human resource policies which manage the relationship with the employee;
- employees' loyalty, motivation and general morale, in the context of their perspective on their level of fit with the organization undergoing change.

Programmes are in place to tackle each of these elements under the umbrella of the strategic intention.

In an organization that is fundamentally intent on change, continuous education and learning are an essential ingredient. The quality of employees and their ability to learn will probably determine the level of organizational success.

First Direct

Tom Ashworth

4

Using processes to satisfy customer needs

Introduction

First Direct is a telephone bank set up by Midland Bank in the United Kingdom in 1989 – it is a re-engineered organization. Strictly speaking, though, First Direct is not a bank in its own right, but operates as a division of Midland Bank, which is in turn wholly owned by the HSBC Group. This chapter is about a review of the organization which took place five years after its launch. In this chapter I will address the following issues:

- How did First Direct evolve?
- What is so special about First Direct?
- Why was it necessary for First Direct to change?
- How was this change achieved?
- What were the effects of the change on the organization?
- What did the organization learn from this and what are the next steps?

The First Direct story

Although the use of terms such as 'process redesign' and 'business re-engineering' were not around at the time, Midland Bank re-engineered retail banking under the name of 'Project Raincloud' in the late 1980s. The texts on BPR, for example

Hammer and Champy (1993), frequently refer to the conversion of an existing business to a radically new form, with all the associated problems of change management. Project Raincloud took an alternative approach. The purpose was to set up a re-engineered business from scratch, alongside the existing business. The project team was drawn from Midland and their IT suppliers. The core banking expertise was drawn from Midland, but as Raincloud evolved into First Direct the majority of employees were recruited from outside.

Final approval for the go-ahead was given by Midland in October 1988, and First Direct opened its telephone lines to customers one year later. In the remainder of this section I will describe the characteristics of First Direct in terms of its size, services, market characteristics, structure and customer base.

The size of the organization

At the time of writing, First Direct has approximately half a million customers and two thousand employees, based at two sites in Leeds in the north of England.

The range of services provided

The services that we offer at First Direct are currently directly aimed at the personal user rather than at businesses. First Direct aims to supply all the financial service needs of its customers, starting with the cheque account and covering savings accounts, Visa, investments, personal loans, mortgages, share dealing, foreign currency, travellers' cheques and a range of insurance products. Most customers start with a cheque account, and recently First Direct has started to sell motor insurance direct to non-banking customers.

By adopting this approach, the range of services they offer has brought First Direct into competition with the major banks, building societies, insurers and others in the personal financial services market in the UK. These competitors, in order to defend themselves against the success of First Direct, are now attempting to set up their own telephone distribution channels.

The characteristics of the market

Retail banking is not, by any standard method of industry analysis, a particularly attractive market. A cheque account will give a customer free access to an immense infrastructure of payment and clearing mechanisms, cash dispensers, cheque books, cards and statements. Having established free personal banking, there is now an understandable resistance to pay for the items mentioned above, and no bank wants to be in a position to be the first to start charging for them. The banks do, of course, charge interest on overdrafts and make money by investing customers' balances. For those customers whose salary each month tends to disappear rapidly, by way of contribution towards a succession of standing orders, direct debits and cheques, the remaining balance available to the bank for investment is too small to pay the interest necessary to cover the associated costs. The banks would lose money on this type of customer.

There are other customers who would tend to spend more than they have deposited (or have arranged to borrow), would pay excess fees, or a fee for the cost of returning a bounced cheque or other payment. No one is ever happy to pay for these charges, although a surprising number regard them as fair, and even as a useful means of ensuring that they keep their spending in check.

In order to be successful in this lopsided market, banks therefore need to cross-sell inherently profitable products to their current account customers. Whilst there are strong brands in the financial services market, the increasing availability of objectively comparable product information (in the form of APRs, commission levels, etc.) means that financial services products are becoming more like commodities. Competitive advantage in this market therefore rests on the ability to deliver exceptional customer service.

At First Direct we have been able to establish a reputation for exceptional customer service over the years (see Figure 4.1), by delivering it unencumbered by the practices and perceived reputations of the high-street banks. Early competitors, reacting defensively, began to add telephone services to their existing branch-based operations. In essence, they had missed out on the benefit of starting from scratch with a new (non-traditional) banking culture.

Within the industry competition is continuously on the increase, as more and more financial service providers are beginning to operate and conduct business over the telephone. Most seem to find it imperative to use the word 'direct' in their name.

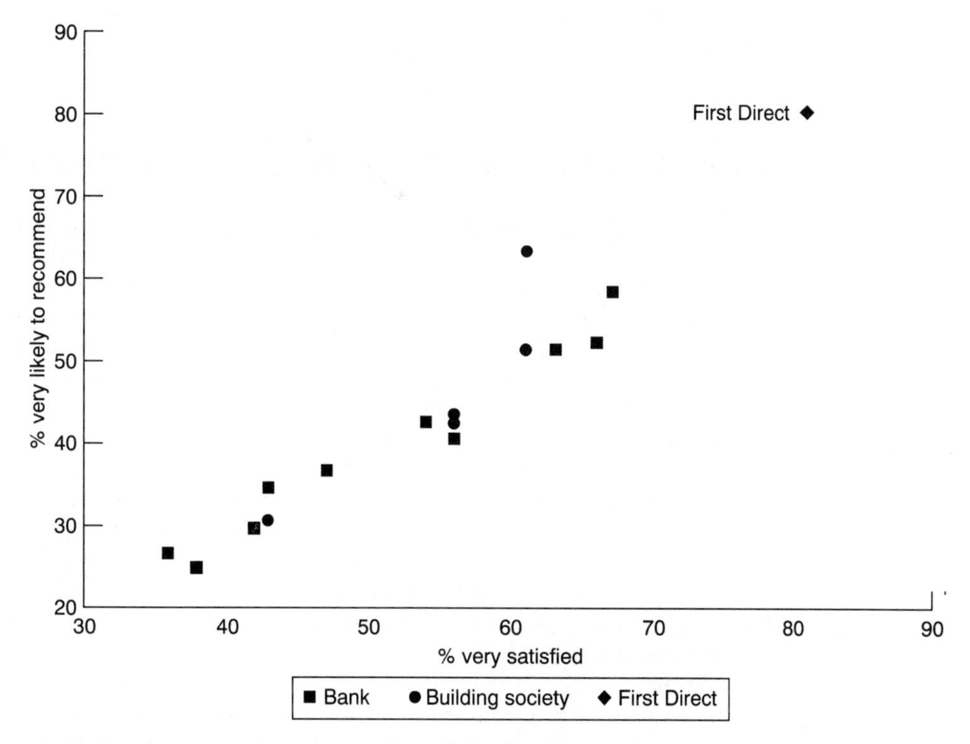

Figure 4.1 UK banking customers – satisfaction v. recommendation.
Source: MORI (1995).

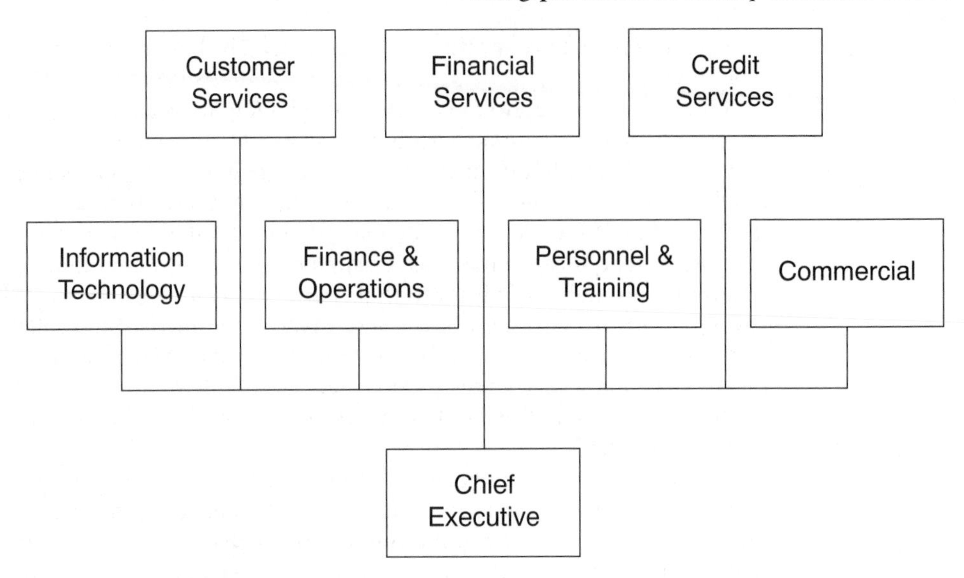

Figure 4.2 First Direct organization structure.

This in turn leads to a confused brand image in the eyes of customers and therefore makes it difficult for the providers to achieve a distinctive identity. Further competition is also likely to rise from the horizon by way of large organizations (such as utilities) who have the necessary data and electronic network infrastructures and who no longer face the traditional barrier to entry, namely to have a high-street branch network.

How the organization structure is represented

A conventional hierarchical diagram would best represent our structure at First Direct. This is often drawn in the form of an inverted triangle, with customer-facing employees at the top, to indicate their importance to the business. Anyone who is not at the customer interface is supporting the people who are. The hierarchical nature of this structure (see Figure 4.2) reflects working practices in the operational areas of the business, where the nature of banking traditionally requires a hierarchical system of various approval authorities. However, where project work is concerned the hierarchy becomes largely irrelevant. There are clear departmental boundaries, but these do not act as barriers to project teams.

The business process review (BPR), which this chapter is all about, was undertaken by the Business Analysis (BA) Team, which reports directly to the IT Director. In many other organizations, under these circumstances, BPR would have been labelled as an IT-led initiative, in spite of the fact that there were no IT people in the BA Team. It is a project-led initiative, as opposed to IT, and this is more relevant for the business.

Within First Direct there are three key operational departments, each headed by a director. All routine customer interaction takes place in these departments, and as we are a customer-led organization these departments include the large majority of our employees:

1. *Customer Services* includes the Call Centre (which can receive up to 25,000 calls per day), an enquiries team and a 'back office' processing team.
2. *Financial Services* handles calls for specialist services such as mortgages, personal loans, sharedealing, foreign currency services and investments.
3. *Credit Services* sets credit and risk policy, and handles calls with customers who are in default on payments, have exceeded overdraft limits or who are experiencing financial difficulties.

These three customer-interface departments are supported by four others:

1. The *IT* department provides and maintains computer systems, in-house software development and the Business Analysis Team.
2. *Finance and Operations* covers financial and management accounting, management information, internal control and compliance, premises support, security and internal mail.
3. *Personnel and Training* provides personnel functions and central training, including induction and management development.
4. The *Commercial* department drives product management, customer and internal communication, customer and market information, and database marketing.

The directors of these departments report directly to the Chief Executive, and together they form the Management Team which is the executive board of First Direct.

The customers

At the time of writing, First Direct has approximately half a million customers; this represents around 1.5 per cent of the current account market in the UK (estimates can be difficult, as traditional banks know how many customer accounts they hold, but not how many different customers that figure represents). New customers join at the rate of about 10,000 per month; all of these customers have previously banked with someone else. Around 30 per cent of new customers join us on the basis of recommendation from existing customers.

First Direct targets relatively affluent segments of the banking market – most are aged 25–44; 80 per cent fit the ABC1 socio-economic groupings (against the market figure of 51 per cent); 65 per cent work full time (market figure 41 per cent); most own or are buying their own home and 35 per cent have household income of more than £35,000.

What is special about First Direct?

There are five areas in which First Direct is seen to be unique. These can be described in terms of its culture, management style, IT systems, internal communication and its operation within market procedures and regulations. Each of these will be discussed in turn.

The creation of a people-centred culture

The culture of the organization is a key determinant factor (if not *the* key factor) in the success of the organization. It can best be described as a people-centred culture. It is a much better description than the now laboured cliché that 'our people are our most valuable asset'. In First Direct's case not only is it true, but it is also believed throughout the organization. Differentiation through service quality, for a telephone bank, depends crucially on the attitude of employees, as transmitted over the telephone. It is difficult to provide an unfailingly polite, efficient and friendly image by telephone if the workforce is unhappy or demoralized, or feels in any way undervalued.

There is no specific culture management activity, rather the culture pervades everything that is done, in the way it is done. In fact, the induction courses for new staff are probably the nearest we get to a culture management-type activity. The greatest concentration of effort goes into training the customer-facing people who have joined First Direct from outside the group. The training is focused on providing excellent customer service, no matter what the circumstances.

The most specific definition of this culture probably lies in the five core values of First Direct – these being *openness, responsiveness, right first time, contribution* and *respect.*

The visibility of the culture in First Direct becomes apparent in the organization's attitude to status. Whilst reporting lines exist and are clear, like departmental boundaries, they do not act as barriers. For example, there is one restaurant at each site, where everyone eats; there are no reserved car parking spaces; everyone is on first-name terms with each other; words which emphasize status differences, such as 'senior/junior' and 'staff' are not used; everyone wears a badge bearing their name and department but not their job title. The most visible aspect of all is probably the absence of individual offices. Not even the Chief Executive has his own office, so there is no chance of communicating status by the usual means of office size and thickness of carpet.

There is probably no single magic ingredient, or even set of ingredients, that produces First Direct culture, although recruitment and selection are certainly elements of the mix. Most new recruits, especially those who have come from more traditional organizations (particularly banks), are struck by the culture and atmosphere as soon as they start – people actually seem to *enjoy* working at First Direct!

An informal and relaxed management style

As befits the anti-status culture, the management style is informal and appears relaxed. Great emphasis is placed on the supportive role of managers, and team leaders are primarily concerned with motivation, coaching and mentoring. However, this style only superficially disguises a high level of focus on tasks.

There is a comprehensive performance management system, which provides the structure to define and quantify individual objectives. These objectives are supported by a set of twelve behavioural skills (including items such as influencing and communication), each rated on a scale from A to H, which are used in defining job requirements and individual development needs.

For managers, the ability to influence the business is based on their own personal effectiveness and is not limited by hierarchical position. Members of the BA Team, coming in from more formal organizations, have to adjust their styles of work to take into account that, for instance, if they want to speak to a director they just go up and speak to him. More significantly, the BA Team can operate on the basis of identifying changes that need to be made, persuading the appropriate decision-maker and getting on with implementation. Formality extends only to the minimum requirements for effective decision-making and project management. Decision-makers want to see positive and committed recommendations rather than lists of options.

Use of innovative IT systems

When re-engineering a branch-based retail bank, our priority was to focus the new business on customers. This sounds like a simple idea, but in IT terms it was a significant project. The big retail banks' IT systems had traditionally been built around accounts rather than customers. Where customers have a relationship with a branch and are known by the staff, this is not necessarily a problem. However, First Direct needed to be able to interact knowledgeably with customers, and hence maintain a personal touch, in an environment where the probability of any one customer (out of hundreds of thousands of customers) speaking more than once to any one First Direct person (out of several hundred) was extremely remote. The key to maintaining a personal level of service in this situation is information.

First Direct had to create an effective IT system that could present the First Direct individual in telephone conversation with a customer, with all the relevant details of that customer's accounts (i.e. cheque, savings, sole and joint, Visa, loans, etc.) on one screen. The end-result is a customer database, with integrated access to Midland's and other external systems, providing comprehensive customer information, and a workflow system which removed the use of paper almost entirely from the main customer interface.

Constantly striving for better internal communications

It is a commonly held belief that most people in most organizations feel that internal communication could be better. This may relate to 'hygiene' information that is indispensable for the correct performance of a job (e.g. prices, interest rates) or to higher-level information which makes people feel better, more valued and more committed (e.g. company mission and goals). First Direct expends a great deal of energy on trying to get all aspects of internal communication right.

Illustrations can be given by way of the following examples. In First Direct there is an internal First Direct newspaper. Each department also has its own newsletter, and some teams within departments have their own news sheets. Each department has an Internal Communication Co-ordinator (ICC) and the ICCs meet regularly. All First Direct people are contactable either by electronic mail or voice messages through the telephone system; every team has regular meetings; the Chief Executive makes presentations to everyone once a year; the state of the business is communicated to all through a Business Barometer system; and there is a programme of cross-departmental communication groups to foster mutual understanding between departments.

As with many other organizations, communication is never perceived to be good enough. We constantly strive to improve the quality of communication, but not simply by increasing the quantity. The secret lies in matching the medium and style of the message to the intended outcome.

Influenced by procedures and regulations of the market

First Direct is bound by the regulations of the financial services market and the requirements of Midland Bank. However, within these limitations First Direct has great freedom to determine, for instance, its own recruitment and remuneration policy. Both are important in maintaining the distinct culture and identity which differentiates First Direct in the marketplace.

Why was it necessary to change?

In 1993, as I have already described, First Direct was indeed a re-engineered bank. After four years of operation, it was seen as highly successful, clearly the market leader in its field, with extraordinary levels of customer satisfaction and no obvious need to re-engineer again at all. However, the gurus tell us that there are three possible reasons for wanting to re-engineer:

1. disastrous performance;
2. forecast of an impending disaster;
3. a desire to leap further ahead of the competition even though they have not yet caught up.

First Direct's motivation, therefore, was undoubtedly the third reason highlighted above, but this was supported by the knowledge that, although the customer interface was all new, a great deal of the 'back office' processing (where a large amount of paperwork still existed) was in a way no different to what was going on behind the scenes of a branch in the high street – albeit an extremely large one. Added to that was the assumption that head-on competition was imminent, yet it was surprising to those at First Direct that this had not happened already.

Change was already a way of life for First Direct people. Indeed, the very flexibility of the organization made it perhaps too easy to change and try out new ways of working. This in turn meant that it could be difficult for people to keep up with the changes taking place. What was required, therefore, was a co-ordinated approach to change across the business, picking up the cross-departmental opportunities and capturing the potential economies of scale. BPR, with its emphasis on customer-facing processes, appeared to offer the right kind of approach to satisfy this need.

The options available

One of the most obvious ways of setting about a BPR review was to engage external consultants. This would seem a logical step as, by this time, most management consultancies were claiming a strong track record in BPR, having renamed and developed their existing approaches to business improvement and change management. Indeed, First Direct was close to starting a consultancy-led process, but in the end decided that an internally led approach would prove to be the best way forward. Lacking the specific expertise internally, they set about recruiting a specialist from outside, which is where the author of this chapter joins the story. The title of the new role was Head of Business Process Management – a mouthful that is only rarely reproduced accurately; it is just as well that job titles are not particularly important in First Direct.

The Business Analysis Team had become an integral part of the IT department, acting as an interface between systems development people and business people. When people in the business wanted a system development, they called for a Business Analyst (BA), who would ensure that user requirements were translated effectively into systems requirements. BA Team members were also closely involved in implementation, particularly at the stage of user acceptance testing. The first job for the newly recruited head of the team, then, was to reposition the BA Team as broadly based business consultants with no automatic role to play in IT projects. Fortunately, at this time the IT development teams were ready to start working directly with their customers (users) in the business; when people in the business want a system developed what do they call for? A system developer.

For long-term wide-scope projects, the Management Team agreed to the new role of the BA Team as consultants and facilitators. This was exactly the right role for the team to lead the BPR project. Some of the existing members of the BA (Business Analysis) Team eventually moved to management jobs elsewhere at this time and successors were recruited externally and internally to match the new role of the team. The main potential problem was that the head of the BA Team reported to the IT Director rather than the Chief Executive. The role of the IT Director had been defined in terms of major change in the business, irrespective of the IT content of that change, so in practice this was not an obstacle to change.

The next issue to consider for the BPR project was scope. We were not looking at an ailing business that needed a radical rethink to survive. We wanted the benefits of radical rethinking in some areas, but did not want to pay the price of major disruption to a successful business. The decision was made, therefore, to pick out a few processes from the existing operation and tackle them individually. This led to the question of which processes, but before we answered that one we had to decide what First Direct's processes were. The business could have been split along any one of three dimensions, which could be represented as the axes of a cube. Like Rubik's cube, we decided that we could split the business along only one dimension at a time. The dimensions were:

- services to customers (mortgages, personal lending, etc.);
- common activities (selling, transferring calls, etc);
- departments (see Figure 4.3).

The natural choice for a customer-orientated organization like First Direct was to work on processes which were directly aimed at delivering the end-service to customers.

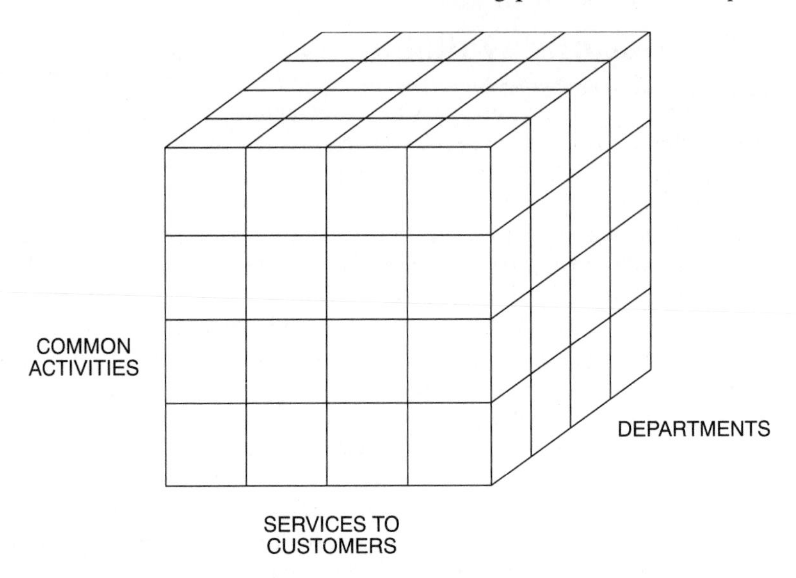

Figure 4.3 Three ways to split First Direct's processes.

How the decision was made

Directors, acting as sponsors for major, cross-departmental projects, represent the views of the Management Team and offer advice and guidance to the project manager, but without a highly detailed involvement in the day-to-day running of the project. In our case, the sponsor for the BPR project was the Customer Services Director, who had experience of major change projects in another financial institution. He and the Head of Business Process Management, who was to be the BPR project manager, developed the method to be used in the BPR project. Final decisions on the structure, scope and timing of the BPR project were taken in consultation with Management Team members, through presentations and discussions at Management Team meetings, with the Chief Executive being the final arbiter. It was vital to the success of the project to secure the commitment of the directors and their agreement on three key issues:

- the approach and method;
- the timing, particularly the start;
- the composition of the project team.

It always seems to be the case that there is never a 'right time' to start a major change project. It is always difficult to release the best people, and there is always something else going on which it would be better to get out of the way first. It was no surprise to discover, therefore, that there was a delay of several months to the start of the project. This proved to be useful, however, as it allowed time for the recruitment of new BA Team members and their introduction to the organization through several smaller projects.

At the end of the day, the directors started the BPR review with commitment and enthusiasm, which was tempered, though, with a degree of healthy scepticism which would only be dispelled when the programme delivered.

How First Direct did it

The following section describes how we achieved our aims in terms of how it was set up, how the project operated and the results.

Organization of the project

The BPR programmee was organized in a number of ways, namely through a steering group, a BPR project team and effective meetings.

The Steering Group

Another decision made in the early stages, which turned out to be highly significant, was to set up a Steering Group for the project. The role of the Steering Group was to set policy and direction, ratify key decisions and monitor the effectiveness of the project.

One distinct possibility would have been for the Management Team to act as the steering group. This would naturally have secured the involvement of the Chief Executive and all the directors. However, it could have turned the BPR into one item among many on a busy agenda and hence actually reduced its profile. We therefore decided to convene a special group which had separate, dedicated meetings even though it nearly matched the composition of the Management Team. Over time the Steering Group comprised:

- the directors of the three main operational departments;
- the Finance Director;
- the IT Director;
- the BPR Project Manager;
- as the commercial implications of the work became apparent, the Head of Product Development and Management (who reports to the Commercial Director);
- the project sponsor, who chaired the Steering Group.

These Steering Group meetings provided the main formal reporting line of the team, but the Project Manager maintained regular individual contacts with the other directors and senior managers.

The BPR Project Team

The majority of the work of the review was undertaken by the BPR Project Team, which comprised the BA Team and seconded managers from the three operational departments. It was decided early on that to achieve ownership of the review and its outcomes by the business and to ensure that the team had the right mix of skills we needed to second several experienced managers to the team.

Some of the members of the BA Team were initially not included in the BPR Project Team but worked on other business projects. This had the unfortunate effect of isolating those individuals concerned from the increasingly high profile that the

BPR project was achieving. As soon as it became clear that BPR could effectively utilize all the existing resources and more, the whole team joined in. This brought the strength of BPR to twelve people for the main part of the project.

The Project Team was created with a wealthy mix of skills which included banking, internal and external consultancy, operational management, organization and methods, and experience from a variety of industry sectors, including manufacturing. The range of personal styles was also quite varied. This resulted in occasional problems of misunderstanding and clashes of style, but these were outweighed by the benefits of having a balanced team, who could be mixed and matched into very effective working groups according to the specific task and the personalities of the business people they were working with.

Meetings

An overlapping pattern of membership of the Steering Group and Project Team helped to provide effective communication, commitment, ownership and overall integrity of the review. The Steering Group met monthly for a three-hour session to review progress and agree priorities for further work. The Project Team met weekly for up to two hours, to review project plans and emerging conclusions – this provided the opportunity to test ideas and make sure that no one had to reinvent wheels that other members of the team had already invented.

One further key meeting was a weekly one-hour session for the sponsor (the Customer Services Director), the IT Director, the project manager and the three most senior members of the project team. This meeting, officially called the project management meeting, but always known as the Thursday morning meeting, was an important bridge between the directors and project team. It allowed the team to 'sound out' the directors on matters of detail and direction at an early stage – and gave the IT Director (who was functionally accountable for the team) and the project's sponsor the opportunity to gain a feel for selected areas of detail and to satisfy themselves that the team's time was being spent effectively. Whenever changes in resource allocation were required, they were agreed upon by the project manager and senior team members and then reviewed at the Thursday morning meeting.

To the reader, this structure may sound potentially unwieldy, but in practice, by applying a minimum of formality to all but the Steering Group, it provided effective management mechanisms to balance the high level of empowerment which was given to the project team.

The tools and techniques used

The myth that their organization is unique is common among managers; they tend to assert that methods used elsewhere 'will not work here, because we're different'. First Direct is no exception to this, but the belief that First Direct is different from other organizations is probably closer to the truth than for many other organizations. Whatever the truth of the matter, it would have been inappropriate to try and apply a standard formula approach to BPR in First Direct.

As mentioned earlier, the method used in the review was developed internally, based on experience of both the delivery and receipt of consultancy-led change projects. Specific principles of BPR were gleaned from conferences and seminars, and in particular from two books – *Re-engineering the Corporation* (Hammer and Champy 1993) and *Business Process Improvement* (Harrington 1991). Hammer and Champy provided the principles and some of the key selling messages; Harrington provided useful techniques, including the process mapping conventions.

It was impossible to resist the temptation to look at a range of process mapping and modelling software. There was an impressive array of packages available, and it would have been easy to get carried away by the sophistication and cleverness of them. However, when considering the real requirements, rather than the 'nice-to-haves', there were four basic needs:

- recording and presentation of process maps;
- presentation graphics for Steering Group meetings and other communication;
- word processing for reports and recommendations;
- data recording and analysis.

These needs were easily fulfilled by standard office automation software (word processing, graphics, spreadsheet, database), with the addition of a basic flowcharting package.

Project management software was used for a time, but it soon became clear that a large amount of effort was going into it and the only valuable output was a Gantt chart. The project management skills of the team, and a short-term horizon for detailed planning, meant that specialist software was of insufficient value. Gantt charts can be produced easily in spreadsheets, if required.

One particular data gathering technique is worthy of mention. Focus groups of customer-facing First Direct people were highly effective in generating ideas for improvements, as well as helping to spread ownership of the outcomes. The focus groups used a brainstorming style to help generate as many ideas as possible.

How the project was communicated throughout the organization

Communication of the BPR project was an important matter, but not as critical as it is for many re-engineering projects. With BPR there is usually an objective (sometimes hidden) to reduce costs, and this is normally achieved through headcount reductions – a tricky message to communicate. The same was true of First Direct, but this was balanced by a significant advantage: the organization was growing so rapidly that it was possible to reduce future headcount from planned levels by slowing down recruitment – no need for redundancies, or even large-scale redeployment.

In the beginning, communication was therefore aimed at the directors and their management teams. These were the people who would be most affected when the project started. Knowing that there would be an initial period of relatively low-profile data gathering and analysis, it was decided *not* to have a big communication effort at the start, as this would have been followed by a period where it appeared, to most people, that very little was happening.

Throughout all of the stages in the project, the main medium used in face-to-face communication was a succession of presentation slide packs prepared for Management Team and Steering Group meetings.

How the processes were decided upon

An early decision had been to define First Direct's processes in terms of the delivery of services to customers. This, however, was a decision made only in principle as to which was the right direction or dimension – the next step was to define and name the individual processes. It was superficially tempting to use the existing products or services as processes, but that would have been to take too much for granted: we could not assume that we were producing the right products or services for our customers' needs. After all, many bank products are purchased because customers have no choice – most of us, for instance, will not be paid by our employers unless we have a bank account. We therefore needed to take a step back – to customers' *needs*.

The identification of customer needs took place during the months of the preparation stage, starting with a draft prepared by the project manager and sponsor, refined through individual discussions with the directors, and finally confirmed by the project team at the start-up workshop (described in more detail in the next section). The definitions were therefore reasonably robust by the time the project started.

As an example of a process, Unsecured Lending seemed a natural example. First Direct has two main products in this area – Personal Loans and Flexiloans. These do not represent customer needs, though: no one *needs* debts and monthly repayment programmes. If we take a step back and ask why, then the need becomes more obvious: people *need* to buy a new car, or they *need* to take a holiday. If they do not have the savings, or choose not to use them for the specific purpose, then one way of enabling them to make such a big purchase is to take out a personal loan. The need, then, is Big Purchases.

The implications of this go far beyond the BPR project – in all dealings with customers we need to remember that (in most cases, anyway) customers are not dealing with us for the sheer pleasure of it. When trying to improve the business we have to look at how we can make it easier for our customers to buy their car, holiday or whatever, rather than just making our own processes more efficient.

The final list of needs was:

- cash flow;
- big purchases;
- long-term provision;
- growth;
- housing;
- making and receiving payments;
- storage;
- protection.

These translated more or less directly into products or services, with one main exception – are credit cards related to making payments, cash flow or big purchases? In the end, credit cards were kept separate, so that the final list of top-level processes was:

- Money Management (covering storage, cash flow, payments and growth);
- Unsecured Lending (big purchases);
- Mortgages (housing);
- Foreign (certain types of payment);
- Insurance (protection);
- Credit Cards (payments, cash flow);
- Investments (growth).

What First Direct actually did

The aims of the BPR project were:

- to achieve bottom-line improvements;
- to create processes and attitudes that ensure continuous improvement;
- to improve our ability to deliver excellent quality of service;
- to improve the way we manage the business.

Figure 4.4 provides an overview of the structure of the BPR project.

Planning and preparation

The preparatory stage took nine months. The duration was determined by the eventual start date, rather than the volume of preparatory work. The main activities during this period were method development, discussions with decision-makers, project planning and recruitment of team members – a lot of detailed preparation, but an equal amount of internal selling. The Management Team was being asked to commit significant resources to the project, and they had to be convinced that this was the right thing to do.

Team set-up

Having obtained the all clear to go ahead and start the project, the full team, including secondees, was gathered together. In other organizations it would be normal for such a project to be allocated a room, but this would have been inconsistent with First Direct's 'no-offices' policy. The team did have a dedicated open-plan area, which provided the benefit of everyone being in one place, yet without the tinge of 'ivory towerism' which can result from project teams locking themselves away from the rest of the business.

What proved to be the most important part of the launch of the project was a two-day workshop for the team members. Many of the team members either were new recruits to First Direct or had not worked together before. Most had had limited exposure to the concepts of BPR, although all had the opportunity to read Hammer and Champy (1993).

The first day of the workshop, therefore, opened with introductions and an exchange of career summaries – it can be very irritating for a team member to spend a lot of time researching a subject in which they later find another team member is already expert. This was followed by an overview of BPR principles and

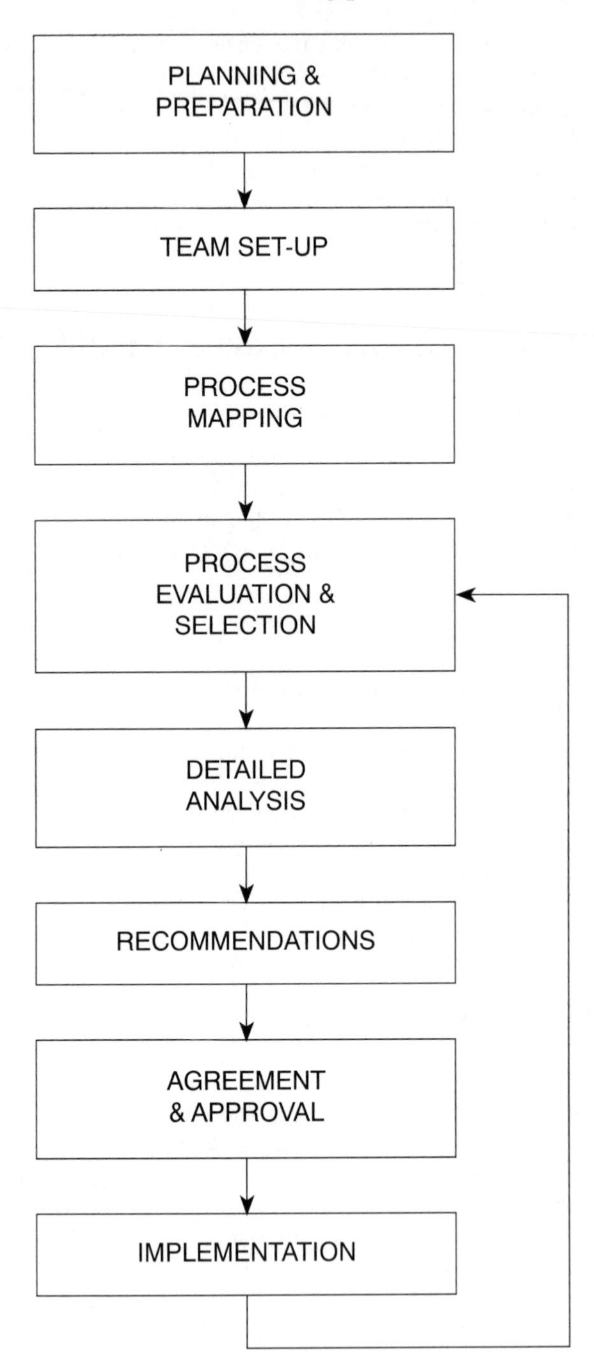

Figure 4.4 BPR project overview.

the outline plan for the project, but the main part of the day was spent on the subject of teamwork and team-building. There is a limit to what can be achieved in building the effectiveness of a new team in a workshop, but the main objective was to make it easy for the team members to discuss team dynamics and interpersonal issues. By

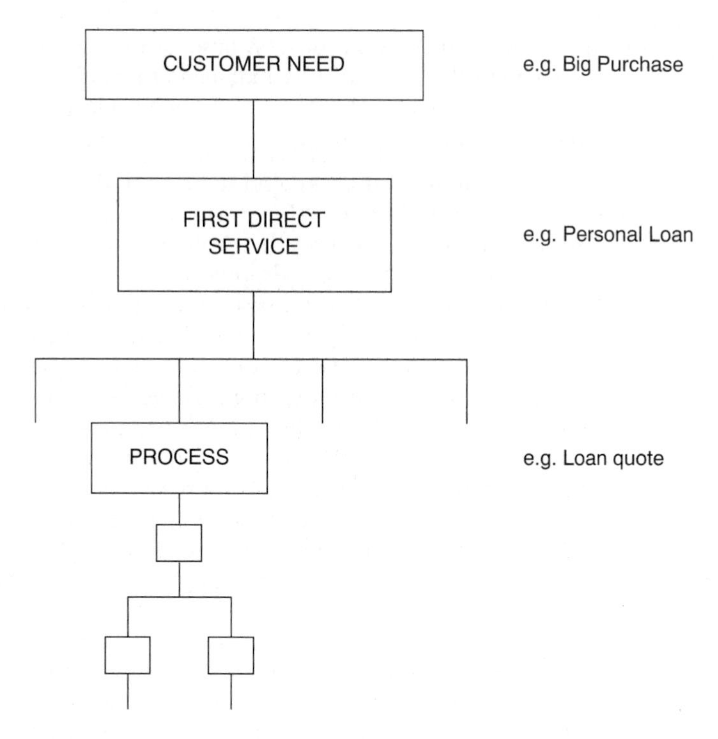

Figure 4.5 Business process structure.

making it a discussion topic and introducing neutral terminology we hoped that any potential problems could be exposed and sorted out quickly, rather than festering until they became obvious, by which time the effectiveness of the team would already have been compromised. It is impossible to know how beneficial this was, but team dynamics did become an issue once or twice later on, and these issues were resolved quickly.

The second day of the workshop concentrated on the nitty-gritty aspects of the third phase of the project, process mapping. The team agreed on the mapping convention to be used and practised mapping some parts of the processes. The team reviewed the high-level process classification and spent some time discussing the conceptual structure of the business processes, which is illustrated in Figure 4.5. The final task was to agree on the allocation of processes to subteams, each of which was led by one of the three most experienced BAs.

Process mapping

At the level below First Direct's main service areas there were some 150 processes. All were mapped by the team over the subsequent ten weeks. Team members' feelings during this phase ranged from excitement, through absorbed interest and confusion, to downright boredom at times. Some of the team enjoyed process mapping, others disliked but tolerated it; all had to do it.

The team members within each group followed the same basic routine:

- an outline of the chosen process based on the existing knowledge of the team;
- review with the relevant line managers to agree the correct details;
- discussions with, and observation of, the people actually doing the job, to find out what was really happening.

In any organization, managers tend to be clear about how work *should* be done, but are often unaware of unofficial 'work-rounds' that people adopt to compensate for inefficient procedures. The process maps were all based on the actual process, where this differed from the theoretical process.

About halfway through the mapping phase it became clear that the theoretical difference between mapping and detailed analysis was not useful. In order to be able to evaluate the effectiveness of some processes we had to engage in large data-gathering exercises, because existing management information was inadequate. For instance, no one knew how many times customers called in to check the balance on their account, because a balance query did not generate a recorded action in the computer system. There were also certain aspects of call timing, such as the duration of the greeting and security checks, which were not collected automatically. The team therefore carried out a programmee of call analysis, by sitting with the banking representatives who take calls and noting the frequency and duration of the various elements of calls.

The culmination of this phase was to be the first Steering Group meeting. The Steering Group members had all been involved individually so far, but diary commitments had not permitted a full meeting. The aim of the meeting was to present an evaluation of the service areas and to decide which should be selected for detailed analysis and redesign.

For the remainder of this section, details of the work done at each stage on two processes (Personal Lending and Mortgages) will be described in order to illustrate to the reader the types of recommendations made and two different variations on the approach to gaining line-management commitment.

Exhibit 1

Personal lending

The most striking aspect of the mapping stage was the complexity of the process within a small part of a department. This was a result of the hierarchy of approval authorities required to ensure adequate control. Seven processes were identified and mapped, including Loan Quotation, Loan Opening, Loan Settlement Figure and Loan Closure.

Mortgages

Most obvious here was the division of responsibility within the area, so that the process moved between two managers rather than being under sole ownership. Nine processes were identified and mapped, including Quotation, Assessment amd Sanction, Drawdown and Account Closure.

Process evaluation and selection

At the start of the mapping phase, the proposed evaluation criteria for the selection of processes to redesign had been agreed with the Management Team. They were, in a rough order of importance:

- *size* – volumes, costs and income;
- *current performance* – how well the process met customers' expectations;
- *complexity* – number of handoffs, bottlenecks, and the potential for simplification;
- *opportunity* – the extent of the potential market for the service;
- *growability* – how well the process could meet existing expansion plans.

It was during the mapping phase that the team attempted to achieve an appropriate balance between analysis and judgement – pure judgement, based on 'feel' could have been used, but it was clear that we wanted a more rational decision on selection of processes; conversely, a thorough quantified analysis of all processes would have taken much longer, the delay would not have been acceptable to First Direct's action-orientated managers and the outcome of a purely numbers-based analysis would have felt too 'mechanical' to be acceptable. The aim, therefore, was to present the Steering Group with:

- a selection of new, and preferably surprising, information;
- an indication of the potential size of improvements to be gained;
- a summary evaluation of the service areas against the agreed criteria;
- an outline project plan for the detailed analysis of the selected service areas (in the hope that we had gained agreement to the first three parts).

The preparation for the Steering Group meeting provided anxious moments for the project team. We had been working for more than two months, and this was to be the first major checkpoint. We wanted to be bold, yet did not want to overpromise, but neither did we want the plug to be pulled because the benefits looked insufficient. Added to this was the fact that any scope for improvement could be construed by the directors as implying criticism of the way they ran their departments. The project sponsor (being the Customer Services Director, since he was running the largest department) decided to confront this issue at the start. He opened the Steering Group meeting by saying, 'Well, the good news is that we are very inefficient, so there's plenty of scope for improvement to come out of the BPR project.' The Steering Group meeting turned out be a great success, with all the teams' recommendations being accepted. It even finished on time.

Exhibit 2

Personal lending

As well as the complexity observed in the mapping stage, evaluation revealed great potential for revenue improvement through more consistent application of low-key selling techniques (First Direct is not a hard-sell operation). It seemed likely that efficiency improvements would release the resource required.

Mortgages

The greatest potential for improvement was in the sales area, with little scope for net cost savings.

The Steering Group agreed that both Personal Lending and Mortgages should be reviewed, with priority given to Personal Lending because of the greater scope for bottom-line benefits.

Detailed analysis

Work recommenced immediately on the selected service areas, with the analysis phase continuing seamlessly (because the activities were similar, but the level of detail was different) from the mapping and evaluation phases. There was some realignment of resources, but the structure of subteams within the review continued.

The activities of the subteams included reviewing management information, observation, analysis of calls, one-to-one interviews, internal focus groups (described in more detail later), customer focus groups (conducted by an independent research agency), reviewing research data and team reviews (where findings and emerging conclusions were shared with, and challenged by, members of other subteams). An early plan for formal generation and evaluation of options for each process was abandoned, as the conclusions increasingly became obvious and recommendations flowed naturally.

Exhibit 3

Personal lending

After mapping the processes, the main gaps in our understanding related to specific types of calls, their content, duration, frequency and time of occurrence. We therefore monitored a sample of calls to quantify all these aspects. We were then able to test out ideas, and refine and substantiate recommendations for improvement.

Mortgages

Here, again, we needed to monitor a sample of calls, mainly to determine how much resource, of what level of qualification and expertise (and therefore cost), was devoted to each type of call – calls vary widely in the level of expertise required to answer them effectively. Options for outsourcing parts of the process to other parts of the Midland Group were also examined.

Recommendations

Each sub-team developed a set of recommendations for improving its selected processes. Each recommendation was quantified in terms of the cost of implementation and the benefits. The aim was to translate the benefits into budget changes, so only direct improvements to income and costs were recorded in quantified form, although all recommendations were formally recorded and included in a project recommendations database.

Exhibit 4

Personal lending

The recommendations included simplifying the matrix used to determine how credit could be allocated across different products to individual customers according to their ability to repay (that is, the mix between overdraft, personal loan and credit card limit); improving IT systems to allow greater flexibility in repayment terms and more rapid approval; better service after quotation to improve sales conversions.

Mortgages

The recommendations included changes to the pattern of outbound telephone calls, to achieve a higher success rate in contacting customers; improved links between mortgage and banking IT systems; and changes to streamline the completion of application forms.

Agreement and approval

The most critical part of the recommendations phase was gaining the agreement and commitment of line managers. The risk of implied criticism was even greater with line managers than with the directors. There was no set procedure for gaining commitment, and the subteams went about it in different ways, which were determined by the preferred styles of the BAs and line managers concerned. In some cases joint working ensured involvement and commitment to the emerging conclusions week by week; in others there were big working meetings when recommendations were formulated and finalized.

Each sub-team had a target Steering Group meeting at which the members were to present their findings and recommendations. As the project progressed, these Steering Group sessions became review and confirmation sessions – all the detailed review and agreement took place prior to the final presentation, except where a decision involving all the members of the Steering Group was required.

As recommendations progressed from 'ideas for discussion' through 'agreed in principle' to 'budget changed', they were labelled appropriately in the database so that a running tally could be kept.

Exhibit 5

Personal lending

This was one of the first subprojects of BPR, and was seen as the 'flagship' that would determine initial perceptions of the success of the process. The timescale was therefore made deliberately ambitious (about six weeks) to achieve results quickly. This meant that, rather than involve line managers gradually over a long period in the development of recommendations, two big meetings were arranged, to include all interested parties and go through all the recommendations in detail.

Mortgages

By contrast, the Mortgages subproject took place over a longer period – recommendations were discussed and developed jointly with the line people at weekly meetings, more or less as the ideas emerged.

Both approaches worked, but the rapid approach for Personal Lending was more risky as it depended on achieving line commitment at a relatively late stage.

Implementation

In many cases, where decisions could be made locally, implementation began immediately, without formal referral to the Steering Group. In fact, the identification and implementation of 'quick wins' had been seen as desirable right from the start, in order to build confidence in the project.

The presentation of findings and recommendations to the Steering Group normally marked the end of the most intense part of each subproject, and the team members became available for the next piece of work. The latter part of each Steering Group meeting therefore focused on the selection of the next service area or set of processes to concentrate on. This normally happened at least one month in advance of the team resource becoming available, so the planning horizon was generally two months ahead. This seems relatively short, but it suited First Direct's flexible style and allowed the outcomes of earlier stages to inform the decisions on later stages.

The major part of the work on implementation would take place after the relevant Steering Group meeting, but always took a smaller amount of resources than the previous stages. Responsibility for implementation was firmly placed with the line managers, yet the project team remained accountable for achievement of the benefits. The team therefore provided as much help, support and encouragement as was necessary to ensure successful implementation. This assistance ranged from an occasional meeting to check progress, through to full-time secondment of a team member to the operational area.

In most cases, line managers undertook implementation and the project team kept in touch through regular checkpoint meetings until recommendations reached the final stage of being implemented and the benefits were recognized in the form of budget changes.

Exhibit 6

Personal lending

A number of follow-up meetings were arranged with the line managers, and implementation followed smoothly, according to the planned timescales of each recommendation. Other initiatives had also been started as part of normal business, and the success of the BPR recommendations became intertwined with those.

Mortgages

The early involvement of line people meant that the handover of responsibility for implementation happened naturally without as many formal reviews as were required for Personal Lending. Many of the ideas for improvement had been implemented before the BPR team had time to record them.

What the problems were and how were they overcome

It had been confusing, and slightly worrying to us, to see a project called 'Re-engineering' on the systems development plan well before the start of BPR. This earlier project had started out with a fairly broad scope and some high ambitions, but in the end became so focused on a small area that it no longer merited its title. Unfortunately, names tend to stick, and the BPR project had to overcome scepticism that BPR would go the same way. This problem was tackled in three ways:

1. There was no initial fanfare to raise expectations, as we knew that results would be some time in coming.
2. The word 're-engineering' was never used in relation to BPR.
3. We achieved results that showed this project was different.

As highlighted earlier, the team was made up of a diverse group of individuals, and it was not clear at the start how well they would 'gel' as a team. The team-building work at the start undoubtedly helped, and minor problems were not allowed to grow insidiously into major problems. Perhaps the major factor, though, was the clarity of the aims of the project. Katzenbach and Smith (1992) cite a demanding performance challenge as the most important factor in effective team performance, and the BPR project undoubtedly benefited from that. There were several occasions when the secondees, in particular, became uncomfortable with the openness and vagueness of subproject aims during the analysis phase; they were surprised by the lack of a precise long-term project plan. There was no easy answer to this, just time, experience and seeing the results emerge.

There were relatively few problems associated with the Steering Group, apart from the difficulty of matching diaries to get them together for the first two months. The most difficult meeting was the one in which the first set of recommendations was presented. We made the mistake of working through the detail of more than thirty individual recommendations – a frustrating and inefficient use of the directors' time. Since that meeting, only the major recommendations have been presented, and this after most of the relevant decisions have been made, with all the required consultation covered outside the meeting.

Making assumptions is a dangerous route to follow, and some relatively minor problems were caused by assuming that within each department there were ideal communications. For example, one decision on a recommendation was eventually reversed, partly because of changing market conditions but partly because one key influencer had not been party to the decision in the first place.

During one subproject, the team members became agitated by the attitude of the people in the business area concerned. 'We only need to mention an idea for improvement, and they've gone and implemented it before we've had a chance to record it as a recommendation!' Needless to say, this was not widely regarded as a problem! The team members concerned quickly saw that they had been instrumental in developing a more active attitude towards continuous improvement, which was certainly one of the aims of the review.

The biggest problem of all actually came at the end of the implementation stage. Generally speaking, line managers and the BPR team had worked together very well. Managers were enthusiastic about the improvements and happy about the quantified benefits, which were based on sound analysis. However, it was, in some areas, very difficult to scale the final hurdle – changes had been implemented but no manager likes to cut his own budget. Even though there was no loss of existing people required, managers were reluctant to lose the 'insurance' factor and take what was seen as a risk – that the anticipated benefits might not materialize. The solution to this was simply hard work – the team had to follow through every recommendation painstakingly with the line managers until they were satisfied and the budgets could be changed.

The things that went particularly well

It was recognized from the beginning that top-level commitment was required. This was certainly achieved, with the initial sceptics won over rapidly. Even though the Chief Executive was not in the Steering Group, he maintained a close interest and was available for support if required.

One factor noticeable by its absence was defensiveness. There were some lively debates over the validity of some recommendations, but these were characterized mainly by rational argument. The team challenged some strongly held beliefs, and these were defended by their holders, but in terms of business benefit rather than personal politics. Even when managers' pet ideas were picked up by the team, the managers were pleased that the review had put some extra power behind them rather than worried that they might not get the credit for their idea.

The Steering Group has featured strongly so far, and certainly must be cited as one of the project's success factors. There was a very high attendance rate, indicating that it was among the Group members' high priorities. One significant benefit of attendance was insight into parts of the operation that the directors did not otherwise see.

The motivation and enthusiasm of the project team remained high throughout – there were some ups and downs, but overall the team worked extremely well. All team members gained new understanding of the business and had the opportunity to be a major influence.

What effects did the initiative have?

The effects can be measured in terms of the scope of the change and the tangible/intangible benefits.

The scope of change

At First Direct the scope of the change was identified in a number of ways, namely: targets, preconceptions, whether the change was radical or incremental, changes in organization and job content and IT systems.

Targets

The BPR project was sold internally on the approach's potential for achieving significant radical change, as espoused by Hammer and Champy (1993). The key factor in such radical change is frequently the demolition of internal barriers – the bringing together, in the form of a multi-skilled individual or a multi-specialized team, of all the elements required to produce an output for the customer without unnecessary hand-offs between people and departments. In many organizations this involves traumatic change for the structure and the people in it. It is important to enter such change programmes with no restrictions on scope, since any expected scope is likely to be exceeded.

First Direct started its BPR with no restrictions. The objectives, agreed by the Management Team, included the statement 'The scope of the review will not be limited in any way'. During the course of the project, the team was never told 'you can't look at that', although it was recognized that certain aspects of the business, driven by regulation and by the parent group, were less susceptible to change than others.

However, as described in the initial section, First Direct was already a re-engineered business significantly different from its branch-based competitors. The key parts of its computer system were new, and the employees were mostly unencumbered by traditional attitudes and work practices. Furthermore, mapping of the processes revealed that there were relatively few hand-offs between departments. For instance, 90 per cent of all customer calls are handled completely by the Call Centre – the first point of customer contact – without reference to other departments. The vast majority of resulting actions are then carried out or passed on by the workflow system.

The end-result of all this was that the BPR project conformed more closely to process streamlining than to business re-engineering.

With the benefit of hindsight, the direction and shape of the review was sealed by the agreement of cost-saving targets for 1996. The targets were set in the knowledge that the approach was to be the selection of individual processes for redesign and the belief that certain parts of the business (mainly the customer interface) were unlikely to yield significant improvements because they were already new. Accordingly, the targets were set at around 5 per cent of the total costs.

The gurus tell us, with their hindsight, that highly ambitious targets (say 40 per cent) tend to be exceeded and modest targets (say 10 per cent) are rarely achieved. The inherent modesty of a small target tends to preclude the really radical and daring ideas which come from totally breaking out of the current mindset – you do not have to break out of the current mindset to achieve 5 per cent or 10 per cent.

Some definite consequences of having a cost-saving target for the following year were:

- That improvements which depended upon a significant systems development were unlikely to help meet the targets because of the length of time involved in such developments;
- That the team automatically focused on tangible, here-and-now benefits that would hit the bottom line almost immediately.

The latter point was reinforced by the apparent wealth of here-and-now opportunities that began to appear.

Preconceptions

There were two main preconceptions about the scope of the project, both of which were to be proved incorrect. The first was that the customer interface was unlikely to be susceptible to significant improvements. It should probably be a maxim of all change initiatives that they should focus on the areas that most people feel cannot be improved very much – such views are often an indication that they have not been critically reviewed in the recent past. The review was able to identify numerous improvements in the way that the conversation was structured during calls, and in the way that the computer system supported the conversation. Because of the very high volume of calls handled, even small time savings in call duration, barely noticeable to individual customers, can result in significant improvement in efficiency.

The second preconception was that the project would be unlikely to identify significant improvements in revenue achievable directly, rather than indirectly through service quality. For example, the streamlining of the approval process for personal loans (with no change to the underlying credit assessment criteria) and improvement of follow-up procedures contributed to a significant improvement in the revenue from unsecured lending. This also highlighted a difficulty in the estimation of benefits achieved in the form of revenue improvement – there are far more potentially confounding variables driving income than there are driving costs. Market conditions, competitor activity, advertising, promotion and pricing all affect income in ways that are very difficult to isolate from other changes. The implementation of BPR changes to personal loans processes came only one month before an improvement in pricing. Fortunately, First Direct does not waste time arguing over who gets the credit in such situations, but we still needed to be able to justify the project, so a certain amount of estimation of income benefits was required. The focus of measurement of benefits and setting of targets remains on cost savings.

Was the change radical or incremental?

As the project progressed, whilst satisfactory progress was being made, there were comments from some Steering Group members about the lack of revolutionary or radical ideas that had been promised at the outset. One response was that we had achieved a lot more than expected without such change, but it was accepted that the potential for step-change had not been fully explored.

All the subproject teams had used creative techniques such as brainstorming in focus groups, and these had been extremely useful, but they did not bring out world-shattering ideas.

Other initiatives linked to the BPR Team have since been started with the aim of focusing on the big changes required for success in the five- to ten-year timeframe, but the BPR project has remained focused on short-term improvements – and there is still plenty to go on. BPR still has the aim of helping First Direct to leap further ahead of the competition, but the original method of process improvement is supplemented by longer-term 'blue sky' thinking by the Management Team.

Process-based organization structure

BPR did not result directly in any significant organizational changes. This was a concern, if only because successful BPR projects are supposed to result in radical change – normally the whole organization has to be restructured and refocused around the newly discovered business processes. These processes, when discovered, are often deemed to be cross-departmental by definition; in other words, if your processes are not cross-departmental they cannot be processes. This is, of course, illogical, because it is based on the assumption that no organization undertaking BPR starts out already structured around its business processes. Our conclusion was that First Direct was, indeed, already structured around its processes.

The reasons for this are fairly simple. BPR, like most useful management ideas and models, is a form of applied common sense. The success of BPR lies in the fact that it is very difficult to apply common sense to an established business, where existing practices are set in the concrete of organizational inertia; BPR provides a means of overcoming that inertia. However, First Direct had been set up from scratch in 1989. The original project team designed First Direct around common-sense principles such as handling the maximum number of customer processes to completion at the customer's first point of contact. In order to achieve that, the IT systems were designed to present to banking representatives all the information they required on one screen; and the banking representatives were multi-skilled to ensure that they

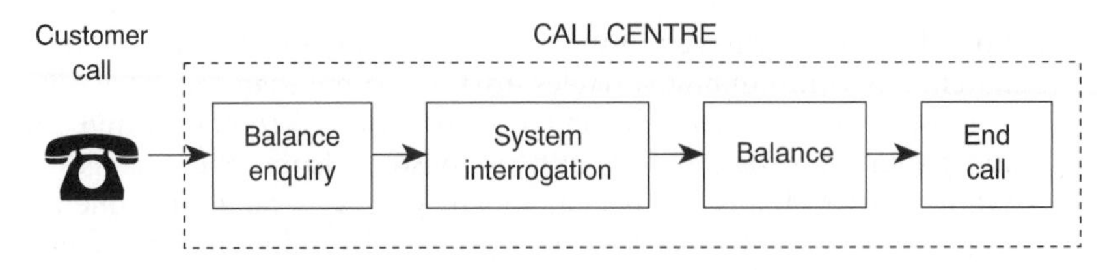

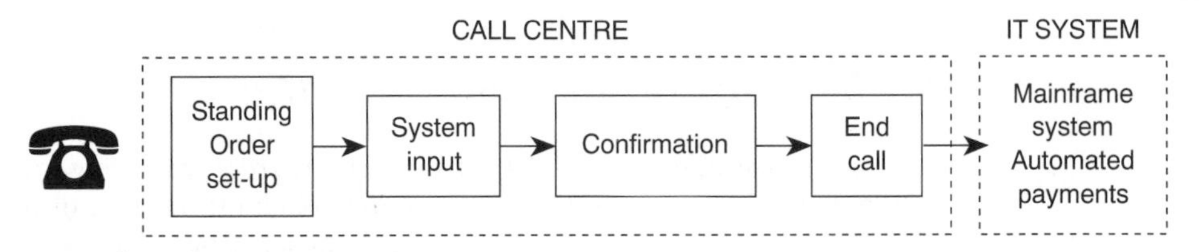

Figure 4.6 Simple processes.

could complete all but the most complex processes without reference elsewhere. Comprehensive systems and multi-skilling are two of the basic tenets of BPR, and First Direct already had them. Some illustrative processes are shown at high-level in Figure 4.6. In these simple processes the direct human involvement is completed during the customer's telephone conversation with the banking representative in the Call Centre. Any further actions are completed automatically by the IT system, or are transferred to external processes, such as the banks' clearing and transfer processes. Ninety per cent of all customer calls to First Direct are completed within the Call Centre.

Much effort goes into multi-skilling the bank representatives, but there are several areas (such as mortgages, personal lending, share dealing and debt counselling) where it is more efficient to transfer the customer call to a specialist. Such processes are illustrated in Figure 4.7. In both cases the call is transferred to the relevant department, where the process is taken to completion without any further transfer.

Overall, the lack of significant organizational change from BPR was because it was not needed, rather than (as we feared for a while) because we had missed something. First Direct is an organization with a balance between process and function: there is potental for further movement towards process, but at its current size it is not yet ready to decentralize some of the major functions such as IT and Finance.

Job content

BPR did highlight a need to shift the emphasis of first-line management in some areas. Team leaders in First Direct are very focused on people management and tend not to have a background in process management. With the particular help of the BPR Team member whose background was in manufacturing, some team leaders in a high-volume processing area have taken on more responsibility for process management, backed up by team coaches. One subproject of BPR has concentrated on the need for process management, and training modules for managers are being developed as a result.

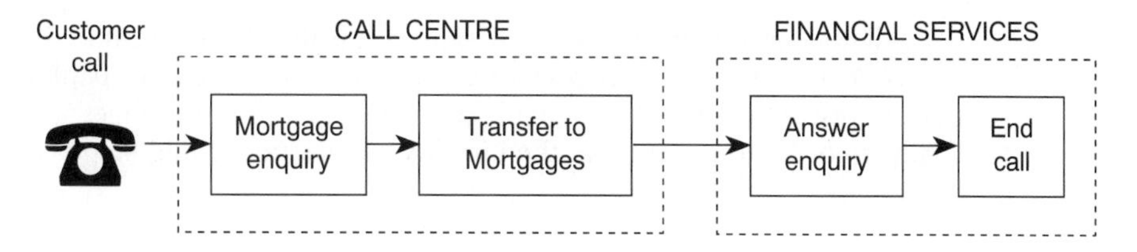

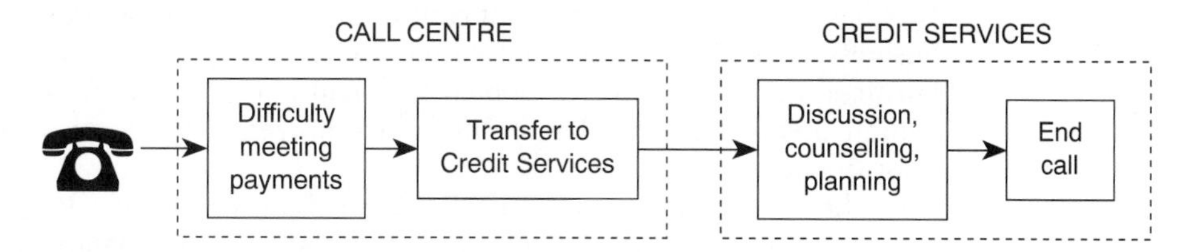

Figure 4.7 Transferred processes.

IT systems

A dramatic and revolutionary change to a business normally requires an equivalent change to its IT systems. One benefit of the non-radical nature of this project was the lack of dependence on IT systems for the majority of the improvements. The expectation that system changes would slow things down also meant that the team tended to concentrate on improvements that could be implemented manually.

The tangible benefits

At the time of writing, the BPR project is not complete, but already the team has clocked up large cost improvements based on working more effectively, with no loss of existing jobs and no detriment to service quality – and with a surprising level of income improvements.

Cost savings have come from improved management of call duration, especially at the point when calls (10 per cent of the total) are transferred from the Call Centre to either Financial Services or Credit Services. This point of handover had not been managed overall across the business before, and so was likely to yield good results. Further improvements are being made in outbound calling, where the team's research and analysis has enabled departments to target their outbound calling more effectively. In one area the successful contact rate has improved from around 30 per cent to almost 70 per cent. Such improvements are translated into the equivalent cost saving and chalked up to BPR, even if the business decides to take the actual benefit in the form of improved service levels or more efforts on selling activities rather than reduced recruitment.

Revenue improvements have resulted from streamlining lending approval, concentrating on the most effective selling techniques and ensuring that customers have adequate spending limits on their credit cards.

All the improvements were designed specifically to exclude any degradation of service. For instance, changes in the standard phrasing used by banking representatives were researched extensively with customers before the changes were adopted generally, in order to ensure that the improved efficiency would be perceived positively.

The intangible benefits

BPR has raised the expectation of continuous change and improvement around the business. This has not been measured, but is clearly evident in some parts of the business. Many ideas were adopted that had lain idle because of a lack of power behind them. BPR provides the necessary power in the form of profile, analysis, priority and resource.

At the start of the review the BA Team had a relatively low, systems-related profile. With several new members joining, the future credibility of the team rested on the outcomes of the BPR project. The success of BPR has significantly raised the profile of the BA Team (now often referred to as the BPR Team), which is regarded as a centre of excellence in the organization for change management and business project management. The measures of this success are a stream of requests to do project work around the business, and a high level of interest from individuals who want to join the team, either on secondment or on the permanent headcount. The managers who were originally seconded to the team have now moved back into line roles, armed with a much wider understanding of the business and improved project working and project management skills.

The profile of the BA Team and the success of the project will help to ensure that First Direct continues to reap the benefits of well-planned and executed change projects.

Lessons learned from the change initiative

The following section highlights areas where the change worked well. It also gives an account of issues that would be handled differently when undergoing a similar initiative in the future.

Areas that worked well

The areas that worked well are the Steering Group, links with line managers, the mapping of processes, focus groups, recognizing the importance of implementation and team mix.

Steering Group

Yet again the Steering Group rates a mention; it ensured a high-level of involvement and commitment from the directors, and it continues to do so. The Steering Group will continue to meet monthly, to monitor and drive change in the business through the BA Team. The Steering Group is now recognized as one of five key management groupings in the business, alongside the Management Team, Operations Management Team, Product Management Group and People Forums. The five bodies have different functions and meet at different frequencies but have overlapping memberships. The Steering Group was also important in providing very visible accountability for the project – even if people sometimes wondered what we were doing, they could be assured that it had the appropriate approval and backing.

The monthly Steering Group meetings had three further benefits. First, the opportunity to make formal presentations to a group of directors was a significant development opportunity for team members. Second, the monthly meeting acted as a natural deadline for all subprojects. There was very little need ever to force the pace when a Steering Group presentation was coming up; if anything, the team members tried to get too much done. Third, knowing that the results of the work had to be presented in summary form helped to maintain a focus on outcomes and significant benefits, as a balance to the tendency to focus on tasks.

Links with line managers

It is a truism in change management that the people who will have to run the changed activities should be involved in their development as a means of ensuring ownership and commitment. The principal means of achieving this were:

- secondment of line managers to the BPR Team, to avoid accusations of 'ivory towerism';
- regular briefing of line managers;
- involvement of line people in data gathering and the development of recommendations;
- joint presentations by team members and line managers of recommendations to the Steering Group.

The links were extended to the directors of the operational areas by briefing them before Steering Group meetings to allow time to solve problems rather than have them emerge during the presentation.

Mapping and analysis

Detailed mapping of the processes at the start provided an excellent means of understanding the way the operation worked. It ensured that the team members had a thorough understanding before starting to develop ideas for improvement. In more than one case, the sheer complexity of the map provided the justification for streamlining. The library of maps has also been useful for people undertaking project work in areas that are new to them.

A significant decision for the initial mapping stage was to keep the maps qualitative – there was no attempt to time and quantify every part of the process at the outset, which would have increased the mapping time by an order of magnitude. Detailed quantification was carried out, where required, in the analysis stage, and proved to be of immense value. Many gaps in First Direct's knowledge about itself were filled by analysis and research carried out as part of BPR. Figure 4.8 shows a typical map, in this case from Unsecured Lending.

Focus groups

A technique used in all of the subprojects was to gather together selections of six to twelve First Direct people into focus groups. These were used at the stage of analysis to help build up an accurate picture of the strengths and weaknesses of the existing process and gather ideas for improvement. Focus groups were also used to test out the draft recommendations of the project team.

Focus group members were usually people working directly at the interface with customers or on hands-on work in non-customer-facing areas. Group members were invariably pleased to have been asked, and joined in enthusiastically. They often provided new insights, and quotes from the groups were effective evidence, if any was needed, for the need to change in some areas.

The format of the sessions varied, but would typically start with an assurance of confidentiality (just in case there was any reticence to imply criticism of managers), then cover strengths, weaknesses and ideas for improvement in a brainstorming style. One of the project team members would facilitate the discussion and another would write up comments and ideas on a flipchart.

Most of the recommendations for improvement that came out of BPR were self-evidently the right thing to do (such as speeding up responses to customers and simplifying processes) or could be tested internally. However, where changes would affect customers in less predictable ways (such as changing the standard call greeting and modifying the security process at the start of calls), the project team called upon the services of First Direct's market research people to seek customers' views through postal questionnaires or focus groups. The customer focus groups were conducted on First Direct's behalf by an agency; groups of customers (and sometimes non-customers) were invited to discussion sessions, and their views on a range of questions were recorded and reported by the agency.

Implementation, planning and follow-through

The importance of implementation was recognized throughout the project, and plans set to ensure that recommendations did not just gather dust once they had been approved. At an early stage, when discussing implementation, nearly every member of the team claimed that they were 'natural implementors', However, when it came to implementation, there was a frustrating lack of progress for some time, mainly because team members moved on to other subprojects and did not spend sufficient time pursuing the results of earlier work.

In truth, several team members had underestimated the doggedness and attention to detail needed; they were far more excited by the next project than by seeing through the last one to the stage of budget changes. The answer was to allocate one individual who was highly methodical and persistent to pursue each recommendation to completion, cajoling team members and line managers as required. As important as the work style of the individual, was the need for this individual to have a good overview of the project, understanding of relative priorities and the respect of the team and line people – this was a role for a senior member of the team.

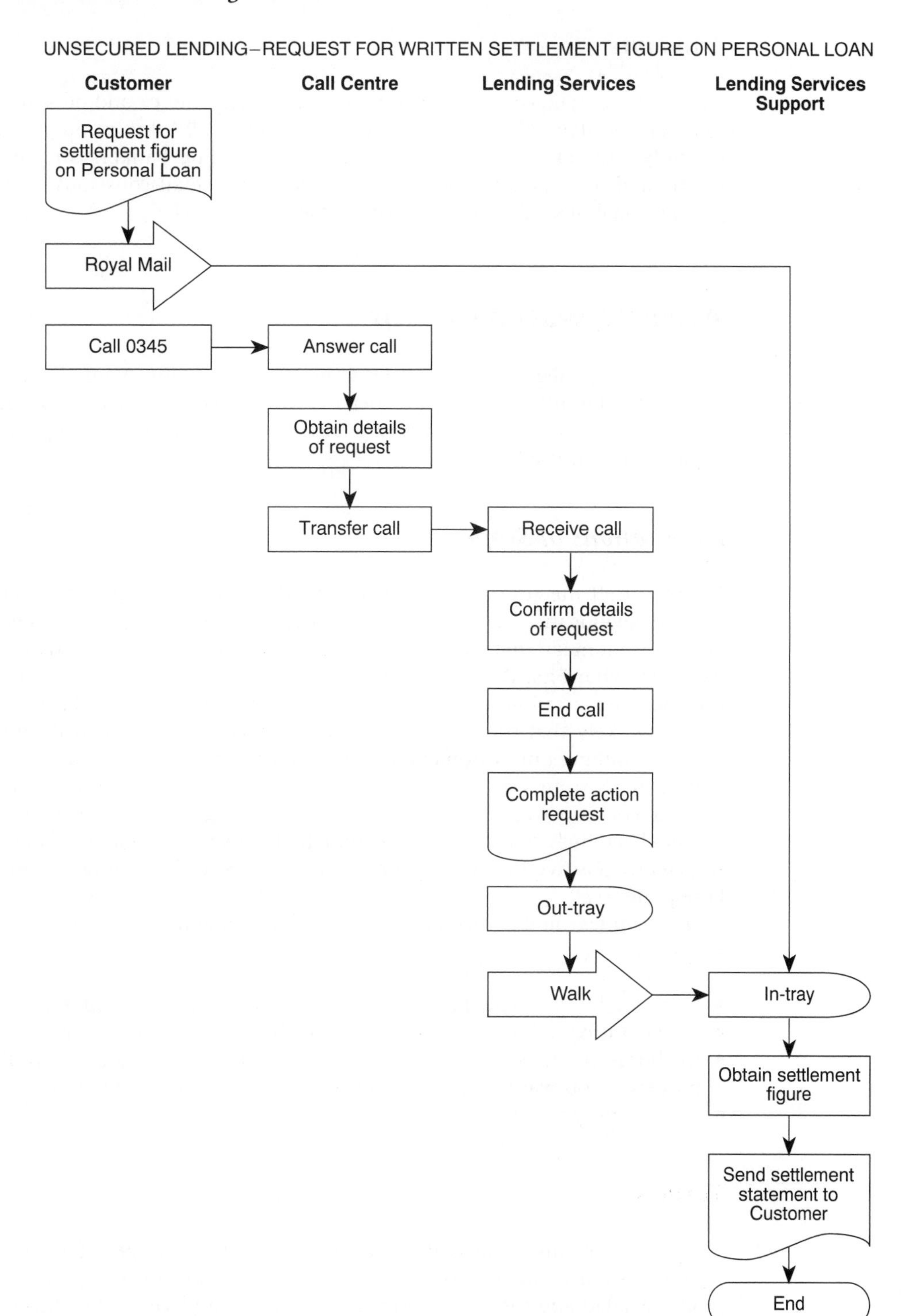

Figure 4.8 Example process map.

Team mix

The eventual make-up of the team, in terms of experience and personality, was to some extent planned, but was also partly fortuitous. For future projects we should certainly attempt to replicate the blend, by including bankers and non-bankers, project and operational people, creative types and detail-conscious types, challenging personalities and team-focused people.

Areas to watch out for

This section highlights areas that First Direct, in hindsight, would have handled or managed differently. They are the need to meet expectations, qualify targets, work as a team, ensure parallel working, manage the decision-making process, and implementation itself.

Expectations of Scope

In spite of all the research done beforehand, we were partway through before it became obvious that we were not doing 'true' business process re-engineering at all. This does not mean that we were doing the wrong thing – the objectives and method were just what First Direct required at the time – but rather that we had built up unrealistic expectations of the type of change that the project would generate. It was highly unlikely that the type of thinking required to come up with radically new ways of fulfilling our customers' needs would be prompted by a detailed examination of the current way of doing things. It is possible that the project would have seemed less attractive at the stage when it was being sold if the 'true' BPR message had not been included. Fortunately, though, the results of what was done have been sufficiently positive that we have not been accused of launching the project under false pretences!

The main learning points for anyone contemplating the launch of a BPR initiative should be:

- to decide in advance what scale and scope of change are required;
- to avoid mixing incremental and radical change in the same project;
- to choose the most appropriate method – avoid detailed analysis of the current process if you want to achieve something fundamentally different;
- to set appropriate targets.

Targets

During the planning stage there were no quantified targets for cost saving or revenue increase; the brief was to go for the maximum. However, business thinking soon prevailed and the cost-saving target was put in place. At first this seemed like pure good news. The per centage was not large but the absolute figure appeared challenging and certainly served to focus the attention of the team. However, the combination of a relatively short timescale and a challenging, but not frightening, target was almost certain to keep the project focused on making incremental changes to the existing processes.

The way to achieve dramatic changes is to set dramatic targets. If the targets are obviously not achievable by 'tweaking', then there is no option but to be radical. The learning points about targets, then, are:

- if you want incremental change, set a target of 5–10 per cent improvement;
- if you want radical change, set a mind-bogglingly difficult target and be prepared for difficult changes.

Teamwork

Having spent a number of years on project work, it is easy to forget how different it is from operational management. The difference is even greater when the project starts out without a clear idea of what sort of solution is required. The secondees from the line first of all had to adjust to being able to plan their own time without any operational constraints, then to working with the uncertainty of not knowing what they would be doing in a few weeks' time. Their reaction to the new situation was initially one of disappointment – the project looked very informal, when they had expected to be impressed by a grand and detailed project plan for at least six months ahead.

The BPR project started with a two-day workshop for the team, which was time well spent. The learning point here is that it would have been more beneficial to have a longer training session to cover the rudiments of project working, even if this was revision for the more experienced team members.

Parallel working

The project team operated as three subteams, each led by one of the more experienced Business Analysts. Within these subteams, in order to cover the broad range of processes required, there was further specialization. This resulted in a number of team members working virtually on their own, with occasional consultation with other team members. A symptom of this arrangement was individuals 'cornering' other team members to tell them about their latest findings. These unscheduled meetings were always interesting, but could tend to make time management difficult.

In future projects, we would opt for covering fewer project areas simultaneously, with the aim of having at least two full-timers on each one where this is practical. This would allow more opportunities for debate and discussion, as well as providing a more pleasant style of work.

Detail and decision-making

Probably the hardest-learned lessons of the review relate to the management of decision-making and the level of detail required for different meetings. The penalties of bringing too much detail to the Steering Group were described earlier, along with the problems caused when a key influencer was omitted from the consultation process. First Direct emphasizes individual accountability for making decisions, based on the right level of prior consultation to ensure that the decision is based on the best information. Some decisions, though, cannot be made by individuals alone, as they require the agreement of several parties. In both cases, the decision-makers need to ensure that they have the support (or are managing the opposition) of key influencers. Great care therefore needs to be taken when gaining decisions on the major topics which emerge from BPR:

1. Do not involve too many people in highly detailed discussions just to make sure that they agree with the decision – that is a recipe for inefficient meetings and wasted paperwork.
2. Ensure that those who work at a detailed level (managers of the operation) have the opportunity to understand the detail and agree with the decision.
3. Ensure that key influencers know about the decision, and give them only as much detail as is required for them to be convinced.
4. Do all the groundwork before key milestone meetings in order to avoid surprise disagreements, which can be an inefficient use of time and have a negative effect on those not directly involved.

Implementation

It is easy to imagine that when the research has been done, recommendations formulated and decisions taken the difficult bit is over and it is only a matter of time before the benefits are reaped. This is a mistake. It is easy for line managers to see a good idea, agree the figures and implement the change; but the most difficult part is actually making the saving. In First Direct's case the criterion was the alteration of budgets and plans to show reductions in planned headcount, but in another organization it could be the redeployment or sacking of staff. Managers who are concerned with delivering a high level of customer service are reluctant to relinquish any safety margin that they may have in achieving service levels. Project team members also tend to underestimate the effort that they will have to put into securing the final achievement of improvements – and are probably less excited by the prospect than by the thought of their next project.

The main learning points are:

- to allow plenty of time for securing final commitment of line managers to cost savings;
- not to 'notch up' savings until the final hurdle has been jumped;
- to be prepared to allocate a suitably dogged and detail-conscious team member to the pursuit of every improvement through to the end, and to compile the results in conjunction with the Finance department.

Summary and conclusions

To summarize, First Direct is the product of Midland Bank's re-engineering of retail banking in the late 1980s. It was set up from scratch with a core of people from Midland and a majority of people from outside banking. First Direct is highly successful, is renowned for its excellent customer service and has a unique culture.

The driver for changing the winning formula was based upon the desire to stay several steps ahead of the competition, who were showing signs of catching up.

A BPR-based approach was used to test for the full potential for improvement while remaining customer-focused and not compromising service quality. Consultants were not used, but expertise was recruited from outside to work with an existing internal project team.

The approach was never intended to redesign the complete business from scratch, but to identify specific areas where significant improvements could be made. However, the early setting of short-term incremental cost-saving targets meant that revolutionary change was unlikely to emerge.

The project team was accountable to a Steering Group, comprising the main operational directors, the Finance and IT Directors and the Head of Product Development and Management. The Steering Group met monthly and provided regular focal points for the monitoring of the project.

The BPR had several important factors which contributed to its success:

- top-level commitment;
- line-management involvement;
- a good mix of industry backgrounds;
- a range of skills and experience in the project team;
- thorough analysis;
- close attention to implementation.

The tangible benefits of the BPR included contribution to large revenue increases and significant cost reductions. Intangible benefits covered the encouragement of continuous improvement, implementation of a number of ideas that had not been given priority previously, an improvement in the overall standard of change management and the personal development of the team members.

The next steps for First Direct

The BPR effectively comprised a series of projects concentrating on different processes. It continues in the form of a succession of projects, some of which cut across the customer processes and come under the heading of 'common activities'. First Direct needs to continue to review and improve processes as long as there are improvements to be made. The continuing growth of the business and changes in the market will mean that there will always be scope for improvements.

There remains the question of whether First Direct should do 'real' revolutionary BPR. Having reviewed the progress so far and checked the organization against the latest thinking in process management, it is clear that there is more work to be done. Although the majority of processes are managed within departments, there are still some significant elements that are managed separately. There is a matrix structure in place to manage these elements, but it will be useful to examine the possibility of complete process ownership and management.

Technological developments may also provide the basis for improvements in the organization; imaging technology and enhanced workflow management are two related areas that look promising.

The key to future success in the personal banking market will be the anticipation of the next big structural change – how long will the telephone remain the principal channel for non-branch banking? While we ponder the answer to that question, we can concentrate on developing the continuous improvement culture that will keep us ahead in the current market.

The Power Tools Division, Robert Bosch Group

Andy Balshaw

5

From outsourcing to insourcing critical processes

Introduction

Robert Bosch Group was founded in 1886, and still has its headquarters in Gerlingen, a small town outside Stuttgart in Germany. The Group has a turnover in excess of £16 billion which is generated through activities in four major sectors:

- automotive equipment;
- communication technology;
- consumer goods;
- capital goods.

In the automotive sector Bosch are original equipment manufacturers of fuel injection mechanisms for gasoline and diesel engines, electric machines such as alternators, drive systems for electric vehicles, and small-power electric motors, systems for passive safety such as airbags and lighting, and mobile communication products such as car radios, navigation systems and driver information systems.

In the communication technology arena Bosch supply and install among other things fibre-optic networks, microwave systems, public switching systems and large-scale private communications networks.

The consumer goods sector consists of several businesses, of which the two larger businesses are: first, do-it-yourself (DIY) power tools (rotary drills, saws, sanders) and professional power tools (demolition hammers, impact drills, and accessories); and, second, a wide range of products such as domestic appliances, refrigerators, freezers and dishwashers.

Finally, the capital goods sector encompasses hydraulic and pneumatic machinery, industrial equipment and packaging equipment. The Group has over 153,000 employees worldwide, of which 91,500 work in Germany. The Group operates directly in over forty countries around the world and has affiliates and representatives in 110 countries. This chapter will focus upon the DIY and professional tools business in the United Kingdom.

The Bosch story

In the UK, Robert Bosch Limited (referred to as Bosch in the rest of the chapter unless otherwise stated) sales were £553 million in 1994, and the company employs 3,200 people. The power tools division is one of five sales divisions in Bosch. The size of the power tools division is more than 13 per cent of the UK's business in terms of turnover, and the division distributes and sells in excess of 1 million items of product per annum. The power tools division currently employs just over 100 people.

The division has five departments. These are external sales, customer services, marketing, after-sales service and technical services. Each department is run by its own manager, and each department reports to the divisional director (see Figure 5.1 for the structure chart). The divisional director reports directly to the UK managing director and indirectly to the head of the power tools division at the headquarters in Germany.

External sales department

This department is responsible for all aspects of the sales and distribution to Bosch customers. Bosch segment their market into two:

- retail outlets and builders merchants, and utilities;
- multiples.

The department as a whole has about fifty people working in it. Of the fifty, thirty people are responsible for the retail outlets. For the purposes of sales to retail outlets and builders merchants the country is divided into five regions, and each has a team of sales executives and a sales manager. The sales executives are allocated a geographical area and, among other things, are responsible for calling on each customer to discuss sales targets, agreeing forthcoming promotional offers, negotiating discounts and discussing ways in which business can be developed. Each region has a sales development person whose main concern is to visit builders' merchants, hire outlets and other such retailers with a view to ensuring Bosch is listed as the premier power tool supplier in each customer.

In relation to the utilities and other large direct customers, Bosch divided the country into two sections. There are two account managers, one for the north and another for the south of the country. Their objective is for Bosch to become an approved supplier and sell our power tools within organizations such as British Gas, BT, electricity companies and local authorities.

For the major multiples Bosch has a dedicated account team of about ten people, headed by an administration manager. This team is responsible for forming strong

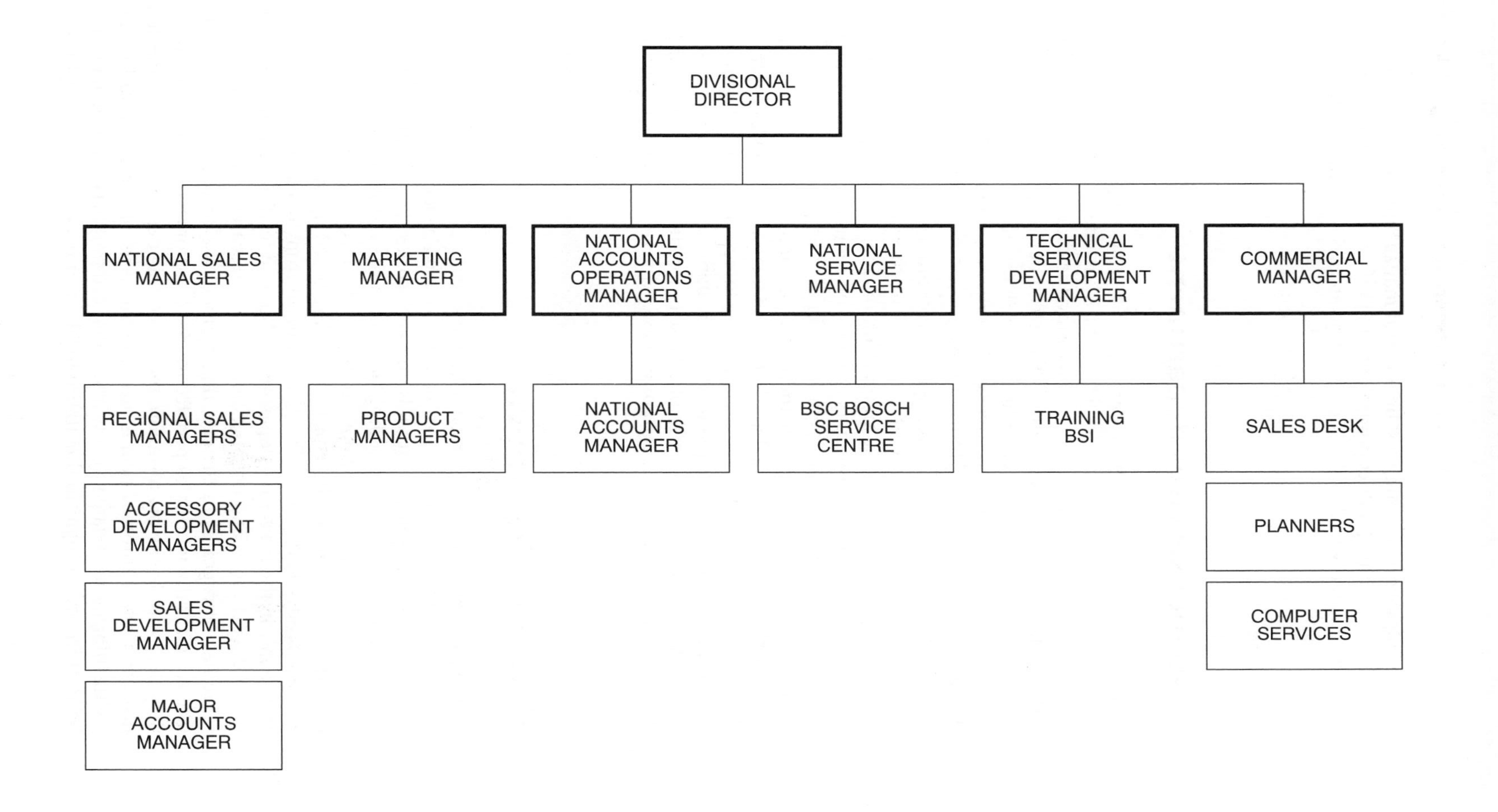

Figure 5.1 Organization of the Power Tools Division.

relationships with the multiples' buyers and management teams, administering each account, presenting product promotions and other offers, negotiating discounts and securing greater visibility for Bosch's power tools in the multiple's outlets and catalogues.

Customer services department

This department of sixteen people covers a wide range of activities. Ten of the sixteen focus upon customer services, which include activities such as taking customer orders over the telephone, processing the orders, actively developing strong relationships with 'their' customers. The customer services teams are also the first point of contact for customers who have delivery, discount or invoice queries. The ten people work in pairs and cover each of the five regions. Their role is to support the sales executives in each of the regions.

A smaller group is responsible for the computer services section. They produce and send out computer-generated reports to the sales force and customers. For example, sales people are sent information on actual sales against targets by customer, region or product. Customers are sent, on request, information on the volume and value of purchases made from Bosch in a given period.

Also within customer services there is a planning section which liaises with the Bosch warehouse, marketing department and factories, as well as external suppliers. This section is responsible for matching sales forecasts and actual demand with call-offs (against contracts) from the factories or suppliers. Their task is made that much more difficult as an over-supply of products for the UK market, which require a three-pin plug, for example, cannot be easily diverted to other European markets.

Marketing department

This department consists of ten people, whose central concern is the management of Bosch's product range. The department has one manager for each product area: DIY and garden tools, professional tools and accessories. The department is responsible for negotiating contracts, including purchase prices, from Bosch factories and suppliers. The department develops promotional concepts which the sales executives can offer to customers. These promotions are based upon market information such as sales trends, market-share figures and input from an external advertising agency. The people in the marketing department also send feedback gleaned from customers on product changes and enhancements to the research and development area.

We have recognized in the past that many of the customers have direct, face-to-face contact only with sales people. To make customers aware of the other people they deal with in the organization, the marketing department publishes a quarterly magazine which profiles people in different parts of the organization, as well as giving information related to new and enhanced products. Thus people who work in head office are brought to the attention of customers.

After-sales service department

This department consists of about thirty people. It provides repairs, both in and out of guarantee, servicing and routine maintenance for Bosch's complete range of products. The department is responsible for planning and ordering spare parts to ensure 98 per cent availability at any one time. The department is also responsible for dealing with customer complaints, repair and technical queries, and, in common with many other after-sales service operations, the department is aware of its contribution to maintaining good public relations. People are responsible for organizing and administering the collection and delivery of repairs to and from the customers premises, the sale of spare parts, direct sales of reconditioned units, and also service training related to, for example, routine maintenance or major repairs. This department also gathers and analyses data on the service provided to retailers and end-users. This is done by means of a customer service questionnaire which asks, for example, about our performance standards and ways in which our service could be improved.

Technical services department

This department consists of six people, three of whom are involved in training staff and customers in the ways of selling and operating Bosch products. The department is also responsible for gaining the BSI Kitemark for products, and gaining and maintaining registered firm status, in conjunction with BS5750, for the Bosch head office in Denham. A customer query hotline for advice on which Bosch product to choose is also handled through this department.

Products and market share

The power tools division has two main ranges of products: DIY and garden tools, and professional power tools. However, the sales of accessories is an increasingly important aspect of the business. The first category includes small cordless drills, screwdrivers, sanders, paint strippers and hedge trimmers. The second category could range from small hand drills to road breakers, i.e. equipment used to break concrete. There are several differences between the DIY and professional tools produced by the organization. The organization manufactures a much wider range of professional tools. There are twenty-seven groups of DIY tools, and each group consists of several models; there is a total of seventy-five products in the DIY range.

The organization produces twenty-four groups of professional tools, and a total of 125 across the various ranges. Professional tools are also built to a higher level of specification, and manufacturing tolerances are more finely tuned. Professional tools are usually tailored for specific uses – for example, Bosch manufactures biscuit jointers and routers for the specialist wood-working trade. DIY tools are used in a wide range of situations, albeit usually in a domestic setting. Also, repairs and after-sales service to professional tools need to be carried out in a time-critical manner as down-time may involve a large financial cost to the user. For example, a construction organization would incur the cost of idle labour and other fixed costs while a road-breaker is under repair.

The market for DIY power tools in the UK was traditionally dominated by Black and Decker, the US power tools organization. The market for professional tools was lead by Makita, a leading Japanese organization. In the late 1970s Bosch's power tools division had a 6 per cent market share of professional tools. At that time we did not have a presence in the DIY market. In 1980 Bosch introduced DIY tools to the UK market. By 1985 we had doubled our market share of professional tools to 12 per cent and had grown the DIY business to a respectable 14 per cent market share from a standing start. At the start of the 1990s we had achieved a 20 per cent market share in the professional arena and 26 per cent in the DIY sector.

Types of customers

Broadly speaking, we have three types of customers: national multiples, other retail outlets, and end-users of the product. The national multiples include organizations such as Argos, B&Q and Homebase; other retail outlets include builders merchants, hire shops, single unit stores and specialist stores; end users include organizational buyers such as the big utilities, local authorities and government ministries. Almost 75 per cent of Bosch's sales of DIY products are channelled through the national multiples. They are, in relation to DIY products, critical stakeholders in our business, and the company could not afford to lose this business. The multiples wield considerable influence as they interface directly with the end-consumer and hence are in a position to influence the consumer decision. We have account managers who are responsible for the major multiples. Much of the remaining 25 per cent of DIY sales passes through regional chain stores and other smaller stores. As the size of the retailer decreases so the level of relative influence in the manufacturer-retailer relationship diminishes. Nonetheless, we pay keen attention to the needs of these customers and this is reflected by the appointment of regional sales managers.

In relation to the professional tool products, the multiples and the regional chain stores play a much less significant role as they account for only a small percentage of the business. The bulk of the sales of professional tools are directed through specialist retailers. These retailers are critical to us as they can play a large part in influencing the professional buyer and pass on word-of-mouth experiences. Professional end-users often buy from specialist outlets primarily because they can purchase all their equipment, including accessories such as drill bits and spare parts, from one source.

Organizational characteristics

At the beginning of the change programme the power tools division comprised about sixty people. Most of the senior managers, the divisional director and the departmental managers had been with the organization for at least five years and worked closely together. Given the size of the organization, most people knew each other well, in a work and personal sense – it could be said that a substantial degree of trust existed between people. The structure of the organization gives each divisional director a great deal of autonomy. Thus, when a divisional director decides to implement changes in his or her division it is usually carried out. Each departmental manager within a division also has substantial control over the way in which her or his particular function operates. Within each function, the style of management used to be control-oriented. Although managers would listen to comments from staff, it was common to find staff being told what needed to be done. The departmental managers and the divisional director all sit on the same floor and hence discuss issues as they arise. The senior managers also hold regular monthly meetings together to discuss each department's performance.

As the proposed changes extended beyond the boundaries of the power tools division, other functions such as IT, warehousing and personnel needed to be brought in to support the changes. The heads of these departments needed to be convinced of the benefit of the planned changes. Any initial doubts about the changes were overcome as the board of Bosch supported all the divisional changes. Gaining the early support of other functions proved important as the changes proceeded.

The management team recognized that a critical cultural change needed to take place in respect of peoples' views of customer service. We were dealing with distributors in a somewhat dictatorial manner. Distributors acceded to our way of working. For example, if Bosch delivered on a Wednesday, then that was the day the distributors took delivery, and requests for deliveries on any other day would in general not be possible under the system we operated. The systems and procedures in the organization were designed to suit Bosch rather than the distributors' needs. In many instances, internal procedures and passing information from one function to another were sometimes slow and inflexible. We realized that in order for the business to move forward people needed to be customer-focused and be able to respond quickly and flexibly to customer needs.

Key drivers of change

By the end of the 1980s the management team at Bosch Power Tools determined that the organization should set two objectives:

- that the organization should achieve number one position in the professional tools market;
- that the organization should consolidate its position as number two in the DIY market.

These objectives were to be measured in terms of the volume and value of sales. However, the organization realized quickly that it faced two major constraints to achieving these objectives:

1. Bosch Power Tools sold its professional and a percentage of DIY products through a two-tier distribution system.
2. In both the professional tools and DIY market, after-sales service was becoming a major competitive issue, and the organization had little control over this area. Thus, in the words of one manager, 'Bosch had little influence on the actual end-user of the Bosch products.'

The structure and operation of the two-tier distribution system

Bosch traditionally had two distribution channels. First, for DIY products, we sold directly to the large multiple retailers. As stated earlier, the large multiple retailers were insignificant players in the professional tools area. The second channel used for all professional tools and some DIY was through distributors. The distributors sold our products to retail outlets all over the UK. The retailers dealt with the end-user. Bosch dealt through about 200 distributorships, who sold on to between 5,000 and 8,000 retail outlets. Hence Bosch was at least two places removed from the end-consumer in this distribution system (see Figure 5.2).

Fifteen sales executives, split into three groups, managed the relationships with distributors. Each group was assigned to one of three regions which covered the country. Each region had a regional manager who reported into Bosch Power Tools HQ. Individual salespeople would visit their set of distributors about every two weeks to discuss, among other things, stock levels, future promotional activity, discounts and actual purchases from Bosch against targets. Information related to future demand would often be fed back to the people responsible for forecasting demand and distribution planning. Typically, distributors would telephone their orders through to our telesales desk. Distributors were responsible for placing their orders by a certain time on a certain day to ensure that they would receive their delivery. Distributors were encouraged to place bulk orders, i.e. forty tools of the same type, which could be packed on a pallet. Orders were delivered usually once a week, and occasionally twice a week, on a Bosch designated day. The delivery system operated for the whole of Bosch UK, not only for power tools. The physical distribution system had been outsourced to third-party hauliers. We contracted on the basis of a scheduled lorry run which would deliver mixed products to particular parts of the country on predesignated days. For example, on a Wednesday a sched-

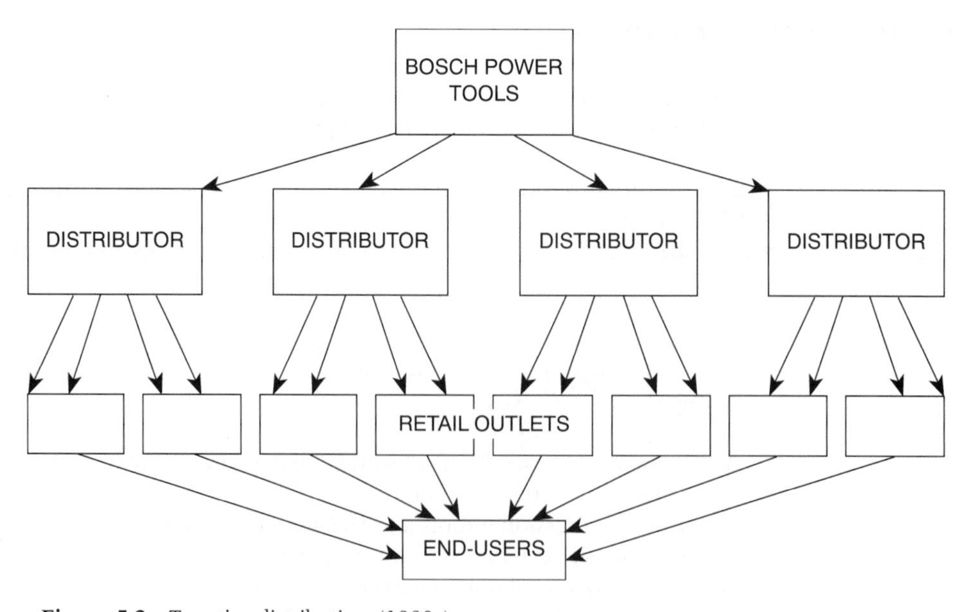

Figure 5.2 Two-tier distribution (1980s).

uled run might cover Birmingham, Coventry and Derby. The lorry would be loaded with products as diverse as washing machines, car radios, spark plugs and drills. Once the run was completed no further deliveries would be made to those areas for a week. Distributors therefore had to maintain high stock levels.

Our warehouse and the systems and procedures that supported the distribution of tools were inflexible to customer requirements. It was highly unlikely that a distributor would be able to take delivery of a Bosch product if it required going outside the 'normal routine' distribution process. Once the product had been delivered an invoice would be raised automatically by a computer system for the product quantity delivered and at the price contracted with the customer. Payment would be received typically after ninety days, with customers being followed up by delayed payment after that. Any shortfalls in delivery due to non-availability of stock would be carried forward as a back order to the customer.

Implications of the two-tier distribution system

In terms of the objectives set by the organization's management team, the two-tier system had major implications. As Bosch dealt with the 200 major distribution outlets in the UK, there were no other sizeable wholesalers or retailers they could sell to. Hence the scope to grow market share profitably was limited. Of the 200 distributors, fewer than forty controlled over 85 per cent of Bosch's sales. Given the size of these distributors they were able to wield substantial power over Bosch. For example, we were expected to give the distributors over ninety days' credit, which increased the cost of working capital. The concentrated high-debt exposure to the larger distributors became painfully apparent when in the late 1980s we lost substantial sums of money as two or three of the larger distributors went out of business. We found ourselves having to offer bigger discounts to distributors so that they (the distributors) could increase their own margins and offer increased margins to the retailers. Thus our own margins were being continuously eroded and the products were being treated as commodity items. Distributor loyalty was often questionable – distributors sold not only Bosch products but also competitors' products. Hence, distributors played one manufacturer against the others to achieve larger price discounts and better promotional offers. Furthermore, we had virtually no control over the discounts and offers being made to retailers and end-users.

There were several instances where we would set up promotional offers for retailers or the end-user. These offers would have to pass through the distributors, who would not necessarily pass on the full value of the offer to the intended beneficiary. Hence, retail customers lost out, and our marketing and sales plans were invariably off target. Unreliable sales forecasts made it difficult for us to manage the achievment of pole position in the professional tools market. The extent to which the organization lacked control over the distribution chain also made it difficult for us to achieve our targets, as distributors would direct their sales forces to maximize their own sales, not necessarily those of our products. As distributors dealt with several brands they could switch the focus given to any brand at their discretion, and without any prior reference to Bosch or any other manufacturer.

We also faced a critical weakness – a lack of knowledge about the second and third tier in the distribution chain, i.e. the retailers and the end-users. The organization neither knew nor understood much about who the 'real' customers were. We were not aware of retailer and end-user needs, how much product each sold or trends in the marketplace from the retailers' perspective. As a manufacturing organization we lost valuable user feedback gleaned by retailers. As the rationale for sustaining the two-tier system became weak and it conflicted with the primary objective of the organization, it became apparent that the organization needed to make fundamental changes to its distribution process. Hence the objectives for single-tier distribution process became evident. We basically wanted:

- to increase market share, which was limited due to the distribution system;
- to generate higher margins;
- to target sales promotions;
- to be able to spread our debt risk better;
- to gain a better understanding of the market by dealing directly with the organizations who sold to Bosch's end-customers.

The problems with after-sales service

The after-sales service affected both the DIY and professional tools businesses. The service came into operation usually some time after the customer had purchased a piece of equipment from a retailer, i.e. when it broke down. As it is required by law and is common practice, we offer a twelve-month guarantee. Thereafter end-users could extend their warranty period or else pay for any repairs when the machine broke down. Typically, the user would have to find the nearest service centre, which was usually a distributor. Alternatively, the user could take the tool to the retail outlet where it was purchased, and the retailer would send it off to a service centre.

Bosch employed six people to provide administrative support for about 130 service centres in the UK. In situations where the distributor was not also a service centre, the tool would need to be sent to a distributor that offered service facilities. Often spare parts would need to be ordered from Bosch prior to the tool being repaired. Once repaired, the tool would be sent back through the chain it travelled through in the first place (see Figure 5.3).

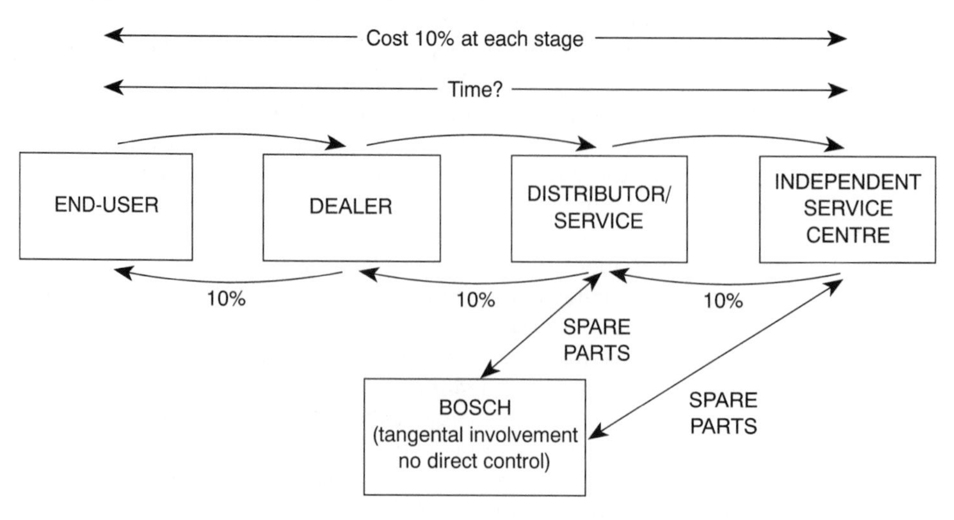

Figure 5.3 After-sales service (pre-1992).

Implications of the after-sales service process

We had little control over the repair times through these external service centres. Often some of the smaller service centres had perhaps one engineer or one mechanic, and if he or she was on holiday or sick the tool would have to await their return and any backlog of repairs before it was dealt with. This could immediately delay the return of the repaired product by several weeks. As the broken down tool passed from one organization to another the attendant paper work and other administrative formalities could add days, if not weeks, to the repair time. Moreover, each time an organization handled the machine it would add perhaps 10–15 per cent service charge on top of any chargeable work. This could be without reference to the owner of the tool, who might have had to pay more for the repair than its purchase price as new.

The quality of the repairs was sometimes inconsistent. Each service centre dealt not only with Bosch products but also with perhaps four or five competitor products. The engineers or mechanics in these service centres might deal with perhaps two Bosch products a week, and perhaps the same product only four or five times a year. As a result, the training Bosch provided to the engineers could well be forgotten by the time a repair needed to be carried out. In a number of instances distributors who were not service centres did not wish to send the broken-down tool to a competitor distributor which was a service centre. Often non-service centre distributorships simply delayed sending the product for repair, which was detrimental to customer service.

There would also be situations where a tool for repair would reach a service centre and they needed to order a spare part from Bosch. Where we had stopped extending credit to the service centre, for whatever reason, the repair could not take place until the credit was restored, which was necessary before the spare parts could be delivered. This led to Bosch receiving complaints from irate customers. We had little control in terms of being able to do anything to improve the situation as the key players in the after-sales service process were outside our direct control.

Options considered for changes to distribution, sales and after-sales service

Faced with the ambitious objectives and implications of the operations as outlined above, the management team reviewed three options. First, there was the choice of leaving the status quo. This would have meant that the objectives would need to be redefined to a lower level and, as this was not something that would be acceptable to the Bosch UK management team nor the head office in Germany, doing nothing was simply not an option. The second option was a halfway house. In this option we would operate on the basis of a mix between direct-to-retailers and distribution. We would pick off the more lucrative retail accounts while leaving the rest to go through the traditional distribution system. This would reduce the number of distributors by roughly half. This option was rejected on three grounds:

1. It was considered too messy to handle because, while the choice of certain distributors and retail accounts was obvious, selecting the marginal distributors and retail accounts was less clear.

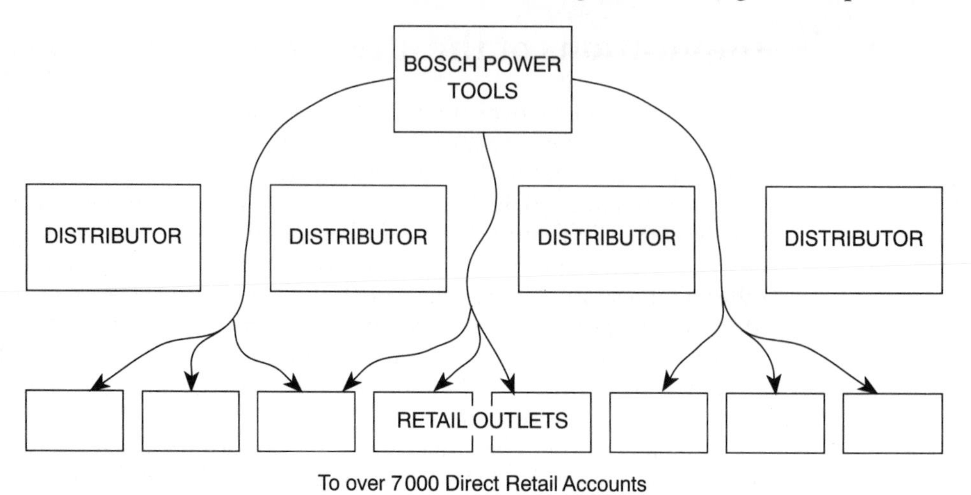

Figure 5.4 An overview of single-tier distribution (June 1992).

2. This was an expensive option as the organization would need to maintain two sets of systems and procedures. Moreover, the organization would not be in a position to reduce the margins it offered to distributors.
3. The distributors that remained with us would be in direct competition with the organization. Specifically, Bosch and the distributors would be vying for similar customers.

This left the organization with one other option, to in-source the distribution process and go direct to all retailers (see Figure 5.4). This decision had an immediate knock-on effect on the after-sales service process – it was highly unlikely that the distributors would be very pleased with the decision to bypass them; hence it was clear that they were unlikely to provide any level of after-sales service. Thus, the decision to in-source the after-sales service process was inevitable.

Moving towards managing the processes

Putting together the team

A team of existing managers was formed to implement the changes. The team consisted of the five departmental managers and a newly recruited marketer. The team reported to the Divisional Director in his role as the change champion.

Each manager was given her or his relevant objective, which was discussed and agreed by all. For example, the after-sales service manager was given the responsibility of transforming the whole service operation from external agents to central internal repairs.

A large amount of analytical work was done at the outset. The marketer was appointed as she had not only marketing experience but also an excellent grounding in statistics. Hence she was given the responsibility of gathering market information and producing a clear plan of potential target customers, their anticipated turnover, a preferred logistical approach and calling frequency and the number of additional staff required. Each manager also had to gather information relevant to her or his own area of responsibility. For example, the manager examining single-tier requirements had to research the benchmark for on-time and frequency of deliveries set by the larger distributors.

However, in certain areas – especially with a major spend like converting part of the warehouse into a modern and fully equipped workshop and the logistics that go with such an operation – costings went backwards and forwards to Germany many times over a period of several months, with minor adjustments and explanations before final approval was 'rubber stamped'.

Motivating and keeping the staff informed

Staff motivation was critical during the early stages of the change, so all staff were kept informed of the change project as it progressed through the approval stages. Nonetheless, when plans were on hold for several weeks at a time while we waited for the necessary approval, peoples' initial enthusiasm and team spirit did naturally decline. The management team felt, therefore, that it was of vital importance to keep the rest of the staff informed at every stage of what was happening and why. Once approval was gained, all the planning and anticipation then became a reality with real-time constraints and deadlines to meet.

Developing a project plan

None of the management team in fact had any experience of changing a sales and service operation on such a large-scale. Hence the project team developed a project plan which acted as a guide to implementation (see Figure 5.5). This included the breadth of activities such as developing stock management systems, creating logistics capability, managing publicity and recruiting appropriate skills. At the start of the planning schedule the project team knew the objectives and the timescales and would report back on a two- to four-weekly basis on progress and whether this matched the project flowcharts and deadlines. The Managing Director was kept informed of progress and helped in removing red tape and administration that could normally slow down such a major project in a large multinational organization.

Changes related to the distribution process

The scope of the distribution process spans the point at which the order is taken from the customer to receipt of payment. Hence this process includes activities such as delivery, warehousing and invoicing. In order to change the distribution process we realized that we had to identify, classify and convert potential into actual customers and provide a service.

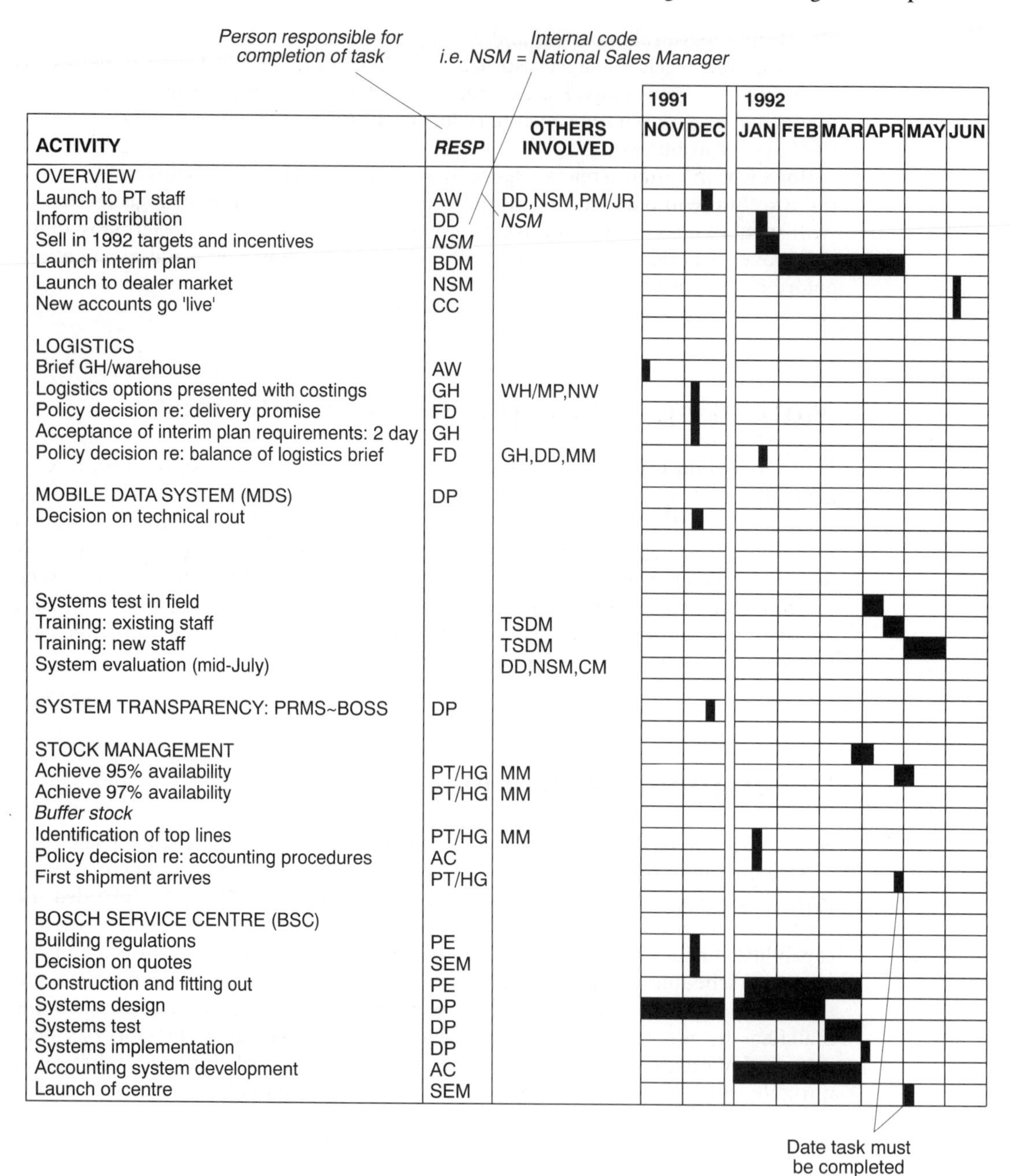

Figure 5.5 Extract of project plan.

Identifying potential retail customers

Bosch needed to identify potential retail outlets. As the organization had no direct dealing with retailers it was not aware of who the retailers were. Those in the distributor network were unlikely to want to give Bosch customers information in any case. Moreover, given the nature of the changes envisaged by the company, confidentiality was critical to the project, especially in the early stages. The organization employed a market research agency to develop a database of potential retail customers who sold electrical power tools that would match our product portfolio. The agency used a variety of sources, including its own mailing lists, external databases and listings in the Yellow Pages. Bosch also asked six salespeople in the regions to gather information from local directories based upon their detailed knowledge of particular areas.

We instructed the market research company and our own sales people to ask a range of questions, including the number of retail branches and staff, percentage turnover of power tools, the brands sold, the distributor(s) they dealt with, the level of service the retailer received from the distributor, a description of the nature of the relationship with the distributor, the terms and conditions they received from the distributor, and delivery, credit terms and service-level expectations. These expectations formed the basis of the measures against which Bosch benchmarked the process. The style of data-gathering interviews was important as questions needed to be asked without raising suspicions about why we were gathering the information in the first place. Hence the style was informal and discursive. All information gathered by the sales executives was passed on to the project team and consolidated with information received from the agency. This information-gathering phase took between two and three months to complete.

Classifying customers

Information relating to potential customers was keyed into a database which was used to identify potential direct accounts. Three categories of customers were developed: A, B and C, based upon the amount of annual purchases, namely £35,000 and over for A, £5,000–£35,000 for B and below £5,000 for C.

Announcement to the marketplace

Once we had a handle on who our potential customers would be we announced our intentions to the industry. Specifically, most of the distributors received personal visits from members of the Bosch management team to explain the new strategy and to reassure the distributors of a continuing relationship, albeit in a changed way. Distributors were given several months' notice so that they could refocus their own business strategies. We also offered help and advice to distributors, although this was treated with a certain amount of scepticism.

Converting potential accounts to actual customers

Our salespeople made appointments to visit each retailer on the database with a view to converting them to buy directly. Each salesperson was provided with a presentation pack which highlighted, among other things:

- the choice of buying packages available to retailers;
- the advantages of each option;
- our policies on promotions, rebates and discounts, and credit terms;
- the benefits, such as increased profit potential and personal communications, of dealing directly with Bosch.

The salespeople made the visits armed with credit application forms, and wherever possible, retailers were signed up on the spot. We also prepared the Bosch 'Direct' Directory, which outlined the way in which the new distribution process would operate. This document set out:

- the different ways in which customers could place orders with Bosch, e.g. by phone or by the sales representative keying in orders on a portable computer from the customer's premises;
- the standard two-day order-to-delivery cycle and an urgent ordering process;
- details and specimens of new documentation that would be used to support the process;
- the ways in which customers could have queries and returns dealt with;
- the terms and conditions of trade, e.g. payment and credit terms.

Agreeing service levels against market expectations

Previously we had delivered to our distributors on a weekly basis and they maintained high stock levels. Based upon data from retailer interviews, we determined that we needed to provide a 48-hour delivery service to retail outlets. To achieve such a dramatic improvement in delivery time we had to hold 97 per cent product availability in the warehouse. We also had to ensure our third-party hauliers were able to support the new delivery time. Members of the project team presented their requirements to our logistics division, who worked out ways in which the target service levels could be achieved. The logistics division went to tender on the requirements and in due course presented the power tools division with a delivery price. Haulier performance is monitored to ensure that they meet the 48-hour delivery period and persistent delays are dealt with firmly.

Changes to the after-sales service process

The key issues to be considered here centre around location, level of service, the design of facilities, organizing the logistic operations, effective communication and the development of systems.

Choice of location

The first choice location was a greenfield site on which a complex could be purpose-built for service activities. The project team selected a location which was in the middle of the country and had easy access to the motorway system so that products could be moved quickly around the country. After detailed analysis of this option, it was recommended to the management team for approval. However, the team was asked to consider the organization's head office in Denham. The property had surplus space which was not being utilized.

The decision was taken to use the space in the head-office building. The rationale was that, as the organization had to incur the costs of the premises, the utilization rate was better if the service centre operated within it. The Denham location was also near to major motorways and trunking routes. As the Sales and Marketing Departments were located at the Denham site, this option enabled the people working in the after-sales process to maintain close contact.

Service levels

The objective of centralized service was to support the new single-tier sales operation. We believed that the central service operation would provide a much higher level of customer contact, customer satisfaction and confidence than the external service centre network.

The new after-sales service operation needed to be of a high quality at a competitive price and also to provide a fast turnaround of repairs. We set a turnaround time of forty-eight hours from receipt of the product to despatch back to the customer and, in the case of a chargeable repair, despatch of the estimate. This would ensure that customers, particularly the tradesman customer, would experience the minimum down-time whilst the product was being serviced.

Due to the central location of the operation we also needed to provide a fast and efficient collection and delivery service. The service promise determined the standard as next-day collection from the customer and next-day delivery back from Denham. The collection operation had to be extremely flexible. We were determined to offer a service that was tailored to the customer's requirements; for example, the company would be prepared to collect tools from a home address, business premises or direct from a construction site.

In order for us to offer a fast turnaround once the product was in the workshop, spare parts had to be readily available. For this purpose we set a very high standard of 98 per cent availability, requiring high warehouse stock levels and detailed planning to ensure that working capital was not tied up in excessive stocks. Only in this way could we guarantee and commit ourselves to total customer satisfaction and ensure that repairs and customers would not be left waiting for spare parts.

A key implication of the 98 per cent target availability was increased costs. We made a decision to accept an increase in the cost of holding stock in order to give customer satisfaction first place. However, to ensure costs are contained and managed effectively a number of stringent measures were set. For example, average stock holding of spare parts should not exceed two-and-a-half months' cover at any time, and individual items that have not sold for six months or more are returned to the factory or scrapped.

The design of facilities

To support the after-sales service process a workshop and administration facility had to be built from scratch in an empty warehouse in Denham. The core management team had no experience of designing and building a service workshop. The project leader for this area (the author), on the management team, was responsible for delivering an operational central service centre, and he decided to carry out extensive research.

The project leader visited Bosch companies and customers in the United States, Scandinavia and around Europe who had carried out a similar change in the past. He interviewed many managers who implemented changes in their organizations. The objectives were to gain ideas and views on how the changes could be achieved and to avoid potential pitfalls when making the changes. Typically, the topics discussed included the design of the workshop, logistics, choice of workshop equipment, the customer's requirements, the customer's reactions to their strategy, ways in which resistance to change were overcome, and the nature of problems encountered and ways in which these were resolved.

Based upon the findings of other organizations, the initial design of the workshop and offices was set out using sketches of the facilities required and the general layout. More detailed technical drawings were then made by a local architect, who also carried out the planning permission application and organized the building contractors.

As the Bosch team members were on site and able to inspect the building daily, one or two alterations to the original plan were instructed as necessary. One particular area that comes to mind was the physical size of the proposed cleaning and degreasing room, which looked fine on paper but had to be reduced in size quite dramatically when observed for real.

As the workshop and offices were nearing completion, the various benches, tooling and office furniture were planned and purchased. We demanded tenders for all purchases and competitive responses were received from various suppliers. The workshop merchandise was inspected and approved prior to installation. Construction of the workshop began in December 1991 and was completed by April 1992. The service centre opened for business in May 1992, one month before the launch of the single tier operation.

Organizing the logistics operations

Once the workshop was up and running we would need to transport the tools back to Denham as quickly as possible from a wide variety of locations throughout the UK and likewise deliver the repaired item direct to the customer. The transport systems that we had in place at the time were not geared up for this type of end-user 'one-off' parcel. We looked to other transport companies and asked three or four famous names to tender for our requirements. The criteria was strict – we needed a fast reaction to a request at the minimal cost.

The logistics operation works in the following way. Bosch provide the carrier with the names and addresses for collection of items for repair by the evening of Day 0. The tools are collected during Day 1 and delivered to Bosch before 10 a.m. on Day 2. Once the tool is in our hands we have forty-eight hours to repair it (although this often takes less than twenty-four hours) and arrange despatch. The carrier calls every working day at 4 p.m. to collect the outgoing repairs for delivery the following day.

Communication

With all these changes taking place around them, staff were concerned about the ways in which they would be affected. Communication was therefore an essential part of the change programme. Given the size of Bosch Power Tools (sixty people at the time), word usually spread quickly around the organization. Our management team conducted regular face-to-face meetings to let staff know what was happening and why. They encouraged staff to ask questions and, as far as practicable, provided direct honest answers.

Likewise with our customers, we gave advance notice of our strategic intentions. A critical aspect of communicating with customers was educating existing and new customers about dealing with us according to the new ways of working. This was communicated in the form of personal visits, personal letters, direct mail, trade press and by proactive calling by the sales team.

We produced a comprehensive document advising all account customers how we would work in a central service environment. The document mentioned earlier, the Bosch 'Direct' Directory, set out among other items of information:

- the scope of the after-sales service process;
- the service levels offered;
- instructions to customers regarding sending a product in for repair;
- examples of the forms that would need to be completed and sent by the customer to the service centre;
- relevant telephone and fax numbers;
- the timings of the new service.

We also offered a variety of training programmes for retailers. These covered Product and Sales training, for example a one- or two-day retailer-specific training, a three-day industrial tools course, or a theme-day sales training course which covered the basics of sales promotions and advice for retailers. We also offered Product Service training. This ranged from one-day tailored courses to a five-day advanced service course. Training programmes were usually run at the Denham site but were occasionally carried out at the customer's site when requested.

Systems

The management team set out to make the central workshop paperless. We did not want customers to receive quotations for repairs which had been prepared by hand and perhaps covered with grease stains. A complete workshop system was therefore required. This was to be produced in-house by one person from Robert Bosch Limited's IT team. This individual worked with the project manager to develop the applications and the supporting databases, and utilized part of the order-input system which was already in place from the sales desk.

The project manager drew high-level flowcharts of the process on paper to show the IT team the major activities which underpinned a tool passing through the workshop (see Figures 5.6, 5.7 and 5.8). The flowchart represented visually an incoming parcel, the unpacking stage, initial diagnosis and all the operational routes the product could take until it was repaired and sent to the customer. The flowcharts became more and more complex as the tool progressed through various options, e.g.

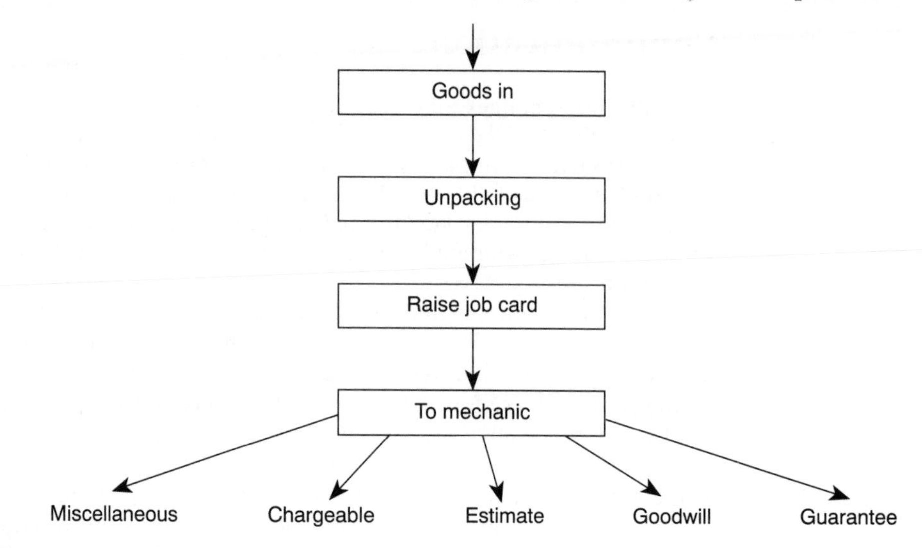

Figure 5.6 Machine to Denham.

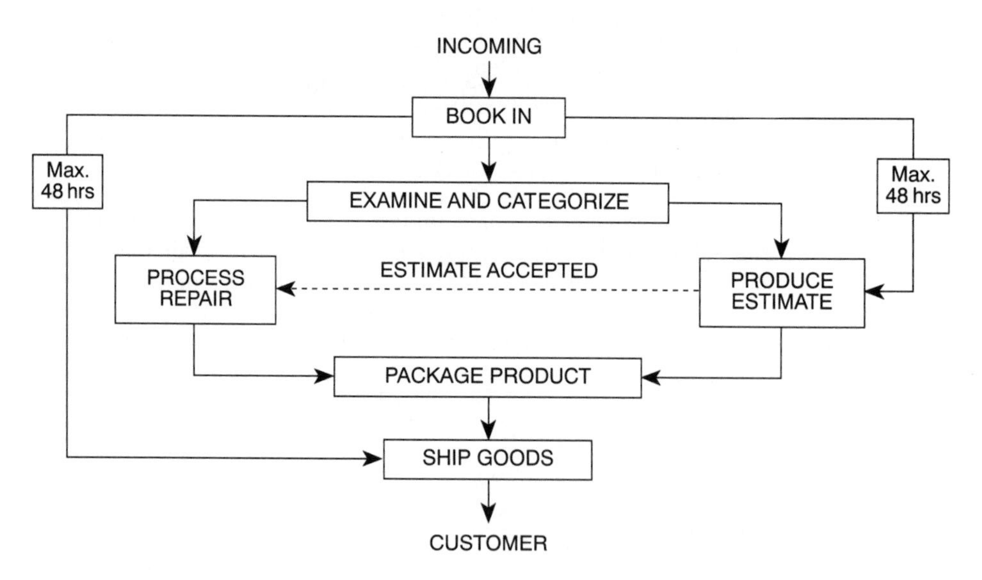

Figure 5.7 The repair process.

guarantee and chargeable, and ultimately forty to fifty charts were produced which captured the process to a level where understanding could be shared between the project and IT people. The IT individual then had to adapt and design programmes to complete these processes.

Implementation and rollout

At this time we had 130 Authorized Service Centres working on our behalf. As the new central workshop was due to open in May 1992 we needed to plan and

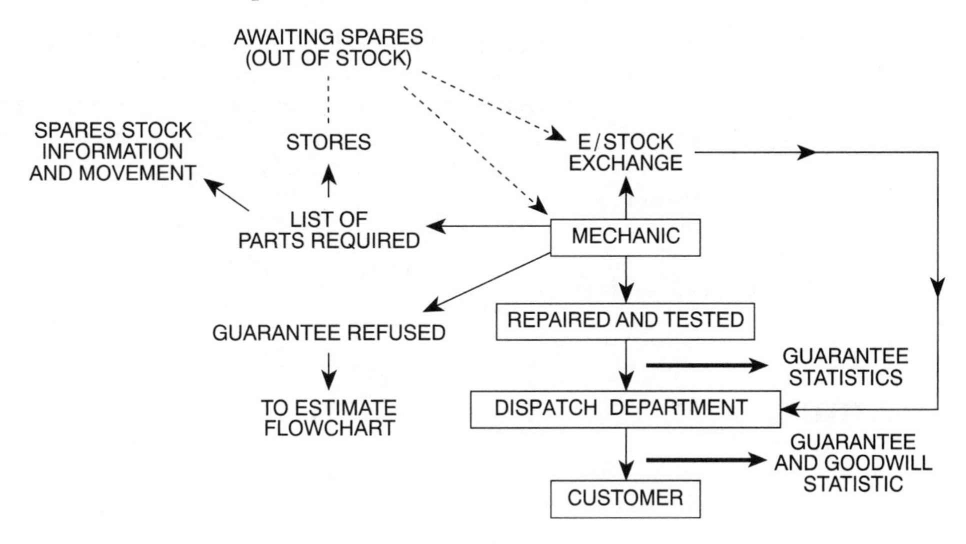

Figure 5.8 Guarantee.

implement the redirection of repairs from these service centres to our own central workshop. It was decided, therefore, that service centres which carried out the smaller number of guarantee repairs would be given notice and phased out on the day of opening. This would give us time to fine-tune our systems and logistics without putting a major percentage of the repair business at risk.

It was decided that any problems encountered would have been sorted out within nine months of start-up and the next phase of service centres could redirect repairs to Bosch. The plan was to reduce the external service network to forty by November 1993, eighteen months from start-up. These remaining forty would cover the less accessible parts of the country, such as the Highlands of Scotland and Island locations, where the logistics operation could not guarantee a fast turnaround at a reasonable cost.

The internal structure had to be changed completely to deal with workshop enquiries, sales of spare parts and general administration. Where the external service agents had previously handled most of the end-user contact, Bosch would now have to manage retailers and end-users.

From an administration and technical staff of six people at head office, the structure would now be fourteen to sixteen, with completely different job functions and responsibilities. It was decided to handle this change with open and honest discussions with our staff to alleviate any job change concerns.

Recruitment was carried out in conjunction with Robert Bosch Limited's Personnel Department, and for the twenty-eight places available in the external sales and central service departments 48,000 applications were processed. The response was overwhelming and time-consuming. In hindsight, a combination of the depressed job market and a broadly worded job advertisement should have caused alarm bells to ring.

We had kept records of all guarantee activity through the service centre network for the previous years, so we knew how much work to expect as products for repair were diverted from the service centres. It was possible, therefore, to plan the recruitment of engineers to coincide with the further diversion of repairs to the central workshop.

Six engineers were recruited initially for the workshop. This was an estimate of the labour required in the first six to nine months of the start-up. The recruits were all from engineering or electrical backgrounds, only one actually having power tool repair experience. The reason behind this was that we have full training facilities and wanted to teach the recruits from scratch. Training therefore commenced two months before start-up.

Although we had every confidence in the new strategy, a local Authorized Service Centre was asked to act as an emergency overflow in case the incoming work exceeded the forecasts.

The impact on the organization

Two tier and external service to single tier and internal service: have the changes brought about success for Bosch?

Results achieved

It is worth reviewing the market position of Bosch at the start of the changes in 1990: 20 per cent in the professional tools market and 26 per cent in the DIY market. In early 1996 the main players in the market commissioned an independent survey of the professional and DIY markets. The results revealed that our position in the professional tools market had grown to 30 per cent in 1995, ahead of our main rival in this sector, Makita, which had 28 per cent. Thus our objective of being number one in this marketplace was achieved.

In the DIY arena the survey showed that Bosch had a market share just below 30 per cent. Black and Decker's market share had declined from nearly 100 per cent in the early 1980s to about 48 per cent in 1995 according to the survey. This made us the second largest player in the DIY market, which was one of our chosen aims. Much of this success is attributed to the changes outlined above (see Figure 5.9).

On an ongoing basis the processes continue to meet the standards set by the customers: 97 per cent of all orders by line are made to the 7,500 retailers within two days; 99 per cent of customer queries are resolved within a day – usually over the phone.

In relation to the after-sales service process, the number of external service centres has been reduced to about thirty-five. In the first year of operation 7,900 repairs were brought in to the Denham service centre; and in 1995 Bosch carried out over 28,000 repairs. Bosch now completes in excess of 80 per cent of all guarantee repairs centrally. In 98 per cent of cases we turnaround repairs within the promised 48-hour target (see Figure 5.10).

Consistency over time

In order to fulfil our slogan 'Excellence comes as standard' the Power Tools Division also adopted a programme of continuous improvement. On a worldwide basis, the

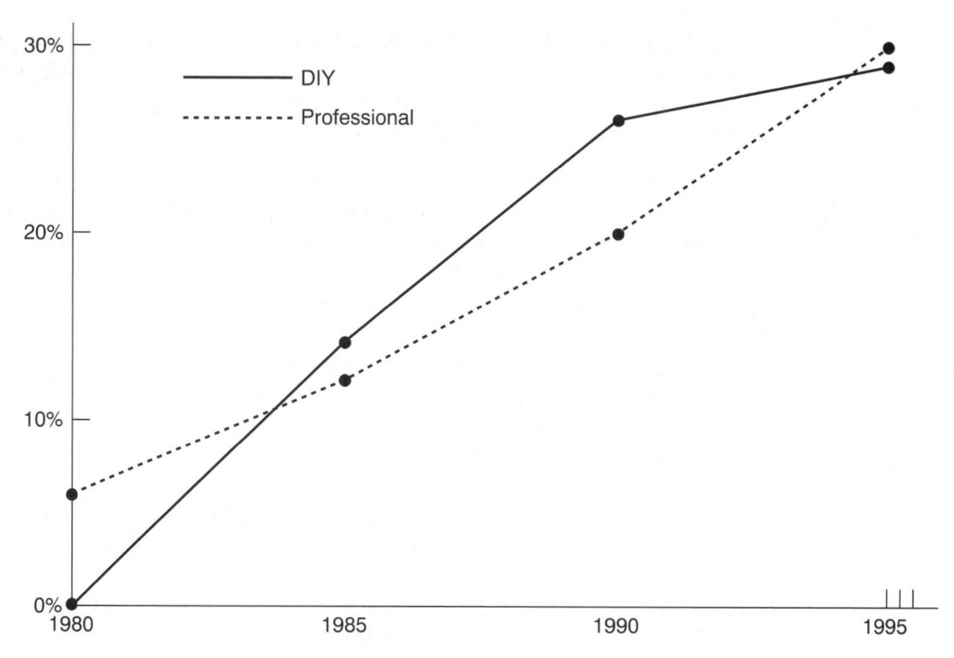

Figure 5.9 DIY/professional market share.

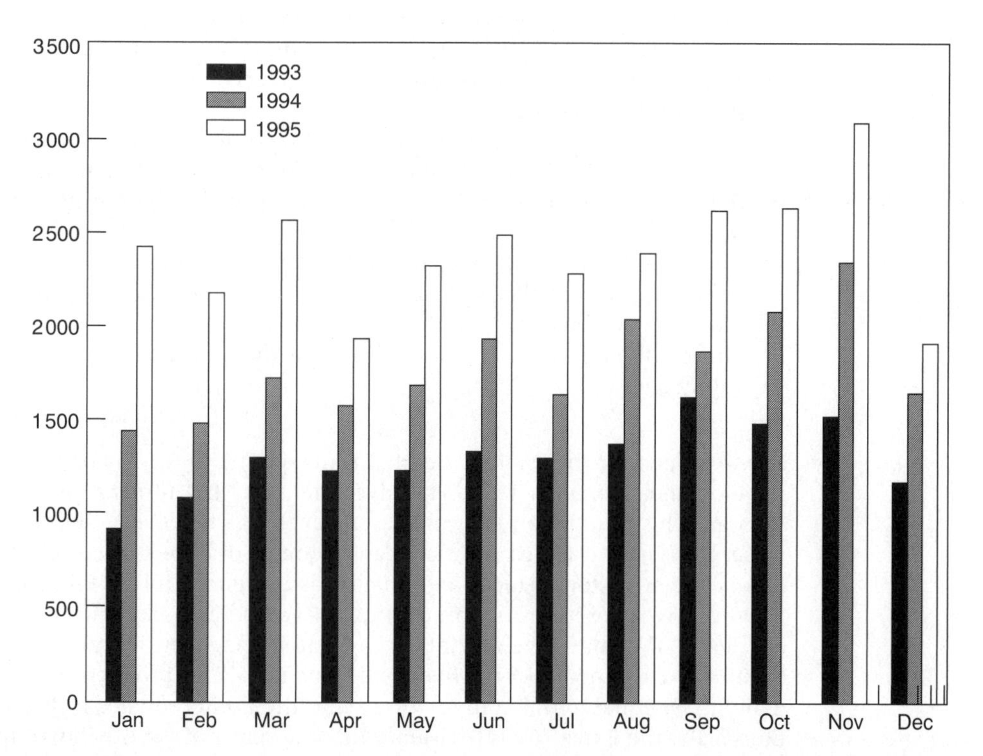

Figure 5.10 Number of repairs (per month) carried out by the Central Service Centre.

Bosch Group aspires to a philosophy which is captured in the acronym QIK. The 'Q' represents Quality, which is related primarily to ensuring high-levels of quality in the product, its components and methods of manufacture. The Group has developed twelve quality principles which are mandatory across the organization:

1. We want satisfied customers. That is why the highest quality of our products and services is one of our major corporate objectives. This also applies to the quality of the work carried out in our name by our trading partners, and in their sales and service organizations.
2. The customer is the judge of our quality. His or her opinion on our products and services is decisive.
3. Our quality goal is always 'zero defects' or '100% quality'.
4. Not only do our customers assess the quality of our products, but also the quality of our services. Deliveries must be on time.
5. Inquiries, offers, samples and complaints must all be dealt with promptly and thoroughly. It is imperative that agreed deadlines be met.
6. Each and every employee in the company contributes towards achieving our quality goals. It is thus the responsibility of every employee – from Apprentice to Member of the Board – to ensure that their work is of the highest standard. Anyone who identifies a problem which may jeopardize quality, but does not have the authority to remedy it themselves, must report the matter immediately to their superiors.
7. All work must be without defects from the beginning. This not only improves quality, but also reduces our costs. Quality increases cost-effectiveness.
8. Not only defects themselves must be eliminated, but also their causes. Prevention of defects has priority over their elimination.
9. The quality of our products also depends upon the quality of sourced parts. Demand the highest quality from our suppliers, and support them in adhering to our mutual quality goals.
10. Even when painstaking care has been taken, defects can occasionally happen. This is why we have introduced numerous and proven methods to identify defects at an early stage. These methods must be rigorously and consistently applied.
11. Ensuring that our quality goals are achieved is an important management duty. When appraising the performance of our employees, particular emphasis is placed upon the quality of their work.
12. Our quality directives are compulsory. Further consumer requirements must be fulfilled.

('Bosch Today Information', 1995)

The 'I' stands for Innovation. Bosch Group spent DM 2.6 billion on Research and Development (R&D) in 1994. The investment in R&D forms about 6.5 per cent of sales and this ratio is bound to increase over time. The 'K' is a German expression – *Kunden orientiert* – which translates as customer-oriented. There is an inextricable link between customer focus and quality, as evidenced in the Principles of Quality. However, we recognize that product quality alone is unlikely to provide a sustainable level of competitive advantage. As one manager in the division commented, 'From the customers' perspective, if the quality of our products is considered generally to be equal to our competitors', what then differentiates us from our competitors?' For the Power Tools Division (and other parts of the Bosch Group outside the scope of this chapter) the answer lies in the quality of service we provide to our customers. The process-oriented changes described in the sections above are central to achieving high quality of service. However, processes can become outdated. We ensure that the quality of service remains consistently close to our customers' expectations through the medium of the Customer Care Plan (CCP).

The CCP was developed by the Power Tools Division. The CCP is contained in a booklet and every member of staff is provided with a copy. The CCP sets out the performance criteria to be met by each area of the organization and the people working in that area. It contains the standard that must be met for each element of the performance criteria, who is responsible for achieving and maintaining the standard and, finally, the measurement instrument to be used. The CCP is structured in a way which ascribes the measures to be achieved to each process.

The CCP concept is explained to customers. Thus the performance criteria and standard measures are visible to the customers. The actual service levels are assessed directly with the customers. Certain customers are asked to complete an assessment form (see Figure 5.11), which elicits their views on issues such as the levels of courteousness, responsiveness and professionalism demonstrated by the Bosch person they deal with; the assessment form also asks the customer to say if they are satisfied with various standard aspects of our service such as timeliness of delivery, accuracy of invoice, speed of information and price information. The form also asks customers to state any complaints. We provide selected customers with a 'Good Service Certificate' (see Figure 5.12): where customers are satisfied with the level of service they receive they sign and release the Certificate to reflect that they were satisfied. Where customers are less than satisfied they can withhold the Certificate. In the latter situation, a full report, giving details of the causes of dissatisfaction and actions taken, is prepared and sent to the Divisional Director.

The CCP has been implemented, so far, with a selection of 100 A-class retailers. A Bosch sales representative visits each of these customers quarterly to gain the customer's perceptions of the service. Any adverse comments must be reported in full to the divisional director, and departmental managers have to speak to the customer and resolve complaints within a week. The objective is to ensure that 95 per cent of the 100 customers consider we have met or exceeded the service standards. Since the implementation of CCP in 1993 the target of 95 per cent has been met in all but two quarters.

In 1994 Bosch commissioned an independent organization, GFK, to conduct a study of the tools market in the UK. Specifically, we wished to determine our image, in comparison with our competitors, in relation to four service areas. These were the external sales force, the internal sales force, delivery service and customer service. The study was based upon a random sample of ninety-seven retail outlets from across the regions and included a mixture of A-, B- and C-class customers. GFK used a combination of two data-gathering devices: structured questionnaires and face-to-face interviews with key personnel from each of the sample companies. The results of the survey showed that we were leading the competition in each service category. The survey also enabled us to identify weaknesses in our service, and working parties were set up to identify ways of dealing with these issues. For example, one issue that emerged was that customers wanted greater contact with head-office management. To resolve this, managers make it a point to visit customers regularly as part of their job function.

CCP

Assessment Form

CUSTOMER CARE PLAN

Please complete this form with your Bosch representative at each meeting. If for any reason we have failed to achieve the established standards in our Customer Care Plan, please raise the matter with your representative and tick the relevant "no" category listed below. Then fill in the section marked, "improving our service to you" detailing what the problem is and, if possible, the way you would like the situation remedied.

On the other hand, if you are pleased with the service you receive from Bosch, tick the "yes" sections accordingly.

Personnel Standards	YES	NO
Courteous		
Caring		
Response		
Reactive		
Flexible		
Supporting		
Professional		
Knowledgeable		

Standard of Services	YES	NO
Timeliness of delivery		
Accuracy of delivery		
Accuracy of invoice		
Speed of information		
Reaction to claims		
Flexibility in problem solving		
Call back response		
Quality of information		
Product availability		
Quality of promotions		
Literature availability		
Customer support		
Technical advice		
Legislative advice		
Training standards		
Representative support		
Call frequency		
Price information		
Demonstration support		

IMPROVING OUR SERVICE TO YOU

I am not happy with the service I have received from Bosch.
I have the following complaints:

What measures would you like taken to remedy the situation?

The Customer Care Plan relies upon accurate feedback from our dealers and representatives. In addition to the criteria listed, are there any comments you would like to make on the standard of service you have received from Bosch in the past month.

☐ I am satisfied with the service I have received from Bosch and I am happy to release the Good Service Certificate to Bosch as a gesture of this satisfaction.

☐ I am not satisfied with the service I have received from Bosch and have retained the Good Service Certificate accordingly until further notice.

Signed:

Name:

Company:

Address:

Account Number:

Figure 5.11 Customer Service Assessment form.

CUSTOMER SEAL OF APPROVAL

This is to certify that

Robert Bosch Limited

____

has met the standards of

____

in respect of

Services, Quality and Courtesy

DEFINED AREAS OF CUSTOMER CARE

PERSONNEL

- Courteous
- Caring
- Responsive
- Reactive
- Flexible
- Supportive
- Professional
- Knowledge

SERVICES

- Timeliness of Delivery
- Accuracy of Delivery
- Accuracy of Invoice
- Speed of Information
- Reaction to Claims
- Flexibility in Problem Solving
- Call back Response
- Quality of Information
- Product Availability
- Quality of Promotions
- Literature Availability
- Customer Support
- Technical Advice
- Legislative Advice
- Training Standards
- Representative Support
- Call Frequency
- Price Information
- Demonstration Support

Signed ________________________________

Position __________________ Date ____________

BOSCH

Figure 5.12 Specimen Good Service Certificate.

Lessons learned

Research and plan the changes

We spent fifteen to eighteen months researching the marketplace, putting together budgets, working out statistically different scenarios and identifying customers' wants and needs. During this period there was a feeling that we were being held back from making the changes as the data gathering was perceived to be getting in the way of implementation. However, in retrospect the information provided a sound basis for developing and committing to the change strategy.

Fine-tune the plan as you go along

No amount of planning can truly represent the reality of implementation. Hence, at times various aspects of the plan needed to be scrapped or amended in order for us to move forward. This required that people and systems be flexible to change direction.

Anticipate the increase in costs and risk to the business

In order to realize the benefits from making the changes, the organization faced an increase in costs. We undertook detailed analyses of where potential cost increases were likely to take place, i.e. logistics, headcount and administration. As 43 per cent of turnover passed through distributors, the change to single tier operations could have had an adverse impact on these sales. Moreover, the increase in costs had to be budgeted for in the face of a potential decrease in turnover during the transition. Management had to be prepared to take a calculated risk and be able to sustain their commitment in case events unfolded against them.

Focus upon critical areas

The organization identified the logistics activity as critical to the entire change strategy. It would have been impossible to provide a credible service with the existing logistics system or a partially completed new system. This area had to be watertight, and received substantial attention. Another area that was identified as critical was the supporting information systems. These needed to be developed, tested and in use so that order entry, invoicing and despatch documentation were integrated. After sales service was another critical area. If we had left this part of our business in the hands of third parties, we believe the single tier sales strategy may have failed. A central supporting after-sales service was therefore essential. The systems were developed to a level that enabled the service to become operational in the timescale set by the business, and further enhancements were made subsequently.

Manage the commitment of other departments

As the scope of the change extended beyond the organizational boundaries of the Power Tools Division, it was essential to ensure that other central departments, such as Personnel, Finance, Credit Control and Logistics were brought into the change. They needed to be committed to making changes to the ways in which they operated in order to enable Power Tools to satisfy its customers. Moreover, their commitment needed to be sustained over the duration of the change.

We could have done the changes earlier

Hindsight is a wonderful thing! We could have made the changes earlier; however, a mix of success and uncertainty regarding the impact the changes might have on the business held us back.

Classifying customers

One of the key issues to emerge was the way in which we categorized our customers. Class C customers were those whose actual turnover with Bosch was £5,000 or below. These accounts were given, relative to A-class customers, considerably less attention. A closer analysis of the names of customers revealed several large organizations were in the C category. We quickly realized that the categories should be based upon 'potential' rather than actual turnover. One organization, for example, had a turnover lower than £5,000 with Bosch because the organization was buying several hundred thousand pounds' worth of products from our competitors.

Summary and conclusions

This chapter examined the way in which Bosch took critical processes – the distribution process and the after-sales process – which had been outsourced to distributors/service centres and brought them in-house. The move formed a key element in the organization's plans to grow in the future. The change is considered to be one of the most significant experienced by the business since its inception. The critical factors that led to the changes being achieved and the lessons learned in hindsight are outlined so that other managers can avoid potential pitfalls when implementing their changes.

Melinda S. Pajak and Rick Solano

6

Implementing information technology to support process redesign in a competitive environment

Preface

Due to the sensitive nature of the information concerning the company involved in the following business process re-engineering initiative, the name of the organization has been withheld. The company is a North American subsidiary of a European car manufacturer. This company is referred to below as an 'automobile importer and distributor' and an 'automotive company'. For ease and simplicity, references will also be made to 'the company'. It is on this basis alone that permission to publish was agreed.

Introduction

In 1992 a subsidiary of one of the largest automobile manufacturers in the world began a business partnership with Perot Systems. This North American-based automobile importer and distributor appointed Perot Systems to maintain its existing business functionality and processing while reducing costs and streamlining processes then in place. The existing functionality included managing the data centre and maintaining software and hardware systems. The company outsourced its data-centre operations to Perot Systems in 1993. This chapter outlines the partnership between the two organizations and how new systems to underpin business and support processes were developed.

The company's story

The global manufacturer and distributor of automobiles supports a large network of dealers in the United States, Canada and Mexico. Competitive pressures forced the North American organization to consider dramatic changes in its business approach.

The company structure

In an effort to become more competitive and increase market share in the US, the automotive company moved from being an organization based on functional areas, to become one focused on the core business processes of marketing, sales, distribution and service. Perot Systems' role was to assist the company in achieving its goals in this transition effort. The subsidiary's management team developed a business strategy and outlined how they would accomplish their critical 1994 objectives. The results of this exercise became the foundation for the future redesign initiative.

Changing times in the automotive industry

Impacted by changing tax laws and the financing structuring, US automobile manufacturers and rental companies modified the way they did business. Previously, car rental agencies kept rental vehicles in circulation for an average time of one year. Once the sleek new car was retired, the rental agency would sell it, acting as a used car dealer. Car manufacturers arranged a programme whereby they would sell a fleet of cars to car rental agencies and offer to buy them back after an agreed period of time, for a fixed price. This arrangement benefited the car rental agencies, who would no longer be forced to operate a used car shop. Moreover, these companies could secure new, clean, attractive cars for their customers.

Obviously, the arrangement benefited automobile manufacturers by ensuring that a certain number of new cars would be purchased. Between 1982 and 1990 this arrangement increased new cars sales by 500,000. The downside of this was that the manufacturers had to offload the returned rental cars quickly. They used automobile auction companies as their main channel to the second-hand market.

Pressures on the dealerships

Dealerships in North America were directly impacted by the decreasing number of new cars sales. Remarkably, profits from new car sales had dropped to practically zero according to a study by a North American Dealer Association (NADA) study. Most of the dealership's profits were accumulated by used car sales. Accordingly, there was a quasi 'shake out' in the industry. Many dealerships closed, sold out or consolidated. The businesses that survived the decline still suffered falling profit margins. Studies confirmed that the service department produced the greatest profits for the dealers.

Currently, car manufacturers in the US have the potential to build 18–19 million cars a year. The demand for new cars, with sizeable price tags, fell from 14.5 million to 12.3 million between 1989 and 1991. A Ford company executive stated that:

> Over-capacity has become so enormous that it will only be resolved with the demise or restructuring of some of today's major manufacturers.
>
> (Automotive News 1991b)

Trends

With the downturn in auto purchases, there was a corresponding decline in the number of automobiles produced. Industry-wide, there were layoffs, closings, consolidations and downsizing of employees. To remain competitive, companies had to acknowledge the trend and pursue the profitable channels for manufacturing, distribution and sales. The company gained its competitive edge by focusing its talent on the dealerships, essentially putting its manpower where it would be most effective.

Since service departments were the top-producing profit segments for most North American dealerships, there was a very good chance that corporate restructuring would be implemented to maximize the service aspect of the car sales cycle. The bottom line was that employees in the manufacturing business seriously considered moving to more customer-oriented service areas.

The link between the automotive company and Perot Systems

The partnership between Perot Systems and the automotive company has quickly progressed to become a relationship that not only supports the present but also focuses on the future. To this end, they launched a technology architecture study to help guide the North American subsidiary through future investments. An overview of a few of the solutions implemented is provided below:

1. Completion of a financial business process re-engineering effort that will assist the North American automotive company's financial department in implementing process improvements.
2. A supplier forecasting system with a graphical user interface (GUI) that utilized an exception-based approach for reviewing suggested supplier orders. This system reduced the number of order review lines by 85 per cent and allows for more accurate forecasting, which has lowered inventory carrying and supplier ordering costs.
3. The development of a customer/prospect database system that utilizes a client/server solution to provide information regarding the collection, management and interpretation of marketing activities.
4. The provision of communications and network services by establishing connectivity between corporate and regional offices so that each user has access to office automation applications and electronic mail.

The Canadian subsidiary of the same global automotive manufacturer had merged its systems development and data centre with its American counterpart. The two subsidiaries consolidated warranty and inventory management processing and transferred the Canadian operation's mainframe processing to the data centre located in the USA.

Formation of other partnerships to provide the best solutions

The partnership chain does not just involve the link between the company and Perot Systems. In fact, Perot Systems has also joined forces with various technology vendors to provide the company with the best price, performance and strategic solution. Perot Systems partnered with Sterling Software to implement an Electronic Data Interchange (EDI) systems solution that will reduce the automobile importer and distributor's reliance on the 'paper trail' in the service, parts and finance departments. The EDI system is ANSI X.12–compatible and enables the company to communicate with parts suppliers and customs brokers in an industry-standard format. Future EDI objectives include establishing communications capabilities with trucking companies and financial institutions.

Perot Systems is also partnering with Radcliffe to provide the company with a complete warehouse bar-code system. The new system provides receiving, put-away, packing and shipping modules, as well as various managerial reporting tools. The aim is to improve the accuracy and efficiency of warehouse operations and thus achieve lower costs and improved dealer service performance.

The organization's characteristics before the change initiative

The company's financial processes and systems evolved over the years from supporting a manufacturing environment to backing a sales and distribution organization.

Over time, these operations became paper-intensive and required a significant amount of manual processing. In 1994 the automobile importer and distributor carried out a BPR study of its financial processes with the objective of improving the performance and systems in this area. The purpose of the financial re-engineering study was to review existing procedures and then to redesign them, providing a streamlined support environment for the financial department.

With the success of the financial re-engineering project organization, and in light of the fact that the company had made a strategic decision to downsize significantly, additional BPR studies were initiated. Operational areas to be re-examined and reshaped included Warranty, Human Resources, Payroll, Area Executives, Compliance and Core Process (CP) 1. The operations of the entire company were divided into subprocesses in order to evaluate the systems most in need of change. CP 1 included initial customer contact such as marketing, sales and advertising. CP 2 encompassed vehicle delivery and parts provisioning. CP 3 efforts supported customer initiatives such as service, warranty and repairs. This new perspective on company functions was the driving force in the initial phase of the company's re-engineering effort. Following the successful implementation of recommended improvements in these areas, the company's senior management considered the feasibility of engaging a full-time BPR staff.

How was the change initiated?

In the warranty department, for example, operational processes were decentralized so that the reduced staff could manage the business. Computer systems helped the employees remaining in the office to shift their mission from warranty training for dealers to supporting the field representatives, ensuring that the reps were 'in control'. Almost simultaneously, the company's Chief Executive Officer (CEO) closed all regional offices and sent account executives into the field with laptops and pagers in a move he called 'turning the corporation inside out'.

The existing IT system

History of the company's office acquisition/requisition process

The Information Technology (IT) system in place at the company for acquiring hardware and software was one of the areas earmarked for modernization and streamlining by executives. The entire office automation requisition system (OAREQ) was selected as a prime candidate for re-engineering. One important result sought in the OAREQ business process re-engineering was to provide customers with appropriate equipment more quickly. The OAREQ department's BPR objectives were as follows:

- to reduce user requests by proactive fulfilment of needs;
- to improve cycle time dramatically;
- to provide a user-friendly interface for customers;

- to eliminate non-value-added work;
- to increase purchasing power;
- to develop and maintain accurate inventory.

Key findings of the process analysis

The re-engineering team conducted interviews with individuals involved in the Office Automation (OA) requisition process and with customers (of the process), another important component of BPR. The BPR consultants formulated process maps of the existing – 'as is' – process, based on important information compiled by the OAREQ team with their customers' input. Some of the key findings of the process analysis were as follows:

1. An unfriendly request system required that each department identify a power user – some one who uses the system frequently, does not refer to the help menu and is fast. The power user would enter the request into the OA requisition system for her or his department. In a significant number of cases, even the power user did not know what items should be selected.
2. The process cycle time was much too long: the average requisition required seven to nine weeks.
3. There was practically no planning within the departments. Items were ordered when needed, eliminating the company's potential purchasing-power advantage.
4. Customers were not always ordering the technology they needed.
5. The existing budgeting and charge-back policies encouraged abuse by customers.
6. Inventory information was not accurately tracked.
7. The existing OA requisition system provided no real value to the process and was difficult for customers to use.

Results highlighted the existing OA requisition system's ineffectiveness in fulfilling customer needs. Lack of planning was identified as the primary underlying problem. Over 80 per cent of requests could be eliminated by accurate planning. With planning, the technology will be delivered when it is expected, and it will meet the future needs of the organization. However, planning will not be able to eliminate all technology requests, and the process of fulfilling the remaining requests must also be improved.

The history of the company's Human Resources department

The Human Resources (HR) department was another group reduced by 50 per cent through a prior strategic downsizing project. A separate re-engineering effort was conducted to improve the operational performance of the much-reduced HR department. For this group, the BPR objectives were:

- to eliminate non-essential HR administrative tasks in supporting both the Canadian and the US organization and operation;
- to refocus HR team efforts to be more consultative;

- to provide better information to monitor corporate HR activities and identify leadership training needs;
- to eliminate non-value-added work;
- to leverage technology to support the new environment;
- to develop a 'road map' to the new environment to account for cultural changes, new technology and the new environment.

Concurrently with this BPR initiative, the US and Canadian headquarters were being merged into one seamless organization. As a result, the scope of this project incorporated a thorough review of the Canadian HR department's functions. This expanded effort was necessary to ensure that any methodological differences were understood and accounted for in the newly designed processes.

Findings from the department

The re-engineering team (hereafter referred to as 'the Team') mapped the department's ongoing functions in the format of process flow diagrams, a useful tool in flagging redundancies and inefficiencies in a process. When these process 'maps' were reviewed it was evident that manual administrative tasks required a disproportionate amount of the HR staff's time and effort.

The overarching reason for the additional manual input was that the department's extant IT system, Orion, did not meet the needs of HR users. As a result, numerous reports, calculations and other management-type activities such as tracking had to be performed manually. Furthermore, peripheral systems used by the HR staff were not integrated with the Orion system, e.g. accounts payable/receivable, employee benefits (including various health plans), flexible spending account administration, 401k funds management, long-term disability insurance, worker compensation and pension benefits. Duplicate data entry was required since the systems did not have a collective point for data entry or shared access. Innumerable forms had to be written by hand for information to be used.

The company's Help Desk

The company's Help Desk was in a process of change over several years before the re-engineering project started. In a ripple effect, changes in other departments – including a variety of business process changes and technology implementations and configurations – placed additional responsibilities on the Help Desk. The level of change was expected to continue steadily; as a result, call loads and the complexity of problems were also expected to increase.

In December 1994 a team was assembled to analyse and re-engineer the company's Help Desk processes. The team began the re-engineering initiative by seeking to answer the following questions:

1. How was the existing Help Desk functioning?
2. How would the Help Desk of the future operate?
3. How would future requirements be handled?
4. What would be the cost of implementing recommendations?

Project goals

The project goals for the Help Desk re-engineering initiative were, first, to analyse the processes in place and, second, to propose cost-effective business processes. It was imperative that re-engineered processes be implemented that would enable the IT team to provide a level of service from the Help Desk to meet or exceed the expectations of their customers. The scope of the re-engineering project was to review and evaluate all processes comprising the existing and expected future functions of the Help Desk. Any external processes with an impact on the Help Desk team's effectiveness were also considered to be within the scope of the study.

Mission statement

Together, the Help Desk and BPR teams constructed a cohesive mission statement, based on existing goals and objectives and ideals for the Help Desk of the future. The mission statement served as a guide throughout the entire re-engineering effort, as follows:

> The Computer Services Help Desk Team's mission is to provide the most professional, accessible, speedy and accurate assistance to our Canadian and US user communities, especially in response to and resolution of their problems, requests, questions, and concerns regarding application software, operating systems, hardware, networks, and telephone systems. Each individual Help Desk team member will be responsible for providing a superior level of customer service, including ownership and resolution of user needs and feedback follow-up. We strive to provide the highest level of first-call resolutions in the Computer Services Help Desk industry.

Current-process evaluation

The BPR team started the re-engineering project by gathering performance data such as volume metrics and incident report (IR) rates. They also interviewed and surveyed the IT team regarding the existing Help Desk process. The Team simultaneously conducted interviews with Account Executives and other Help Desk users/customers. Data from these sessions, combined with observations of the help desk operations, were used to compile the 'as is' process flow diagrams.

Help desk community

The Help Desk user community comprised a wide-ranging level of computer literacy and specific, company-specific and industry experience. Prior to the re-engineering project, the company had hired a subcontractor; subsequently, new employees were employed to support Help Desk activities.

The Help Desk team leaders compiled a minimum proficiency matrix with the basic information required to perform necessary functions due to several instances where 'first-call' resolutions had not occurred because the Help Desk staff had not been exposed to all potential problems. This requirements aptitude list was useful for long-term planning because it served as a checklist for new-hires as well as a training roster for existing employees.

Support community

The re-engineering team understood that the Help Desk relied on a 'support community' of outside departments where the Help Desk staff could go for assistance. The response of the support community to problems which Help Desk employees had 'escalated' to them was a major determinant in the satisfaction of the Help Desk's customers. Because of the impact of the support community on the Help Desk, representatives from several support groups were included in the re-engineering process, as follows:

1. *Mainframe-based*: the mainframe-based support community consisted of a few onsite personnel and a group of individuals in an offsite support team.
2. *PC-based*: the PC-based support community comprised all onsite personnel, primarily former Help Desk staff members.
3. *Communications/local area network (LAN)*: the communications/LAN team included various network engineers and security administrators.
4. *Database administration (DBA)*: the DBAs were split between onsite and offsite personnel. IMS and CICS support was provided by offsite support, while LAN-based DBAs were located onsite.

User community

The user community comprised consultants, employees from Canadian operations and individual users. Interviews with individuals having first-hand experience with the Help Desk process were invaluable in determining recommended areas of improvement. Though this group understood the difficult job requirements placed on a Help Desk agent, employees who had to deal with the Help Desk complained that it worked more like a call distribution service than an office providing answers or assistance.

Some issues discovered by the re-engineering team in their initial assessments stemmed from operational limitations. One example was support of the Account Executives (AE) on location, commonly referred to as 'in the field'. The AEs, spread across four time zones in the USA and Canada, were increasingly affected by batch runs of systems. A more thorough understanding of the AEs' positions and reliance on their laptop applications would enhance the Help Desk's level of service by making the latter more sensitive to the AEs' problems.

Comments on the customer service skills, phone etiquette and professionalism of the Help Desk personnel ranged from 'very good' and 'compassionate', to 'terrible' and 'devoid of empathy'. In general, the consensus was that as Help Desk agents developed a more empathetic relationship with the user and got to know and understand their situation their professionalism improved. Regardless of whether the problem was completely resolved, the user had a better impression of the experience.

Systems and tools

The Help Desk's problem management system is mainframe-based. Although this 3270 dumb terminal environment provides the staff with the capabilities of a problem-tracking system, the productivity enhancements of a GUI front end are not available. The only 'tools' used to track issues or outstanding problems are verbal communication or e-mail. Transition data exists only as a compilation of notes and lists in a ring binder. There was one, seldom-used, Windows workstation in the area, used only for a Windows-user problem. Using this workstation meant the agent was forced to move physically across the room to resolve the problem, which added time to the call resolution. In summary, the Help Desk systems automation was limited to highlighted messages and rolling screens on a few of the MVS consoles and 3270 workstations dispersed through the room.

Business philosophy

The central theme of the newly formulated mission statement was that the new Help Desk process will be customer-oriented. The Help Desk team must understand who their customers are, what they do and how they do it in order to serve them expeditiously and efficiently.

The BPR team helped the Help Desk group derive several other positive results. The re-engineered Help Desk staff's approach was to be proactive and preventative in helping the user community. Problem resolution would be placed firmly in the hands of the Help Desk agent. To better support their own customers, the Help Desk agents desired enhanced communication and support systems with the support community. An important recommendation from the BPR study was substantial integration of the Help Desk team into the overall Systems Life Cycle and Roll-out Planning process.

The new operative structure: organization and hardware

The new structure consists of three-person AE teams where each member represents proficiency in service, sales or parts. The creation of these teams was part of the initial restructuring effort which the BPR study built upon. In the new infrastructure, AEs dial in to the corporate office, downloading data and e-mail while they work. The portable computers possess fax capabilities and printers which allow field reps instantly to allocate vehicles which dealers request and to assist them with sales, service and warranties.

The 200 field employees now access a corporate intranet for various daily tasks. They carry text pagers which run on PCs. The field representatives use a mail system that is compatible with text pagers as well. Conference calls are facilitated with an (800) freephone number – a useful tool for a widely distributed Team.

Leveraging high-ticket items such as long-distance calling helped to pay for the quick transformation. The automobile importer and distributor expanded its voice data system to allow calls to other locations worldwide for just pennies a minute instead of dollars.

Communication: what did you say?

Many organizations often underestimate the power of communication during the implementation stage of a BPR project. In some organizations only one method of communication, such as memos, is employed. The effective small-group format where employees express feedback and verbalize their concerns may be more successful. The familiar environment supports active employee participation and provides a means for quickly addressing discontent and thereby managing (or thwarting) resistance. A successful communications strategy must include a variety of informational activities.

Transition strategy: a communications affair

The company finance BPR study strongly recommended hosting an employee fair as part of the transition strategy. The two-day event could provide an ideal opportunity to introduce and explain reasons for changes. At the fair, employees would be presented with a consistent, straightforward method to accomplish change and experience a common message with the intent of raising employee morale.

A subsequent recommendation was to establish a Human Resources Information Bureau as a single-source provider of information for employees. Many of the questions arising from the introduction of new policies would most likely be similar among employees. The bureau would provide a focused method to gather these questions and respond with a common message. In addition, human resource issues must be pushed back into the Human Resources group to allow other departments to focus on their core processes.

In reality, the corporate intranet served as a central repository for corporate information and performed a similar function to what had been proposed in the BPR study. Employees now had a central point of contact for current information. Moreover, the intranet became a resource for obtaining strategic information about the company's direction.

The benefits from implementing the re-engineered finance processes and supporting system were realized once the individuals supporting the changes understood that the changes were necessary to achieve the company's goals and success. Therefore the employees had to be involved in the change process.

The process team approach

The company established 'process teams' for each of the processes to be re-engineered. Although the overall Transition Strategy is managed by a transition leader, ownership of the processes is supported by the appropriate process teams. The teams are made up of company and Perot Systems employees, comprising the blended team approach. This approach ensures that the re-engineering ideas and concepts are infused (and accepted) throughout the company's culture. The teams are led by existing members of the individual project's Core Team. Their charter is to develop detailed project plans for the transition of each of the processes including policy changes.

Evaluation

The Transition Strategy provides a vehicle to monitor the success of an individual project, such as finance. The transformation of the finance area can be deemed successful only if the finance 'customers' benefit from the new environment. A process entitled 'Climate Monitoring' is one method used to judge customer satisfaction. The process utilizes focused, anonymous questionnaires to provide feedback for design and implementation of continuous improvement action plans. Ongoing actions may include technical training, communications training, team-building, goal-setting, time management, or recommendations for additional equipment, skills or other tools necessary to accomplish a desired level of service.

Training and education

The education involved in the finance group transformation included training on the new SAP (software accounting package) application software, as well as instruction on the optimum ways to transition from a specialist to a generalist environment. Currently, many organizations are utilizing skills-matching applications to aid in the development of training or redeployment strategies. A skills-matching application identifies areas of skill inefficiencies by comparing the skills required in a re-engineered environment with those of the existing environment. The current skills of finance employees will need to be assessed and a skills-matching software can be utilized to identify a training plan for each employee.

Consequences

With the Financial Systems Implementation split into phases, the automotive company will advance towards its goal of migrating applications from the mainframe computer to a client/server environment. Successful system implementation involves many components, one of which is for users to work closely with application developers. From requirements definition to acceptance testing, teamwork ensures a common understanding and expectation of the goal.

During the construction activity for the financial re-engineering project, developers converted data, built interfaces and reports, and fine-tuned the applications. The user-team members in turn prepared training modules, policy materials and acceptance test plans.

Testing came next. User-team members trained other end-users in the applications and business process changes while the development team members tested the integration of data conversions, interfaces, applications and reports. The user acceptance test served to bring users and developers together in parallel testing of the new systems against current production systems.

Parallel testing utilized the live production environment, data and systems. At the completion of parallel testing, the existing production systems could be archived and dismantled as part of implementation as the new systems are put in place. Although the new application systems would be running in production during the testing activity, implementation would include any final code migrations, the archiving of current mainframe data and systems, and preparation of a Phase II Implementation Plan.

The existing financial system

Included in Table 6.1 are some of the findings from initial analysis completed on the Financial re-engineering project. Other findings inherent in many other systems

Table 6.1 Findings from the financial re-engineering project

Discovery	*Example*
Lack of System Integration • duplication of effort (rekeying) • data integrity problems • excessive report generation to aid reconciliation	Payroll not interfaced to General Ledger
PC and associated tools not widespread	Planning/budgeting data entered from hard copy forms Purchasing – productivity tools not available for purchasing personnel
Information not timely; no on-line real-time access	Accounts Receivable cannot determine customer balances until month end
A lot of 'heads-down work' required – less time available for analysis	Concentration of time in tax filing instead of tax planning for savings
Reconciliation efforts needed due to rekeying	Manual interface from Fixed Assets Payroll and Banking to the General Ledger
Processes require excessive approvals	Purchasing requires a minimum of six signatures for purchases less than $20k, seven for greater than $20k
System reporting is weak	Mainframe information is rekeyed into spreadsheets to create monthly reports for main company
Paper driven from the source	Paper requests required to bill a dealer for a purchase, to have a check cut for taxes, etc.
Company Finance Department made up of solution-oriented people	Overcome organizational and system obstacles to get the job done – Purchasing department, General Ledger Consolidation
No back-up departmental personnel to support current processes	Payroll department – one accountant and two clerks
Poor utilization of current systems • training • lack of policies and procedures	Input into 1099 system from Parts
Non-finance-related activities have been absorbed by the finance department	Asset tagging performed in fixed assets versus at receipt

included excessive duplication and manual data entry, excessive approvals and other 'red-tape' actions. Also noted was a feeling of being overwhelmed with the day's work and not having much time for planning and analysis.

Summary

The company examined its core work processes. Cost containment was the first focus. The Team used more methodology than technology to change factors that affected selling a vehicle. Customers 'in need' were identified, for example a new purchaser with high claims data.

Another high-impact, high-exposure area was the Human Resource department, now half its former size. Using technology, the collective company/Perot Systems business engineering team reduced the number of existing tasks from 392 to 124. This move empowered company employees to update records personally in their online file, and freed them to consult and monitor the organization without having to perform clerical tasks. This effort had to be completed in concert with the Canadian operation's counterparts to ensure that new processes accounted for existing regulatory differences.

Data centre cross-training leads to improved performance

In 1993 the North American data centre operations consisted of ten employees who worked the graveyard shift. Now, five cross-trained employees support the systems as well as two other revenue-producing accounts. Employees from the combined accounts questioned the existing process and brainstormed ways to do it 'better, faster and cheaper'. The synergy resulted in a lower cost per unit and a reduction of as much as two hours in the time it takes to run a job. The bottom line: the automobile importer and distributor saved money.

With the support teams afield, the number of warranty employees dropped from thirty-nine to six. One of the six remaining warranty specialists stated that onsite business engineering consultants showed him how to 'think' differently during the warranty process decentralization. 'It took three months for the combined efforts of Perot Systems and the company to get the new process on track,' the specialist explained, 'where we had spent one year on TQM, but hadn't implemented things.'

Hardware support

Fortunately, the hardware in place at North American operations was the systems integrator's choice: Windows NT. Though it is somewhat in vogue, Windows NT proved to be the most versatile system for the company's needs. As the company's North American and Canadian operations were consolidated, the client/server system allowed for joint database customer prospecting and e-mail. Now, the entire company requires only one support team. Another added benefit is that long-distance costs are noticeably lower.

In conclusion, one analyst stated:

> as our company crests the technology horizon, the theory 'the sum of the parts is greater than the whole' is tested daily. The pains of downsizing are gone, and for stalwart company employees, there is no such thing as 'business as usual'.

Drivers for change

New system, new process

Drastic changes in the organization demanded changes in several internal systems. Managers in the finance department decided to implement a new software accounting package (SAP) which necessitated changes in the way the department would do business in the future. In October 1993 managers at the automotive company started to re-engineer their financial business process.

Tried and true: up-front planning saves time

The company immediately recognized not only that it could benefit from automating what was in place following SAP implementation, but also that it would secure additional benefits by examining other existing processes which would interface with the new accounting system. It made sense to leverage and streamline activities connected to SAP while implementing the SAP, rather than to modify activities afterwards. This project was the automotive company's pilot re-engineering project, undertaken with Perot Systems' involvement. Re-engineering at the company has since evolved into an enterprise-wide endeavour.

The company's approach: change, then accommodate change

Prior to June 1994 sales had been plummeting. Consequently, company executives conducted a major restructuring effort. The end-result was the downsizing of the entire company by nearly 43 per cent. In addition, management decided to merge the Canadian and the North American operations into a single organizational unit. The end-result was that some departments in the Canadian operation were pared to 20 per cent of their original size.

After the downsizing took place, the company plunged into improving operations and reshaping the business. Its goal was to change in order to remain competitive and recapture market share. Management's philosophy was to 'grow' dealerships and to implement an effective partnership with the dealers. This design would, in turn, be a better process for the retail customer. The rationale was that if the company ensured that dealers were well stocked, well served by their representatives and the corporate office, and more in control of inventory and practices, the dealers, in turn, would sell more vehicles.

During this transitional period, company executives re-engineered the warranty administration department, a high-impact, high-exposure area. The warranty department had recently downsized by nearly 80 per cent from thirty-nine people to six. Those six people were in a very unenviable position: they had no choice but to accept re-engineering. Unless the new team examined their functions and re-engineered the ongoing processes, the responsibilities and output of almost forty people were not going to change. That implied that the six employees would either have to work around the clock, or they would fail.

Success breeds success

The innovative ideas generated by the warranty administration business process re-engineering initiative encouraged company executives to continue re-engineering other processes. Though the implementation of many of the study's objectives was rocky, the executive committee wanted to achieve additional successes with other departments. To this end, Perot Systems, acting as the change agent, continued to perform additional studies with the automotive company's team.

In starting the subsequent efforts, the BPR team identified the warranty group as a microcosm of the rest of the organization. The Team recognized that the 'panic' they had seen in the warranty group regarding management's goals, objectives and expectations, with fewer people to carry on those tasks, was imminent in many other departments.

This opportune realization presented enough justification to continue re-engineering on an enterprise-wide scale. In support of the leaner, more efficient organization, the Chief Information Officer (CIO) was also in favour of the enterprise-wide re-engineering project. It would be unwise to conduct such a massive re-engineering for the entire company at once. To accomplish the sweeping changes envisioned throughout the organization, the CIO needed 'support champions' from his management. People with industry experience coupled with re-engineering know-how would accomplish this bold objective.

Plan and prioritize

Company executives and Perot Systems consultants agreed that the best way to accomplish the mammoth task of enterprise-wide re-engineering would be to prioritize areas and processes according to customer satisfaction and fulfilment. Re-engineering would occur first in areas with the highest priority. Priority would be given to processes with high financial impact or which directly affected customer satisfaction. The automobile importer and distributor's customers were defined as the dealerships and, ultimately, the actual vehicle owners.

Business areas, departments and processes were each categorized as belonging to one of three priority levels. In 'Priority 1' (P1) areas, re-engineering projects would begin immediately. While the P1 projects were being conducted, Perot Systems trained the automotive distributor's personnel. The CIO envisioned that as the P1 projects were completed and the P2 projects initiated, the level of Perot Systems' involvement as a consultant would taper off to a small core of individuals assisting in multiple re-engineering projects and continuous improvement activities. The bulk of the re-engineering analysis and implementation would be performed by company managers.

Even so, the predominant philosophy of leading BPR executives was that the BPR consisted of more than just the study and recommendations. Their idea was that the BPR was finished only when the recommendations and practices had been implemented and effectively utilized, and the organization was then ready for another re-engineering effort. A company executive commented that the BPR study was the point at which some consulting firms 'end' their involvement. Perot Systems' role involved more than simply doing the process analysis and providing a final presentation with recommended future actions. The BPR team intended from the start that the effort would include implementation, and they proceeded accordingly.

The K to K initiative: unanimous executive agreement as a high-priority study

An example of a P1 initiative was the K to K project. The K to K name refers to the proximity of the customer to the company employee. The K to K project began in

June 1995 when the re-engineering consultants polled the leadership team members of the company and gave a presentation of the enterprise re-engineering plan, asking them what additional areas they saw as having major opportunities for re-engineering in the short-term. Executives who were CP leaders, reporting directly to the president, overwhelmingly opted to do the K to K project from a selection of various departments and priorities for the BPR study. The consensus was achieved through a process where the CP leaders met with a BPR consultant, discussed the issues and then voted. The results were reviewed at a meeting with the CP leaders, who represented different areas within the company.

The reorganization of the automotive company resulted in a different focus, changing a department orientation to a process orientation. Thus, the 'vehicle distribution' department became a 'delivering the goods' process. A subprocess of 'delivering the goods' was parts and vehicle transportation and parts inventory.

What is a successful customer?

Convincing a CIO or CEO of a company that is years ahead of its competition that the company needs to re-engineer the way it does business is not as easy as it would be to convince a company that is less successful or behind the competition. Company executives in the latter category understand the need for change. With a successful company, it may be difficult to understand that there is good reason to change anything. Even so, some forward-thinking companies never look back and are always cognizant of the need for improvement.

At the beginning of the re-engineering effort, the automobile importer and distributor was struggling. Market share was below 3 per cent in the USA and car sales were markedly diminishing. The situation at this particular company was not such that it was difficult to convince the CIO or managers of the need for change. Previously 50 per cent of the workforce had been cut – up to 70 per cent in some cases. Company workers knew that they needed a change. For example, most people understood that fifty workers could not handle the same workload, with the same operations and procedures, as a previous staff of 100.

The automotive company executives and employees were looking for radical changes in how they conducted business. Employees were determined to move ahead of the competition. They wanted to improve productivity and consequently market share, not just maintain the status quo. The staff knew the re-engineering effort had to be successful and they backed it up 100 per cent.

Internal support to 'champion' the effort is instrumental to a successful BPR

The BPR team leaders met with the company's executive team of CP leaders to find a 'user' to be involved in the re-engineering process who possessed strong backing from the leaders. Rather than letting the re-engineering team take the view that they are the leaders of the change, they knew that the change leader should be a representative from within the area undergoing the study. The company leaders knew they needed to re-engineer, and realized they needed assistance to accomplish the daunting task. As such, they were willing to select and support a CP leader as the re-engineering champion. The champion/user role demanded full-time concentration throughout the six-month study and subsequent implementation efforts.

The champion kept the leadership involved by providing relevant information whenever and wherever possible. The user was well respected by the executive committee and, as one leader indicated, was a 'top-notch communicator' as well. The user had worked in the US organization for three years and had previously been employed with the company's Canadian operation.

The user brought focus and clarity to the BPR effort for K to K which involved forecast accuracy, flexibility in production and dealer allocations. This allowed executives to focus on a finite number of issues, and helped to narrow the scope of the study rather than making the re-engineering 'everything to everybody'.

Improvement measures determine success

How are improvements measured and how is success determined? In addition to financial savings, improvements can be gauged using performance measures such as cycle time. Success could mean improved responsiveness to a customer's order or money saved in processing an order.

At the US branch of operations, the CIO wanted to expand the business customer base and market share without adding any people. The re-engineering team's objective complied with that of the CIO. Instead of burdening sales staff with redundant or non-value-added activities, the focus of the re-engineering effort was on performing strictly value-added activities.

Agree on performance measurement from the start

Part of developing the initial business case is to determine the way data will be presented to the company executives, the re-engineering sponsor (also referred to as the champion and the user) and the employees affected by the changes. Sometimes status reports suffice. Often final reports and analyses are seen as just another report or just another management fad.

An underlying principle for the combined company/Perot Systems team is that the re-engineering 'customer', the actual automotive company employees, was an integral part of the entire re-engineering process. This included facilitating meetings, brainstorming sessions, and presenting information to senior management and junior employees. Company IT managers actively participated in the change; their involvement in and dedication to the final outcome of the business re-engineering objectives were cemented by their participation in the re-engineering effort from the ground up.

A notable point was made by one of the re-engineering team members: 'there was never a "watershed" presentation to company executives.' That way, executives would understand what was being accomplished, how, when and at what price. There would be no surprises when it came time to fund BPR implementation following the data and recommendation provided throughout the initial BPR study phase.

The blended team works

The blended team approach exemplifies a win–win approach to completing a re-engineering project. On site, Perot Systems and company IT consultants are a team. When the appropriate time comes to make recommendations to the chairman, the company IT consultants, including the BPR project champion, actively participate, while Perot Systems' consultants remains on the periphery. This strategy is explained to company executives and the IT consultants from the start of the project. The expectations and reasons for working jointly on the project are spelled out fully in the 'kick off' phase, if not sooner, such as during the initial study or business case preparation.

Training

In preparation for implementing the many recommendations from the BPR studies, Perot Systems, at their customer's request, developed a training class tailored to the company's project. Managers at various levels spent two and a half days learning about what business re-engineering really means, what kinds of changes to anticipate, and how this process would ultimately affect the way the company, and therefore the employee, does business.

The BPR initiative

Concurrent re-engineering projects

In 1994 the automobile importer and distributor had seven BPR projects underway: Warranty Administration – US operations; Warranty Administration – Mexican operations; Field team, field organization; HR; Compliance; Payroll; and Credit. Not all seven projects were at the same stage of development at the same time, so there was not necessarily a ratio of one consultant per undertaking. While the Warranty Administration re-engineering effort was being implemented for the US branch of operations the other projects were in progress at the 'engagement stage', meaning they were in progress.

Consolidated teams

As previously mentioned, the re-engineering teams were integrated with the automotive company and Perot Systems membership. Perot Systems worked jointly with the company IT managers, either working side by side with them, as in field operation engagements, or reporting directly to them and keeping them informed of progress on a daily basis. In this case, a joint project team was also what the company's CIO wanted. The unified approach, with the BPR consultants working closely with the company's IT managers, served as valuable training for the latter.

Their knowledge and on-the-job training provided the experience necessary to continue the enterprise-wide engineering effort in a phased approach. The company's managers could see, first-hand, the successes of their efforts, as evidenced in improved corporate sales and performance records.

Changing roles – changing mindsets

The transformation of the company's IT managers' roles and responsibilities was not without problems. Since the role of consultant was entirely new to IT re-engineering 'trainees', there was much to learn and a new way of thinking to adopt. Prior to this, company managers were individual performers, more focused on their own goals, programmes and performance statistics than on the entire company's performance. These managers were not accustomed to conducting projects. Furthermore, their perception of their responsibilities differed from the CIO's notion of the mid-level manager's future role.

Once engaged, the CIO was behind the effort 100 per cent. Interestingly, despite the opinions of several of the automotive company's managers, the CIO was accessible to BPR consultants and established an open-door policy. While he relinquished enterprise-wide BPR responsibilities to two managers directly reporting to him, he was very interested in the status, problems and accomplishments of the re-engineering projects. In that respect, he became an extremely supportive member of the Team.

A successful BPR takes time, dedication and resources

One result of having a senior champion as the project sponsor was the bringing together of a 'core design team'. This team was composed of executive-level representation of the overall re-engineering effort. The group met monthly and demonstrated visible support for the re-engineering effort.

Many of these team members had full-time positions elsewhere in the company. Communication occurred as necessary by phone and electronic mail. Initially they met weekly, daily or monthly, then, as the project progressed, more on an as-needed basis. The five team members who were 100 per cent dedicated to the re-engineering effort worked and then would present the ideas to the other team members as necessary in Mexico and elsewhere.

Re-engineering is a full-time effort and requires 100 per cent dedication. The engagement will fail if only 10 per cent of management's time is allocated to a BPR project as the project scope would then require two years to complete. The bottom line is that the users will not wait and sales would continue to fall.

The consultant's role

One of the reasons the CIO planned to phase his own managers into the BPR consulting capacity and phase out Perot Systems consultants was financial. After the top-priority projects were completed, the CIO agreed to retain a minimal number of Perot Systems staff to guide the remaining re-engineering projects. One Team member anticipated that, realistically, the company would probably require five or six consultants dedicated to ongoing re-engineering efforts.

Industry expertise required

One prevalent issue when hiring consultants to undertake a re-engineering endeavour is the question of whether or not they are industry experts – indeed whether they have any industry knowledge. That particular question was not an issue with the automobile importer and distributor BPR project. The Perot Systems consultants were not asked to provide the ultimate answer and it was crucial to working with the company that this was clear from the outset.

Perot Systems had a role to play in guiding and assisting the company in re-engineering its finance department. The focus was on improving processes, eliminating unnecessary activities, upgrading technology and working with company managers to gain insight into how they might improve their own jobs. The employees are regarded as the 'content' experts in the automobile industry. A 'blended team' approach in this case provided the ideal cross-fertilization of ideas about and understanding of what to change and how to change it. Perot Systems consultants provided a structure and framework, as well as some external expertise from other industries and projects.

The HR re-engineering project – results from interviews

During the first phase of the project, all HR staff members in the USA and Canada were interviewed by Perot Systems in order to gain an understanding of the existing processes and systems used to perform their functions. These processes were mapped and approved by the HR leadership. These mapped processes established a benchmark for the re-engineering phase which followed.

The initial HR meeting – crucial communication regarding the BPR project

The HR director led a BPR kick-off meeting with the entire HR staff and representatives from other organizations within the company that would potentially be affected by decisions made during the re-engineering process. The HR Director, as BPR sponsor, encouraged everyone's support and gave the combined BPR team authority to accomplish the following objectives:

1. To develop a project plan to the new environment:
   - culture;
   - technology;

- process;

2. To minimize HR administrative tasks in supporting North American organizations;
3. To refocus HR team efforts to be more consultative;
4. To provide better information to:
   - monitor corporate HR activities;
   - identify leadership training needs;
5. To eliminate non-value-added work;
6. To leverage technology to support the new environment.

The results of the BPR improvements were significant: the BPR team reduced the number of tasks performed by HR staff members by 68 per cent. This reduction was achieved by the use of technology, by eliminating non-value-added tasks and reassigning functions to their true process owners.

Implementing HR BPR findings

The re-engineered process maps were used by the BPR team to develop a Functional Requirements Document. This document, which contained specifications, was sent to selected HR software vendors. The BPR team facilitated demonstrations from the various vendors. HR participants were then invited to rate the functionality of the package. At the conclusion of the demonstrations, the results were presented to leadership in the HR and Information Technology departments to use in making their selection of a software vendor. Following vendor selection, the BPR team 'transitioned' installation to the technical team. Perot Systems was responsible for software and hardware installation and data conversion. The BPR team continued to support HR leadership in the change management phase of the project to ensure a successful implementation of the new HR system.

Results from Core Process 1 initial interviews

As with results from the HR BPR effort, themes from interviews with the project managers and team members for CP1 echoed findings from previous studies, such as:

1. Decision-making and functional overlap with other organizations;
2. Conflicting perspectives between Market and Production;
3. Lack of clear leadership goals;
4. No consistent feedback;
5. Lack of communication between groups within CP1;
6. Criticality of an objective and 'pure' market voice;
7. Necessity of requests;
8. Provision of:
   - fulfilment of more requests;
   - information to those who 'should' ask;
   - earlier market input to decision-making process;
   - more timely and priority-based responses.

The future Help Desk

The future Help Desk process can be viewed from three perspectives: operations, systems development life-cycle, and training. The BPR team, in cooperation with the Help Desk team, sought to change the traditional views of the Help Desk. One important initiative was to introduce a career path for Help Desk team members to achieve future personal growth.

Help Desk operations

Operations is the most important function of the Help Desk. The people, procedures and supporting technology must work together to assist the customer successfully, whether the customer is a Canadian dealer, or an Account Executive representative, or someone else affected by the company's operations. The Help Desk of the future must have the capability of providing 'at-the-fingertips' access to all relevant information regarding a customer's problem, resolution, history, systems environment, etc. To achieve this, the professional Help Desk agent will need to possess a high level of customer service and representational skills in addition to proficiency in the company's systems environment.

Help Desk systems monitoring

The Help Desk operations of the future will rely heavily on automated systems monitoring tools. These tools will have predictive qualities and problem-broadcast rules to provide early warning or notification to the end-users/customers and Help Desk support staff. While the monitoring and broadcasting can be accomplished via tools, there will always be a need for the professional Help Desk agent, who must interact with customers with specific problems, questions and requests.

Help Desk training

Training is an instrumental part of the new Help Desk process. Studies confirm that the more knowledgeable the Help Desk agent is, the more capable she or he will be of providing first-call resolutions. The broad knowledge base of the company Help Desk, combined with specialization and cross-training, should provide versatility to the staff in dealing with customer systems.

The training set contains three categories of disciplines. These are:

1. Customer Services Professional Training: dealing with people, phone etiquette, follow-up skills, prioritization and management reporting.
2. Technology Training: keeping abreast of the latest in technologies which they are expected to support; PCs, the Windows Environment and Productivity Tools, Trouble-shooting and Problem-Solving.
3. Applications Training: being involved in the development group's systems life-cycle.

Communication is key – the future Help Desk

The Help Desk of the future will function in a proactive, bi-directional communication style, rather than the reactive, single-direction mode whereby the user informs the Help Desk of problems. The systems monitoring tools mentioned above will announce general systems and operations conditions through automated voice messages.

The future process is designed to provide information to the customer in a variety of ways, rather than simply via direct interaction with a phone agent. If the automated method fails, the customer will transfer to an agent who specializes in handling specific customer groups. The direct connection between the customer and the specialized agent is handled through a menu option in the automated voice messaging system.

Help Desk statistics and performance metrics

Statistics and performance metrics of the Help Desk will also change in the future. The information will be much more accessible to a broad spectrum of personnel. The information will be on a more real-time basis, and will be integrated with a system to allow graphical presentation. Temporal measurements such as call volume, response time, hold time, resolution time, etc. are captured as events occur and immediately recorded. As the queue of callers for a particular category of problems increases, agents specializing in other areas will be alerted to assist in accepting calls.

The customer will be able to provide feedback to the Help Desk through the automated voice messaging system. This has features which allow it to elicit and record answers to customer satisfaction questions. Scores are automatically tabulated and made available for management reporting.

Help Desk systems development life-cycle

The future Help Desk agent will be directly involved in the design, test and user acceptance phases of the systems development life-cycle. This is important since the agent will eventually provide support for that system end-user. The agent will verify the accuracy of help guides or manuals developed for the application. Enlisting the help of the Help Desk agent to review these materials can provide invaluable feedback to the development team. Any improvements to the applications help material will decrease the number of phone calls to the Help Desk.

Help Desk performance measurements

Part of the change management process is continuous improvement. To measure process performance accurately, metrics need to be established and monitored. The 'metrics', or performance measurements, are based on industry standards and the reporting requirements of the management team. The overall goal is to gather information as feedback into the decision-making process in order continuously to

Table 6.2 Examples of Help Desk performance measures

Area of activity	*Achievement*
Total calls received per day	Total calls abandoned
Total Help Desk incident reports (IRs) per day	Percentage of IRs resolved by Help Desk phone agent
Total batch production IRs per shift (3rd)	Percentage of first-call resolutions
Average time to closure	Number of outstanding IRs
Clarity	The language used in the Help Desk products and services should be concise and clear
Suitability	Procedures should be developed in a way that considers the environment in which they will be used
Correctness	Similar to above More associated with situation appropriateness
Efficiency	Knowledge of the customer drives the language used to accomplish problem-solving objectives
Completeness	What is the number of 'incoming call-backs?' Resolving the problem rather than the symptoms Doing it right the first time
Consistency	No matter which agent a caller speaks with, the answer should be the same There should not be a disparate skill level among agents

monitor and improve performance. Some of the elements of performance measurement are shown in Table 6.2.

In addition to measurements, there are statistics tracking online systems availability and network availability. The automotive company monitors 'up time' in the following countries: Brazil, Canada, Germany, Mexico and South Africa. There is a direct correlation between the performance of systems, networks and applications, and the number of calls the Help Desk receives.

Best in class statistics investigation benefits the K to K project

Since the K to K effort was worldwide, the Team anticipated that there was perhaps something to be gained by investigating 'what's out there'. To this end, they visited a 'sister' subsidiary in the UK and examined its supporting hardware and software systems, trying to ascertain what this company did and how it did it. Likewise, they investigated several other top car manufactures, including Mercedes, Toyota, Land Rover and Cadillac. They discovered that not one of these companies was using a commercial, off-the-shelf package. With that knowledge, the Team focused their attention on the systems that other importers used, potentially so that the automotive company could make use of and adopt one of them. However, after additional analysis and further consideration, the conclusion was that the company needed to develop its own, home-grown system.

Other organizations were highly cooperative with the study by the company's re-engineering team's. According to a Perot Systems associate, there was 'a pretty good spirit of cooperation within the industry'. Representatives from these other companies discussed systems and concepts such as customer order and a vehicle pool concept. In effect, the Team conducted a benchmarking study insofar as they were comparing the same information across companies, although not with comparable data.

The impact on the organization and its people – after the change initiative

Directional shift: operations and technology

In serving its customers better, the North American automobile importer and distributor designed a multi-phased rollout of a business solution to put technology in the hands of people working in the field. The field representatives were equipped with instant voice and data communications with corporate offices and host-based systems. This, in effect, provided the field service representatives with the ability to order, supply, negotiate and otherwise support the customer almost instantaneously. Needless to say, empowerment in making decisions, acting and reacting responsibly was a critical BPR recommendation implemented in the field as well as in the company's internal operations and management.

The business solution involved placing key account executives into the field. The field representatives are supported by small expert teams to facilitate rapid response and high service levels for customers, which for this company were both dealers and car owners. This approach required a dramatic reorganization of the business, including closing zones or 'regional' offices. The automobile importer and distributor defined and implemented the key mobile computing and communication technologies required to make this strategy successful.

The field teams are organized as shown in Figure 6.1. Each team member has a standard set of hardware and software to allow connection to the company business centre. This technical suite is currently deployed and operational for 200 people in the United States and Canada. It consists of the hardware and software shown in Table 6.3. The field computing device connectivity is being rolled out in three phases. During Phase I, the systems communicate via dial-in to CompuServe at 14.4 Mbps. This provides access to all current corporate systems. During Phase II, CompuServe will be replaced with a modem pool to enable remote LAN access at 28.8 Mbps, and it will finally be upgraded to wireless during Phase III in 1996. In addition to these

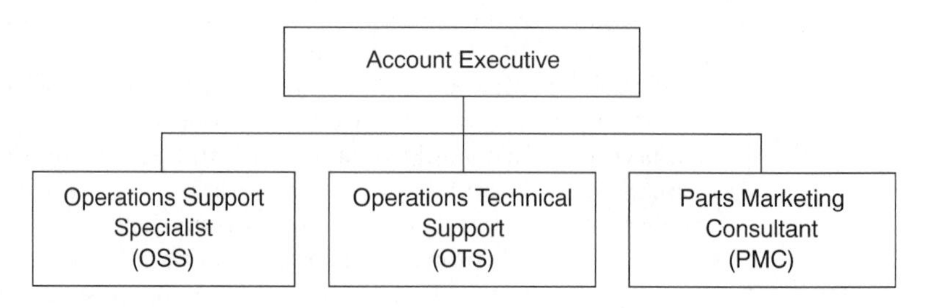

Figure 6.1 Key account field team structure.

Table 6.3 IT to support the field team

Hardware	*Software*
IBM ThinkPad model 755C, 510 MB hard drive, 20 MB RAM, and active colour, plus 14.4 Mbps modem to be upgraded to 28.8 Mbps by mid-1995	Microsoft Office Professional Suite
Text Pager	NFS/FTP software to enable TCP/IP file transfer capability
Fax/scanner/copier machine	MS Mail with both X.400 and memo capability
Mobile printer	GUI applications developed using FoxPro, Access and Cognos Powerplay, as appropriate
Voice mail	Skyward enables people to type text messages on a computer to send out (individually or to distribution lists) to the field
Cellular phone	Currently evaluating Windows 95 functionality as possible operating system candidate; if Windows 95 is not selected, Perot Systems will implement Windows for Workgroups

Note: FTP = file transfer protocol, GUI = graphical user interface, NFS = network file system.

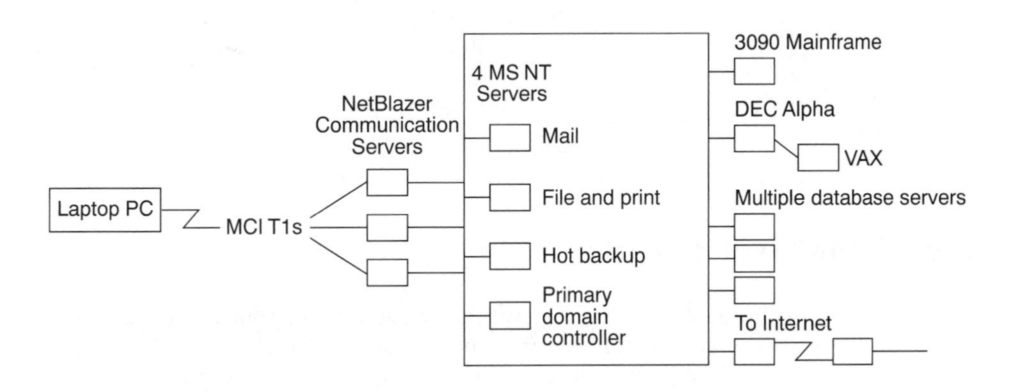

Figure 6.2 Wide area network configuration.

technologies, the automotive company incorporated video conferencing and video PC conferencing abilities to a subset of the 200 field sales personnel.

The company and Perot Systems jointly designed the network configuration capable of handling the connectivity requirements and transaction volumes expected from the mobile field workforce. The future wide area network (WAN) configuration is shown in Figure 6.2. In response to badly needed technological upgrades, Perot Systems furnished the applications development and operations to support the automobile importer and distributor's business. Consequently, Perot Systems assumed responsibility for the ongoing maintenance and support of the Account Executive system beyond its contribution in the areas of design and implementation. This level of involvement varied depending on the requirements for the different projects. One critical attribute of this project was defining and successfully integrating a highly complex, multiple-vendor solution on time and within budget.

Directional shift: functionality

A key discovery made in the K to K BPR study was the vehicle pool concept uncovered through meetings with other company executives. The concept of pooling vehicles in close proximity to dealerships would enable the dealers to trim down their inventory.

The pilot studies done as part of the BPR proved that the pool concept functioned and operated. In order to get to that step, the BPR team completed a requirements document and invited other groups, including the systems design team, to review the document and provide feedback. The next phase of the project was completing the General Design Document and defining the systems needed to support the defined processes. Part of this phase was selecting several key elements of the re-engineering effort and beginning to pilot them. The pilot project was started in May 1996 in Georgia. Another pilot study in Chicago, Illinois, should be complete during 1997.

Algorithms were tweaked, enabling vehicles to be delivered in the appropriate timeframe. This involved the accuracy of the order to the factory, a change in the vehicle delivery process, the realm of the K to K project. Vehicles for a customer could be delivered in two days, and inventory could be replaced in five days. These numbers represent an improvement of almost 100 per cent.

Some consider the dealer as the company's customer; others consider the purchaser as the ultimate end-customer. Although not all company employees and executives agree on the definition of the 'customer', everyone downstream from the manufacturing process benefits from changes made in the vehicle distribution process as a result of the BPR study.

Key learning points

The involvement and enthusiastic support of company management helped make the re-engineering effort a smooth and successful one. Re-engineering studies of several individual departments paved the way for more in-depth and complex re-engineering projects. The plan as laid out earlier remains in effect. Projects with the highest priority for exposure and impact on the customer were implemented first, followed by re-engineering efforts for other departments.

The automobile importer and distributor grasped the need for change, and, importantly, understood that change would not occur overnight. Company management determined that they would tackle the various re-engineering efforts with a gradual approach as resources permitted and need dictated. From the outset, management planned to devote the necessary personnel to implement the project. Of necessity this meant that the employee would not be able to conduct business as usual in whatever capacity she or he had previously been employed. Underlying the company attitude was a steady, determined commitment to achieving the final goal of the re-engineering effort.

Another integral factor in the company's successful re-engineering effort was the eagerness of management to learn about the concept, benefits and 'how-to's' of the re-engineering process. One of the company's IT managers was selected as the re-engineering 'proponent'. That manager attended training offered by the renowned

Michael Hammer and studied the practices of creative thinkers such as Edward DeBono. In conjunction with the consultant expertise provided by Perot Systems, the proponent hosted an onsite class for company managers and employees taught by Perot Systems analysts. The class went beyond an introduction to the concepts of business re-engineering and focused on specific activities of the automotive company.

Reflecting the cooperation of the company/Perot Systems Team, two company employees who were focusing on re-engineering analysis attended the quarterly Perot Systems BPR meeting in Dallas, Texas. This participation provided the company with an insight into the current research, techniques and latest findings employed by re-engineering experts. The conference offered an ideal opportunity for Perot associates to acquire information, ideas and impressions from 'the Customer', while exposing the automotive company's re-engineering specialists to other techniques and experiences from projects discussed at the meeting.

The initial plan was to utilize the talent of experienced re-engineering experts and then eventually to train company staff and use them to support the continued re-engineering projects. This was the strategy used by the company and has proven to be the route to continued success. At the same time, as the company's re-engineering staff have followed through on successive re-engineering projects, they have ascertained the need for their expertise in other projects. In the spirit of a true partnership, the company hired a key Perot Systems associate to continue assisting in the BPR studies and implementation of crucial BPR initiatives, ensuring continued success.

As with most major change efforts, in retrospect certain aspects could have been handled differently and perhaps more expeditiously. Two salient factors in the initial re-engineering project would have smoothed the effort. First, in the Field Operations re-engineering project, roles and responsibilities were not clearly defined. The staff were primarily located at the head office, with regular hours and well-established routines. The new role engendered by the re-engineering project differed vastly from that of the office environment. The staff were to be deployed in the 'field' and were to interface directly with customers, dealers and other industry personnel.

Coupled with the change of environment was the changed mode of operation. The field representatives also had to learn how to operate new technology. The fact that many of the field representatives required advanced technology to support the new method of operation, even though some of them may not have been technically experienced, is the second factor that could have been implemented differently in the re-engineering effort. Even after training courses, it was apparent that the field representatives were much better trained on the system than they were in the process.

In the future, the re-engineering effort would benefit by including a skills summary indicating the requisite skills people would need to operate high-tech equipment. Individuals also would benefit from knowing what was expected of them in the new position and could evaluate the future scenario accordingly. If they had been given a choice, some of the field engineers might have opted to change positions. On the other hand, many of the field representatives with little or no prior computer experience have excelled in learning the new systems and processes and continue to bring a fresh perspective to their positions.

Benchmarking statistics would have been extremely useful in creating more efficient processes. Comparisons with other companies both in and outside the industry would be helpful in determining just how far to go. At a minimum, it would be useful to establish a baseline to determine the current metrics and to create a standard to measure future changes. The automotive company could have used data in both categories in assessing the degree of success in the initial effort.

Summary and conclusions

The partnership between the company and Perot Systems has been highly successful. The hopeful attitude of the company's employees, coupled with their resolution to make change happen so as to become a more prosperous company, was an important factor in the partnership. Employees at the automotive company did not perceive Perot Systems as the people with the black hats who were going to cut expenses – and, most likely, jobs.

Several major changes in the company preceded the enterprise-wide re-engineering effort at the automotive company. The approach was one of 'change, then accommodate change' in some managers' minds. In any case, the re-engineering projects were well planned and executed. When the Perot Systems manager was asked what single factor was most critical in ensuring the success of the re-engineering project, he called unequivocally for a 'champion for change' in the organization, one who unswervingly supports the study with vision for the improved interfaces, systems and communications.

Much still remains to be done at the company, however. The effort has proceeded more slowly than initially planned. However, the approach is solid and well focused and the company is pleased with the results to date.

Due to the delay in implementing some of the projects, the initial assumptions and conditions upon which conclusions were drawn have changed in several instances. Before embarking on a re-engineering project for which the study has been conducted some eighteen months previously, the company's re-engineering specialists must thoroughly review and evaluate statistics to ensure the approach most appropriate to existing systems and processes.

Ashley Braganza and Andrew Myers

7

How can organizations be successful in implementation?

Issues to consider

What are the key issues that need to be addressed in order to achieve a successful change initiative? The survey undertaken by Cranfield School of Management at one of its annual BPR symposiums (as described in Chapter 1) has documented some useful evidence as to what organizations have accomplished when undertaking a re-engineering initiative. It indicates the importance they attach to a number of key issues and the level of difficulty they perceive in achieving positive outcomes to these during the implementation of a project.

The study undertaken at Cranfield set about analysing critical success factors or key issues when implementing BPR. These factors are shown in Table 7.1. These factors, which are basically drawn from the current literature and conversations with practitioners in the field, were identified to quantify the relative importance that each participant attending the symposium attached to them in the implementation of a re-engineering initiative. In order to measure this, scores were registered on a seven-point scale (ranging from 1 = not important to 7 = very important). Participants were also asked how difficult it was to achieve each of the factors. A seven-point scale was again used here (ranging from 1 = not difficult to 7 = very difficult).

The mean scores for each of the criteria shown in Table 7.1 above were calculated.

Table 7.1 Critical success factors in relation to BPR

Steering group	Cross-functional BPR team
Cultural change	Attitude change
Behaviour change	BPR pilot
Process modelling tools	External consultancy
Internal communication	Chief Executive commitment
Functional director buy-in	Cost-benefit analysis
Identifying intangible benefits	Changing the roles of functions
Changing reward systems	Changing individuals' assessments
Providing staff with different skills	Reducing headcount
Changing reporting lines	Introducing team working

The results show the level of importance and difficulty each individual respondent attached to each criteria. These importance and difficulty dimensions are displayed in Figure 7.1. On inspection, the items would appear to link up in the figure into five definable groupings, namely induction; providing skills; changing roles and systems; commitment; and culture, attitudes and behaviour.

Induction

Undertaking a cost-benefit analysis and setting up a cross-functional steering group have been highlighted by a number of the theoretical arguments in the literature. We have defined such issues as 'induction'. They are issues that should be fairly straightforward to achieve and are therefore not thought of as critical issues. One could, however, describe them as 'hygiene'-type factors; in other words, if they are not developed from the outset, problems may be encountered in later stages.

Providing skills

A second grouping includes changing individuals' assessments, providing staff with different skills and introducing teamwork. Respondents indicate that these are important issues, yet they are rarely dealt with in any depth. However, it is likely that if the assistance of external consultants was sought, a number of these issues would have been dealt with.

Commitment to the project

A lack of commitment could be a potential threat to the success of a re-engineering project. A conflict of views and poor communication of intentions within the organization would make one question the serious commitment of an organization to such an important initiative.

The importance of the role of the CEO has been well documented in the literature. The Cranfield survey supports this, but gaining CEO commitment, although important, is not a sufficient condition for the effective implementation of a re-engineering

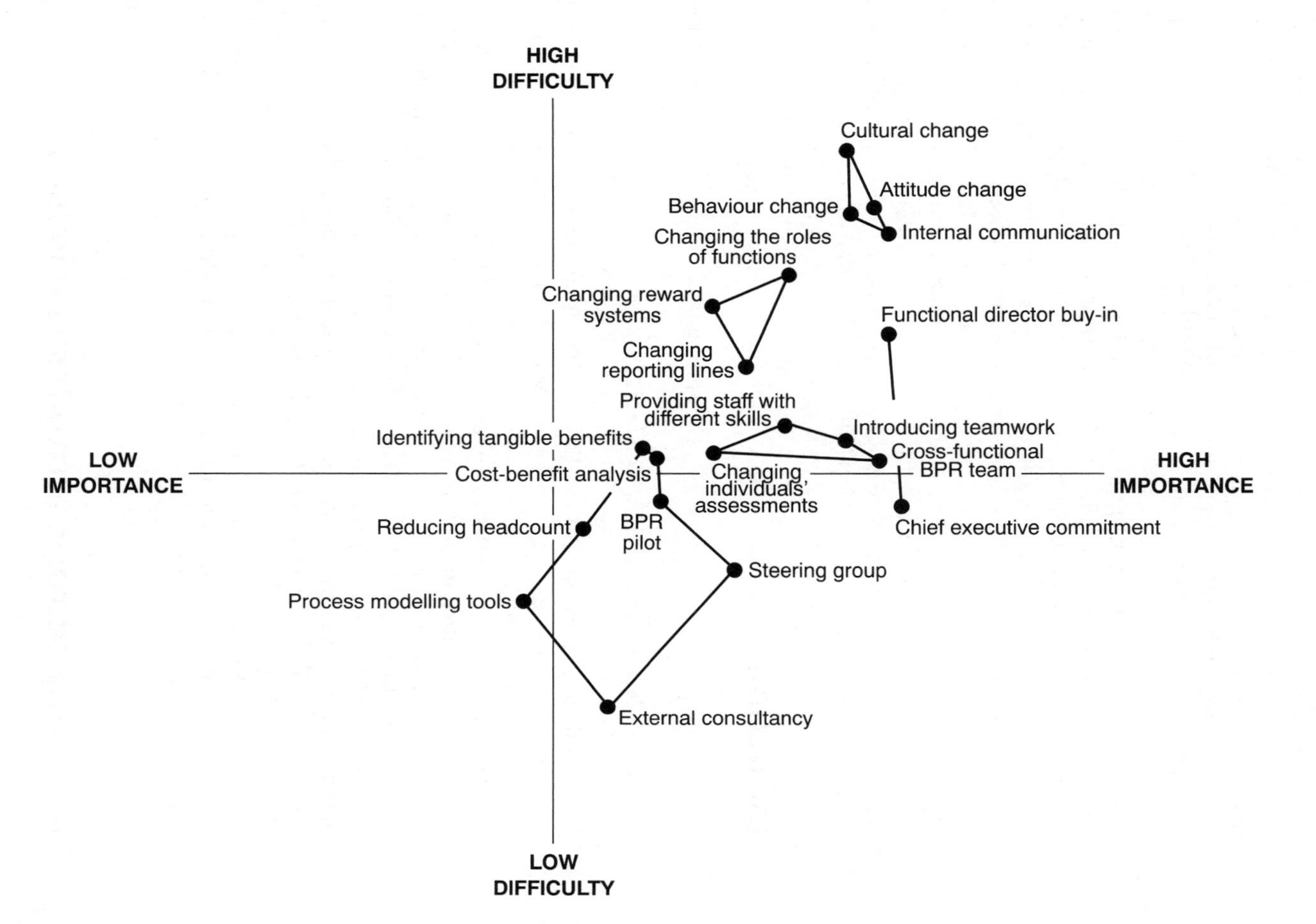

Figure 7.1 Critical success factors.

initiative. A lack of commitment to such an initiative may also arise if managers find it difficult to accept the changes proposed. A lack of support at different levels within the organization is likely to be problematic, more so if the discussion centres on whether the change is to be incremental or radical. If consensus is not obtained the likelihood of the re-engineering initiative not achieving its expected outcomes is much greater: 'Without a clear, shared view about the proper level of radicalism early on, management expectations will vary . . . making disappointment likely and confusion inevitable' (Heygate 1993: 80).

At higher levels within the organizations taking part in the survey, there seems to be a fairly high-level of awareness of re-engineering. Does this mean that there is commitment to the re-engineering initiative? There was a significant perceived gap between the relative ease of gaining the CEO's commitment when compared to gaining the same degree of commitment from the functional managers. Such managers may feel that if the organization is moving towards a process approach they may potentially lose 'parts of their empire'. In such circumstances they are likely to defend their patch. This highlights a potential problem that managers have to combat when attempting to re-engineer. It could also have implications in the long run; how long can the CEO sustain commitment to the re-engineering initiative when the managers may be somewhat dubious or against it? It is therefore necessary, in the early stages of the implementation process, for functional managers to 'buy in' to the initiative. A shared view is fundamental to success.

Changing roles and systems

The Cranfield survey also shows the relative importance of changing the roles of functions, reporting lines and reward systems. Achieving such changes is also shown not to be an easy task. The success of the re-engineering initiative is likely to depend to a great extent on these factors, mainly because they will have an effect on how individuals and functions are likely to perform, and also on the part they play in influencing the attitudes and behaviour of people within the organization, which, in turn, could impact upon the ensuing culture of the organization.

Kerr and Slocum (1987) recognize that reward systems are not a remedy. They identify, in a qualitative study of fourteen organizations, that changing reward systems provide a powerful method of adapting the behaviour and attitudes of employees. They conclude that organizational cultures can be changed gradually through changes in performance criteria and reward systems. Reward and recognition mechanisms 'reinforce the values and norms that comprise corporate culture' (Kerr and Slocum 1987: 106).

Changing culture, attitudes and behaviour

The survey results show that it is difficult to transform the culture and change peoples' attitudes and behaviours, and that it is important to do so. This supports what is already known from the literature. As cultural change is often viewed as the main determinant of a re-engineering initiative, it is therefore necessary that the initiative is effectively communicated to everyone within the organization.

Effective communication often elicits trust from the employees. Peters and Waterman (1982) state that employees react more quickly and better to change when they feel that the organization has created a culture that they relate to and can be part of. Kerr and Slocum argue that changing the culture of an organization is not straightforward:

> Culture itself is rooted in the countless details of organizational life. How decisions are made, how conflict is resolved, how careers are managed – each small incident serves to convey some aspect of the organization's culture to those involved. Given the pervasiveness of culture, it is not surprising that managers are frequently frustrated in their attempts to change it.
>
> (Kerr and Slocum 1987: 106)

One could therefore argue that re-engineering may not be entirely successful as changes in the organization's culture are not fully realized. Achieving changes in culture, attitude and behaviour is perhaps more likely to be influenced by factors such as changing reporting lines, skills and team-working. As re-engineering is about cross-functional change, it is not unreasonable to assume that when the CEO and functional managers have committed to the initiative, changing the roles of the functions, reporting lines and skills is likely to make implementation that much more successful. Once these changes have been adopted, the culture, peoples' attitudes and behaviour are likely to change, but it has to be recognized that this could be a lengthy process.

Indicators

The results of the Cranfield survey highlight some useful indicators for other organizations contemplating a re-engineering initiative. Key issues need to be well managed when implementing a re-engineering initiative:

- gaining the commitment of functional managers and the management team;
- effectively communicating the change process and its effects on individuals within the organization;
- changing the reward systems/structures;
- shifting reporting lines from a vertical direction to a more horizontal one;
- providing employees with a wider range of skills;
- using teams to satisfy the needs of customers.

Too often the focus appears to have been on changing the culture of an organization. Where the above issues are considered, change could be introduced much more successfully.

Lessons learned from the cases

The previous section gives critical success indicators for organizations undertaking a re-engineering initiative. Although this is a useful source of information, it does not go into depth as to what is specific to a particular organization. To the reader, what should be evident from the cases, which was not apparent in the survey reported in the previous section, is the importance of people in the change process – keeping them informed, understanding how it can impact on them, understanding their possible anxieties, etc. Not taking people's feelings or the impact of the change on them into account could also explain why some initiatives have been unsuccessful.

This section summarizes the key learning points or messages from each of the cases. The learning points vary between the cases, as the context described in the preceding chapters for each change is different.

At **Texas Instruments** Janis identified a number of key learning points centred around the team. The lessons learned and pointers for those wishing to undertake a similar initiative are as follows:

- have a diverse team, not only in skills, but in personality;
- you must have a strong, humble, open team leader;
- be prepared to deal with the team dynamics;
- be aware of the pessimists and opportunists that may be disguised as team members;
- be on the lookout for team members sent with the objective of derailing the team;
- plan for the unpopularity of the re-engineering team;
- plan celebration points;
- define roles for team members;
- be prepared for the team, as well as individual team members, to move through the change cycle at different rates and different times;
- the outsiders can be equal participants or facilitators depending on the situation and the culture;
- be prepared for the natural team transition points in the project;
- celebrate and capitalize on failures;
- the business, not the team, must get the credit for all the victories;
- the best you can hope for is about 70 per cent of what you set out to accomplish, but be prepared to recognize and acknowledge the 30 per cent you do not get.

The lessons learned from **Rank Xerox** were mainly to do with managing the change process itself:

- create and deploy a unified vision;
- constantly review the management process;
- apply process change methods;
- implement quality initiatives;
- empowerment is a force for a change;
- process performance measurement is essential;
- measurement acts as a basis for monitoring change.

The areas that worked well for **First Direct** centred around:

- an effective steering group;
- development of positive links with line managers;
- the mapping of processes;
- the use of focus groups;
- recognition of the importance of implementation;
- a good team mix.

Tom also identified areas to watch out for:

- assess the expectations and how these are to be met;

- qualify the targets;
- recognize the importance of working as a team;
- develop parallel working;
- manage the decision-making process and implementation well.

At **Robert Bosch** the lessons learned over time include the need to:

- research and plan the changes;
- fine-tune the plan as you go along;
- anticipate the increase in costs and risk to the business;
- focus on critical areas;
- manage the commitment of other departments.

At **the automotive company** the key messages arising from the change initiative were:

- when employing outside consultants, operating as a partnership is essential to the initiative's success;
- be actively involved and supportive of the initiative;
- recognize that change will not happen overnight – change, then accommodate change;
- gain commitment from and work with various functions;
- ensure that the message is communicated effectively;
- ensure that people will be sufficiently trained in the new environment;
- have a champion for change.

So what?

Why should managers decide to take their organizations through the pain, frustration and trauma that is experienced when implementing BPR? The cases, specifically the benefits gained by the organizations, discussed in the earlier chapters provide part of the answer. Many authors recount examples of organizations that were able to secure their survival or substantially improve service levels, decrease cycle times or substantially increase market share and profitability substantially, or achieve sustainable competitive advantage. These are substantial benefits, and it could be argued that managers will be judged increasingly by their ability to deliver such benefits.

Hence managers need to be able to maintain and enhance their organization's performance. In retrospect, organizations shifted from a functional to a process orientation as a major flaw became evident in an attempt to cope with today's pressures. Yet we are led to believe that process organizations will be able to cope better with future pressures. How can managers be certain that the process organizations they create today will not become as ossified in the future as the functional organizations they replace.

We are continuously reminded that we live in an epoch of continuous change. However, the nature and drivers of the changes are also changing. For example, even until a few years ago it was possible for an organization to identify its competitors clearly. Yet, in industry after industry, the traditional boundaries of competition are blurring. Take the financial services sector as an example: a few years ago managers from a large bank would perceive their competitors to be other large banks or building societies. Today the banks compete with Marks and Spencer, a clothing and food retailer, for personal loans and pensions; Virgin, the airline to beverages organization, for personal equity plans; General Motors and high-street retailers (many of whom are their customers) for credit cards and product-related loans such as car loans. In the cola industry, until recently Coca-Cola considered Pepsi as its major rival. In the UK today Coca-Cola competes for consumer taste buds against Sainsbury's, one of its customers. The speed with which information is acquired, processed and converted to meaningful action is having a major impact on organizations. Tesco, the UK's largest food retailer, introduced loyalty cards for its customers. The organization is potentially able to gather and analyse the purchases of individual consumers and offer discount vouchers on products that match the consumer's preferences. Clearly the loyalty cards could have a longer-term impact on the manufacturer–retailer relationship. For example, many of the discount vouchers are for brand products, yet large retailers could substitute brand discount vouchers with those that supported their own 'house' label. Mass customization comes to the retail grocery trade.

Given that today's organizations operate in a rapidly changing environment, what future changes face managers? Only the brave (or foolhardy) would venture to suggest what they thought would be the top five issues organizations are likely to face in the next five years. Perhaps, then, organizations face a future that is best described by words such as 'the unknown', 'uncertain', and 'unanticipated'.

Managers need to create organizations that can endure unknown and unanticipated situations. These organizations are likely to be able to exploit the opportunities created by changing circumstances. A process-based organization provides a potentially sound foundation upon which to build a flexible organization. We refer to such an organization as the 'conscious-action organization'. We use the word 'conscious' as we wish to convey the notion that such an organization would have a sense of shared purpose, that it would be alert to the most subtle changes in its external and internal situation, and that it would have the capacity to reflect upon these changes in order to reach a reasoned conclusion. We use the word 'action' to indicate that the flexible organization needs to bring to bear energy, influence, performance and motion to convert the outcomes of the project to benefits and results for the organization. Our initial research based upon the work of Morgan (1986) indicates that the conscious-action organization would display three features.

The first feature is the relationship between the whole and the parts of the organization. In essence, the aim is to create an organization in which each process is able to satisfy the needs or expectations of a stakeholder in the business. Stakeholders include, among others, customers, employees, suppliers and regulators. In a world with no resource constraints, the ideal organization would consist of a set of self-contained processes, each of which had its own unique activities. Each process would have a process owner with control over all the resources in the process. However, as all organizations face increasingly demanding constraints upon resource utilization, re-engineering presents managers with an opportunity to design processes that co-ordinate all the activities necessary to satisfy the stakeholder. All the activities need not necessarily take place in the process or within the organization. Thus, while some activities may remain centralized – e.g. accounts payable and training – and others are outsourced – e.g. logistics and IT developments – these activities would be integral to each process. The outcome of this feature is that all the activities (parts of the organization) necessary to satisfy stakeholders are brought together virtually into a set of processes (the whole organization).

Consider the distinction between the whole/parts relationship in the conscious-action organization just described and that in the functional organization. The functional organization is fractured into activities which are focused around expertise. Thus no individual activity can deliver the organization's products or services to its customers or satisfy the needs of other stakeholders.

The second feature is the capacity to specialize and generalize. By this we mean that individuals need to be specialists in their particular sphere of activity. Yet they need to be sufficiently generalist so that they can deal with another activity should they be required to do so. This feature is found in certain roles today; for example, bank clerks are able to serve as cashiers, open accounts, process loan applications and issue travellers' cheques. At more senior levels this feature manifests itself in the ability to understand the implications for one activity of decisions taken in another activity. This feature needs to be built into the processes at two levels. First, within each process a marketing manager should be able to understand the implications of a particular campaign upon manufacturing and logistics so that she or he are prepared to meet increased demand. Second, between processes the implications of changes effected in one process are passed on to other processes. Moreover, the shape, extent and location of areas of specialization and generalization need to change over a period of time to reflect the pressures driving the organization.

Again, the distinction between this type of organization and the functional organization is manifest. Each function performs a unique activity and these are carried out by experts. Spare capacity in one area cannot be transferred easily to another which is short-staffed. The focus upon one dimension, specialization, also leads to comments such as 'this is not my job' and 'this is my customer'. Also, there is a greater propensity to focus upon what is correct for one function, and managers often make decisions which are wholly consistent within their function but have adverse consequences elsewhere in the organization.

The third feature is the pattern of connectivity. This feature encapsulates the effective management of information flows and knowledge across the organization. The capacity of organizations to deal with hitherto unknown challenges may be hindered by poor management of information. A telling illustration is the number of electronic mail messages managers receive each day. We discovered that one manager received over 250 messages in the course of one week; that was after his secretary deleted those she considered non-essential! This manager estimated that fewer than fifteen of the 250 would be of interest to him, and that five would be important. Yet the time it would take him to find the five made it impractical to look. In another organization 'really important memos' were sent by paper – not electronic mail. It would be easy to blame the technology which makes apparent the symptom of the problem. The underlying cause is that managers have given insufficient thought to creating patterns of connectivity.

Managers need to create patterns of connectivity so that information can be absorbed by any part of the organization, at all times, and individuals have a level of awareness which allows them to assess which information is most relevant. This implies that people need to be sensitive to and understand different parts of the organization. Before patterns of connectivity can be put in place, several questions need to be answered, such as how important is this information? To whom in the organization would it be useful? And when would it be useful? While this feature is not a call to control every aspect of the organization's information flows, managers need to identify critical pieces of information and ensure these are dealt with sensibly.

The capacity to innovate rests upon the continuous conversion of information into knowledge, as knowledge is critical to meaningful action. Managers need to create patterns of connectivity at the level of a single process and between processes. Clearly, once an organization successfully acts upon knowledge in one process, this knowledge should be transferred to other processes. Consider the example of a well-known multinational company. This organization designed a manufacturing process that spanned several functions, including raw material acquisition, manufacturing, plant operations, warehousing (raw materials and finished goods) and delivery. The manufacturing process was implemented in different geographic regions. One region found a more efficient way of dealing with the quality of raw materials. As the organization had no way of transferring such knowledge between processes the benefits remained isolated in one region. Patterns of connectivity act as an integrative mechanism which facilitates the co-ordination and control of otherwise potentially complex and detailed operations in the organization.

The cultural, systems and structural issues that would be unique to the conscious-action organization still need to be understood. Yet organizations are pursuing one or more feature intuitively, for example multi-skilling, and cross-functional teams. By understanding and co-ordinating the work being done in each feature, the organization is more likely to gain benefits.

It would be a pity for organizations to attempt re-engineering and become one of the four which fail rather than the one which succeeds. The experiences and lessons in each case will give managers insights and ideas to reverse the ratio so that fewer than one in five fail. Successful BPR will take organizations beyond strategic advantage; it will take organizations to the higher plane of flexibility.

List of contributors

Ashley Braganza

Ashley Braganza has been with the Cranfield School of Management in the Information Systems (IS) Group since May 1991. He is involved in all major business process redesign (BPR) initiatives at Cranfield. Ashley was appointed the director of a seven-day management programme on BPR. He has established a major industry-funded research project in the area of BPR. He is also the director of an annual BPR symposium for senior managers. Ashley is retained by a number of organizations, advising them on BPR issues.

He joined the IS Group in 1991 to research the managerial aspects of electronic data interchange (EDI). The key areas of responsibility were the financial and commercial aspects of EDI. Ashley managed two studies which formed a key part of the EDI project. First, the supply chain study, which examined the impact EDI has on the flow of goods through a typical supply chain. This included BP Chemicals, Procter and Gamble, and ASDA. Second, an international payments study. The purpose of this study was to work with two major European banks (ABN AMRO Bank and Union Bank of Switzerland) and about twenty multinational corporates to identify future payment services banks could provide using EDI and other state of the art technologies.

Since joining Cranfield Ashley has collaborated on a project to win a European Commission contract on EDI and Financial Operations. This pan-European project (twelve EC and six European Free Trade Association (EFTA) countries) involved examining the current position of electronic banking and financial EDI, and their development over the next five years. Ashley examined six countries: UK, Switzerland, Austria, Greece, Ireland and Iceland.

Ashley completed an MBA at the Strathclyde Business School. He elected to specialize in corporate strategy and finance. His MBA thesis was an examination of mergers and acquisitions in the single European Market. Prior to that he completed the Chartered Institute of Bankers examinations. Ashley is currently working towards a PhD. His research focuses upon the 'people' aspects of BPR.

Andrew Myers

After completing his first degree at the University of Hull in 1985, Andrew Myers worked as a researcher at Cranfield. In his years at Cranfield he has gained experience in research design, methodology and analysis. He has worked on a number of cross-cultural research projects which have subsequently been published in academic and practitioner journals. He has also undertaken attitude and behaviour studies for a number of organizations.

Andrew is now working independently and one of his current areas of interest is BPR and its influence on people. At present he undertakes contract work for the human resources department at Cranfield, where he is also studying for his PhD.

Tom Ashworth

Tom is Head of Business Process Management for First Direct. His role is to improve the effectiveness of First Direct by challenging the way things are done, championing new approaches, and managing change projects. He started his career with British Airways, after gaining a degree from the University of Aberdeen. In the course of the subsequent ten years with the airline, Tom worked as an operational manager at overseas airports, returned to head office to take up a systems analysis role in a new marketing area, and then managed yield control for British Airways' domestic and Mediterranean routes, before becoming an internal management consultant.

He then worked in external consultancy, first with PE International, then with Crane Davis Ltd. His consultancy experience, specializing in service organizations, covers strategy development, change management, cost management, business planning, management training and development, quality and marketing.

Andy Balshaw

Andy has been an employee of Robert Bosch Ltd since 1980, holding positions in their Domestic Appliance Division and their Power Tools Division.

Andy's current responsibilities are the general management of after-sales for the Power Tools Division and as Business Development Manager within a region of the sales team. Andy has been instrumental in the planning and implementation of a recent strategy to bring after-sales service 'in house' at their Denham headquarters and phase out external service agents.

Within the same timescale he also sat on the Power Tools Divisional Board as part of the team which brought about single-tier sales distribution from its original two-tier distribution. He is an active member of the Bosch Power Tool Divisional Board and holds a Diploma in Management and a Diploma in Marketing.

Janis Jesse

Janis Jesse is the Director of Business and Strategic Services of Texas Instruments (TI). She has also served as the process owner of the Solutions Provisioning Process in Texas Instrument's Information Systems and Services Group and is on the Information Systems and Services Leadership Team. As Director she is responsible for Business Process Re-engineering, Business Process Improvement, Benchmarking, Office of Best Practices and Strategic Development work across all of TI. As Process Owner her responsibilities included managing the re-engineering effort to dramatically reduce cycle time for delivery of information technology to the businesses of TI. Duties on the Information Systems and Services Leadership Team include guiding operations and future direction of IT at Texas Instruments.

Prior to her current assignments, Janis spent three years on the much publicized Semiconductor Order Fulfilment Re-Engineering Team. This team achieved dramatic results from cycle time and variability reduction in the largest business unit of Texas Instruments.

She is a key contributor to institutionalizing business processes in all the business units and at the corporate level in Texas Instruments.

Melinda S. Pajak

Melinda Pajak has been a consultant with Perot Systems Corporation in Reston, Virginia, since June 1990. She is currently working as a program manager in telecommunications. As a member of Perot Systems' Business Re-engineering team within the Reston office, Melinda consulted on projects and spearheaded communications in that department. Melinda was formerly the internal communications manager at Perot Systems, editing and managing the corporate newsletter and other means of on-line communications for the corporation.

Melinda holds BA degrees in Rhetoric/Communications Studies and Psychology from the University of Virginia. She is currently working towards a Masters degree in Communications at George Mason University in Fairfax, Virginia.

Cedric Williams

After receiving a degree (BSc) from London University, Cedric Williams joined an orthopaedic engineering company with roles in inventory control and purchasing. In Rank Xerox Limited headquarters' information systems he progressed through systems analysis and systems management roles. Later he moved to an internal consultancy group working in Rank Xerox locations throughout Europe and, subsequently, in Xerox manufacturing and design centres in England.

Over the past four years, Cedric has concentrated on understanding, developing and implementing business process re-engineering and business process management in Rank Xerox (UK) Limited.

Note: Rick Solano's details withheld by request.

Further reading

Ascari, A., Rock, M. and Dutta, S. (1995) 'Re-engineering and Organizational Change: Lessons from a Comparative Analysis of Company Experiences', *European Management Journal* 13(1), pp. 1–30.

Alderson, W. (1965) *Dynamic Marketing Behavior: A Functionalist Theory of Marketing*, Homewood, IL: Richard D. Irwin.

Automotive News (1991a) 'AuctionNet Grows Rapidly in Its First Year', *Automotive News* 5412 (23 September), p. 79.

Automotive News (1991b) 'Program Cars Lure New-Car Dealers to Auction in Record Numbers', *Automotive News* 5412 (23 September), p. 80.

Barczak, G., Smith, C. and Wilemon, D. (1987) 'Managing Large-scale Organisational Change', *Organisational Dynamics* 16(2), pp. 23–35.

Bartlett, C. A. and Ghoshal, S. (1990) 'Matrix Management: Not a Structure, a Frame of Mind', *Harvard Business Review* (July–August), pp. 138–45.

Beckhard, R. and Harris, R. (1987) *Organizational Transitions*, 2nd edn, Addison Wesley, Reading, Mass.

Belmonte, R. W. and Murray, R. J. (1993) 'Getting Ready for Strategic Change', *Information Systems Management* (summer), pp. 23–9.

Benjamin, R. I. and Levinson, E. (1993) 'A Framework for Managing IT-enabled Change', *Sloan Management Review* (summer), pp. 23–33.

Blumer, H. (1970) 'Methodological Principles of Empirical Science', in N. Denzin (ed.) *Sociological Methods: A Sourcebook*, Butterworths, London.

Braganza, A. and Myers, A. (1996) 'Issues and Dilemmas Facing Organizations in the Effective Implementation of BPR', *Business Change and Re-Engineering, The Journal of Corporate Transformation* 3(2), pp. 38–51.

Bresnen, M. (1988) 'Insights on Site: Research into Construction Project Organisation, in A. Bryman (ed.) *Doing Research in Organizations*, Routledge, London.

Bryman, A. (ed.) (1988) 'Introduction: "Inside" Accounts and Social Research in Organizations', in *Doing Research in Organizations*, Routledge, London.

Buchanan, D. A. and Huczynski, A. A. (1985) *Organizational Behaviour*, Prentice-Hall, London.

Bulmer, M. (ed.) (1977) *Sociological Research Methods: An Introduction*, Macmillan, London.

Bulmer, M. (1988) 'Some Reflections upon Research in Organizations', in A. Bryman (ed.) *Doing Research in Organizations*, Routledge, London.

Burke, W. W. (1992) *Organization Development: Principles and Practices*, Little, Brown & Co., Boston.

Butler Cox Foundation (1991) 'The Role of Information Technology in Transforming the Business', *Research Report 79* (January).

Chait, P. L. and Lynch, A. J. (1995) 'Re-engineering Revisited: Achieving Seamlessness', *Prism*, (2nd quarter), pp. 23–9.

Clemons, E. K. (1995) 'Using Scenario Analysis to Manage the Strategic Risks of Re-engineering', *Sloan Management Review* (summer), pp. 61–71.

Columbus Despatched (1991) 'Automakers Endangered, Ford Exec Says', *Columbus Dispatch* (28 September), p. F1.

Copper, R. and Kaplan, R. S. (1988) 'Measure Costs Right: Make The Right Decisions', *Harvard Business Review* (September–October), pp. 96–103.

Coulson-Thomas, C. (1992) *Transforming The Company: Bridging the Gap between Management Myth and Corporate Reality*, Kogan Page, London.

Crompton, R. and Jones, G. (1988) 'Researching White Collar Organizations: Why Sociologists Should not Stop Doing Case Studies', in A. Bryman (ed.) *Doing Research in Organizations*, Routledge, London.

CSC Index (1994) *State of Re-engineering Report*, Executive Summary.

Dahler-Larsen, P. (1994) 'Corporate Culture and Morality: Durkheim-inspired Reflections on the Limits of Corporate Culture', *Journal of Management Studies* 31(1), pp. 1–18.

Davenport, T. (1993) *Process Innovation: Re-engineering Work Through Information Technology*, Harvard Business School Press, Boston.

Davenport, T. and Nohria, N. (1994) 'Case Management and the Integration of Labor', *Sloan Management Review* (winter), pp. 11–23.

Davenport, T. H. and Short J. E. (1990) 'The New Industrial Engineering: Information Technology and Business Process Redesign', *Sloan Management Review* (summer), pp. 11–27.

Davenport, T. H., Eccles R. G. and Prusak, L. (1992) 'Information Politics', *Sloan Management Review* (fall), pp. 53–65.

Deal, T. (1986) 'Cultural Change: Opportunity, Silent Killer or Metamorphosis', in R. Kilmann, M. J. Saxton and R. Serpa (eds) *Gaining Control of Corporate Culture*, Jossey-Bass, San Francisco.

Deal, T. and Kennedy, A. (1982) *Corporate Cultures*, Addison-Wesley, Reading, Mass.

Denzin, N. (ed.) (1970a) *Sociological Methods: A Sourcebook*, Butterworths, London.

Denzin, N. K. (1970b) 'Triangulation; A Case for Methodological Evaluation and Combination: Introduction', *Sociological Methods: A Sourcebook*, Butterworths, London.

Dichter, S. F., Gagnon, C. and Alexander, A. (1993) 'Memo to a CEO: Leading Organizational Transformations', *The McKinsey Quarterly* (1) pp. 89–106.

Drucker, P. F. (1988) 'The Coming of the New Organization', *Harvard Business Review* (January–February), pp. 45–53.

Duck, J. D. (1993) 'Managing Change: The Art of Balancing', *Harvard Business Review* (November–December), pp. 109–18.

Dunkerley, D. (1988) 'Historical Methods and Organization Analysis: The Case of a Naval Dockyard', in A. Bryman (ed.) *Doing Research in Organizations*, Routledge, London.

Easterby-Smith, B., Thorpe, R. and Lowe, A. (1991) *Management Research: An Introduction*, Sage Publications, London.

Ernst & Young/ICL (1992) *Process Innovation – The UK View*, London: Ernst & Young.

Galbraith, J. R. 'Strategy and Organization Planning', in H. Mintzberg and J. B. Quinn, (eds) *The Strategy Process: Concepts, Contexts, Cases*, 2nd edn, Prentice Hall, Englewood Cliffs, N.J.

Gilberto, P. A. (1993) 'The Road to Business Process Improvement – Can You Get There From Here?', *Production and Inventory Management Journal* (3rd quarter), pp. 80–6.

Greenwald, J. (1992) 'What Went Wrong?', *Time* (9 November), p. 42.

Gulden, G. K. and Reck, R. H. (1992) 'Combining Quality and Re-engineering Efforts for Process Excellence', *Information Strategy: The Executive's Journal* (spring), pp. 11–16.

Hagle, J. (1993) 'Keeping CPR on Track', *The McKinsey Quarterly* (1), pp. 59–72.

Hall, G., Rosenthal, J. and Wade, J. (1993) 'How to Make Re-engineering Really Work', *Harvard Business Review* (November–December), pp. 119–31.

Hall, R. (1993) 'A Framework for Linking Intangible Resources and Capabilities to Sustainable Competitive Advantage', *Strategic Management Journal* 14, pp. 607–18.

Hambrick, D. C., Geletkanycz, M. A. and Fredrickson, J. W. (1993) 'Top Executive Commitment to the Status Quo: Some Tests of its Determinants', *Strategic Management Journal* 14, pp. 401–18.

Hammer, M. (1990) 'Re-engineering Work: Don't Automate, Obliterate', *Harvard Business Review* (July–August), pp. 104–12.

Hammer, M. and Champy, J. (1993) *Re-engineering the Corporation: A Manifesto for Business Re-engineering*, Nicholas Brealey, London.

Hammer, M. and Stanton, S. A. (1995) *The Re-engineering Revolution: The Handbook*, HarperCollins, NY.

Harrington, H. J. (1991) *Business Process Improvement*, McGraw-Hill, New York.

Harrison, D. B. and Pratt, M. D. (1993) 'A Methodology for Re-engineering Businesses', *Planning Review* (March–April), pp. 7–11.

Hendry, J. (1995) 'Process Re-engineering and the Dynamic Balance of the Organisation', *European Management Journal* 13(1), pp. 52–7.

Heygate, R. (1993) 'Immoderate Redesign', *The McKinsey Quarterly* (1), pp. 73–87.

Heygate, R. and Brebach, G. (1991) 'Memo to a CEO: Corporate Re-engineering', *The McKinsey Quarterly* (2), pp. 44–55.

Huczynski, A. (1987) *Encyclopedia of Organizational Change Methods*, Gower, Aldershot.

Imai, M. (1986) *Kaizen, the Key to Japan's Competitive Success*, McGraw-Hill, New York.

IMPACT Management Bridge Joint Venture (1991) *Business Process Redesign: A Guideline to Best Practice*, ed. M. Dale.

IMPACT Management Bridge Joint Venture (1993) *Business Process Redesign Case Study Report*, ed. M. Dale and C. Palmer.

Janson (1992–3) 'How Re-engineering Transforms Organizations to Satisfy Customers', *National Productivity Review* (winter), pp. 45–53.

Juran, J. M. (1974) *Quality Control Handbook*, McGraw-Hill, New York.

Juran, J. M. (1993) 'Made in USA: A Renaissance in Quality', *Harvard Business Review* (July–August), pp. 42–50.

Kanter, R. M. (1989) *When Giants Learn To Dance*, Simon & Schuster, London.

Kaplan, R. B. and Murdock, L. (1991) 'Rethinking the Corporation: Core Process Redesign', *The McKinsey Quarterly* (2), pp. 27–43.

Katzenbach, J. R. and Smith, D. K. (1992) 'The Delicate Balance of Team Leadership', *The McKinsey Quarterly* (4), pp. 128–42.

Keidel, R. W. (1994) 'Rethinking Organizational Design', *Academy of Management Executive* 8(4), pp. 12–30.

Kelderman, J. (1991) 'NADA on Warranty Compensation', *Automotive Executive* 63 (September), p. 34.

Kerr, J. and Slocum, J. W. (1987) 'Managing Corporate Culture Through Reward Systems', *Academy of Management Executive* 1(2), pp. 99-108.

Kidder, T. (1981) *The Soul of a New Machine*, Little, Brown, Boston.

Kilmann, R. (1995) 'A Holistic Program and Critical Success Factors of Corporate Transformation', *European Management Journal* 13(2), pp. 175–86.

Kilmann, R., Saxton, M. J. and Serpa, R. (eds) (1985) *Gaining Control of Corporate Culture*, Jossey-Bass, San Francisco.

Kotler, G. (1992) 'Approaches to change', *Training & Development* (March), pp. 41–2.

Kotter, J. P. (1978) *Organizational Dynamics: Diagnosis and Intervention*, Addison Wesley, Reading Mass.

Lawrence, P. R. and Lorsch, J. W. (1969) *Developing Organizations: Diagnosis and Action*, Addison Wesley, Reading, Mass.

Leavitt, H. J. (1964) 'Applied Organizational Change in Industry: Structural Technical, and

Human Approaches', in W. W. Cooper, H. J. Leavitt and M. W. Shelley (eds.) *New Perspectives in Organization Research*, Wiley, New York.

Lee, S. K. J. (1992) 'Quantitative versus Qualitative Research Methods: Two Approaches to Organisation Studies', *Asia Pacific Journal of Management*, 9(1), pp. 87–94.

Legge, K. (1984) *Evaluating Planned Organizational Change*, Academic Press, London.

Lewin, K. (1958) 'Group Decision and Social Change', in E. E. Maccoby, T. M. Newcomb and E. L. Hartley (eds) *Readings in Social Psychology*, Holt, Rinehart & Winston, New York.

Likert, R. (1967) *The Human Organisation*, McGraw-Hill, New York.

Lippitt, R., Watson, J. and Westley, B. (1958) *Dynamics of Planned Change*, Harcourt, Brace, New York.

Lofland, J. and Lofland, L. H. (1984) *Analyzing Social Settings*, Wadsworth, Blemont, Ca.

Martinez, E. V. (1995) 'Successful Re-engineering Demands IS/Business Partnerships', *Sloan Management Review* (summer), pp. 51–60.

Marx, K. (1976) *Capital: A Critique of Political Economy*, Penguin, Harmondsworth.

Miles, M. B. and Huberman, A. M. (1984) *Analyzing Qualitative Data: A Source Book for New Methods*, Sage, Beverly Hills, Ca.

Miles, R. E. and Snow, C. C. (1978) *Organizational Strategy, Structure and Process*, McGraw-Hill, New York.

Miles, R. E., Coleman Jr, H. J. and Creed, W. E. D. (1995) 'Keys to Success in Corporate Redesign', *California Management Review*, 37(3), pp. 128–45.

Mintzberg, H. (1991) 'The Innovative Organization', in H. Mintzberg and J. B. Quinn (eds) *The Strategy Process: Concepts, Contexts, Cases*, 2nd edn Prentice Hall, Englewood Cliffs, N.J.

Morgan, G. (1986) *Creative Organization Theory: A Resource Book*, Sage, London.

Morgan, G. and Smircich, L. (1980) 'The Case for Qualitative Research', *Academy of Management Review* 5(4), pp. 491–500.

Morris, D. and Brandon, J. (1993) *Re-engineering your Business*, McGraw-Hill, New York.

Ostroff, F. and Smith, D. (1992) 'Redesigning the Corporation: The Horizontal Organization', *The McKinsey Quarterly* (1), pp. 148–67.

Pall, G. A. (1987) *Quality Process Management*, Prentice-Hall, Englewood Cliffs, N.J.

Parker, K. (1993) 'Re-engineering the Auto Industry', *Manufacturing Systems* (January).

Parnaby, J. (1994) 'Business Process Systems Engineering', *International Journal of Technology Management* (special issue on Technology, Human Resources and Growth), pp. 497–508.

Peters, T. J. (1991) 'Strategy Follows Structure: Developing Distinctive Skills', in H. Mintzberg and J. B. Quinn (eds) *The Strategy Process: Concepts, Contexts, Cases*, 2nd edn, Prentice Hall, Englewood Cliffs, N.J.

Peters, T. J. and Waterman, R. (1982) *In Search of Excellence*, Harper & Row, New York.

Plant, R. (1987) *Managing Change*, Gower, Aldershot.

Porter, M. (1980) *Competitive Strategy*, Free Press, New York.

Prahalad, C. K. and Hamel, G. (1990), 'The Core Competence of the Corporation', *Harvard Business Review* (May–June), pp. 79–91.

Punj, G. and Steward, D. W. (1983) 'Cluster Analysis in Marketing Research: Review and Suggestions for Application', *Journal of Marketing Research*, 20, pp. 134–48.

Quinn, J. B. and Paquette, P. C. (1991) 'Technology in Services: Creating Organizational Revolutions', in H. Mintzberg and J. B. Quinn (eds) *The Strategy Process: Concepts, Contexts, Cases*, 2nd edn, Prentice Hall, Englewood Cliffs, N.J.

Raskas, D. F. and Hamrick, D. C. (1992) 'Multifunctional Managerial Development: A Framework for Evaluating the Options', *Organizational Dynamics* (autumn), pp. 5–17.

Rockart, J. F. and Short, J. E. (1989) 'IT in the 1990's: Managing Organizational Interdependence', *Sloan Management Review* (winter), pp. 7–17.

Sadler, P. (1991) *Designing Organizations*, Mercury Books, London.

Savage, E. W. and Lycoming, T. (1991) 'Total Quality is Total Change', *Journal for Quality and Participation* (September), pp. 100–7.

Schein, E. H. (1988) *Process Consultation: Its Role in Organisation Development*, vol. 1, 2nd edn, Addison Wesley, Reading. Mass.

Senge, P. M. (1990) 'The Leader's New Work: Building Learning Organizations', *Sloan Management Review* (fall), pp. 7–23.

Silverman, D. (1985) *Qualitative Methodology and Sociology*, Gower, Aldershot.

Smith, A. (1976) *The Wealth of Nations*, University of Chicago Press, Chicago.

Solomon, R. C. (1976) *The Passions: The Myth and Nature of Human Emotion*, Anchor Press/Doubleday, New York.

Tapscott, D. and Caston, A. (1993) *Paradigm Shift: the New Promise of Information Technology*, McGraw-Hill, New York.

Templin, N. (1991) 'Sales of Used Rental Cars by Big Three Depress Other Second-hand Auto Prices', *Wall Street Journal* (6 January), p. B1.

Teng, J. T. C., Grover, V. and Fiedler, K. D. (1994) 'Re-designing Business Processes Using Information Technology', *Long Range Planning* 27(1), pp. 95–106.

Terlaga, R. (1994) 'Minimizing the Risks in Re-engineering: A Socio-Technical Approach', *Information Strategy: The Executive's Journal* 11(1), pp. 6–11.

Turner, B. A. (1988) 'Connoisseurship in the Study of Organizational Cultures', in A. Bryman (ed.) *Doing Research in Organizations*, Routledge, London.

Turney, P. B. B. and Anderson, B. (1989) 'Accounting for Continuous Improvement', *Sloan Management Review* (winter), pp. 37–47.

Used Car Merchandising (1991) 'Auto Auction Industry Faces New Popularity, New Problems', *Used Car Merchandising* (October), pp. 7–10.

Venkatraman, N. (1991) 'IT-induced Business Reconfiguration', in M. S. Scott Morton (ed.) *The Corporation of the 1990's: Information Technology and Organizational Transformation*, Oxford University Press, New York.

Want, J. H. (1993) 'Managing Radical Change', *Journal of Business Strategy* (May–June), pp. 21–8.

Ward, J., Griffiths, P. and Whitmore, P. (1990) *Strategic Planning for Information Systems*, John Wiley & Sons, Chichester.

Webb, E. J. (1970) 'Unconventionality, Triangulation, and Inference', in N. Denzin (ed.) *Sociological Methods: A Sourcebook*, Butterworths, London.

Yin, R. K. (1989) *Case Study Research Design and Methods*, Sage, London.

Zelditch, Jr, M. (1970) 'Some Methodological Problems of Field Studies', in N. Denzin (ed.) *Sociological Methods: A Sourcebook*, Butterworths, London.

Zuboff, S. (1988) *In the Age of the Smart Machine: The Future of Work and Power*, Basic Books, New York.

Index